Reclaiming Reality

Reclaiming Reality

A Critical Introduction to Contemporary Philosophy

ROY BHASKAR

VERSO

London · New York

Published by Verso 1989
© Roy Bhaskar 1989
All rights reserved

Verso
UK: 6 Meard Street, London W1V 3HR
USA: 29 West 35th Street, New York, NY 10001-2291

Verso is the imprint of New Left Books

British Library Cataloguing in Publication Data
Bhaskar, Roy, *1944*
    Reclaiming reality: a critical introduction to contemporary philosophy.
    1. Philosophy. Realism
    I. Title
    149'.2

ISBN 0 86091 237 X
    0 86091 951 X Pbk

US Library of Congress Cataloguing in Publication Data
Bhaskar, Roy, 1944
    Reclaiming reality: a critical introduction to contemporary philosophy/Roy Bhaskar.
    p. cm.
    Bibliography: p.
    ISBN 0 86091 237 X.–ISBN 0 86091 951 X (pbk.)
    1. Philosophy, Modern–20th century. I. Title.
B804.B48 1989
149'.2 dc 19

Typeset by Leaper & Gard Limited, Bristol, England
Printed in Great Britain by Bookcraft (Bath) Ltd

Contents

Preface

The commonwealth of learning is not at this time without master-builders, whose mighty designs, in advancing the sciences, will leave lasting monuments to the admiration of posterity: but everyone must not hope to be a Boyle, or a Sydenham; and in an age that produces such masters as the great Huygenius and the incomparable Mr Newton, with some others of that strain, it is ambition enough to be employed as an under-labourer in clearing the ground a little, and removing some of the rubbish that lies in the way to knowledge.[1]

The philosophers have only *interpreted* the world, in various ways; the point is to *change* it.[2]

The essays collected in this volume all seek to *underlabour* – at different levels and in different ways – for the sciences, and especially the human sciences, in so far as they might illuminate and empower the project of human self-emancipation. They attempt, that is to say, for the explanatory–emancipatory sciences today, the kind of 'clearing' of the ideological ground, which Locke set out to achieve for the prodigious infant of seventeenth-century mechanics. Such sciences, which only partially and incompletely exist, will not only interpret but help to change the world. But they will do so rationally only on the condition that they interpret the world aright.

These essays seek only to reclaim reality for itself. To reclaim it from philosophical ideologies – such as empiricism or idealism – which have tacitly or explicitly defined it in terms of some specific human attribute, such as sense-experience, intuition or axiomatic ratiocination, for some or other restricted – individual or group – interest.

The perspective which allows us to reclaim reality for itself I call 'critical realism'. This is introduced in Chapter 1, where I discuss the so-called 'new realism' currently in vogue in some erstwhile socialist circles. Chapter 2 shows how the critical realist, or as I have also called it the transcendental realist, account of natural science can be derived by an immanent critique of the dominant contemporary philosophies of science. Chapter 3 considers the work of two of the most influential philosophical schools of the twentieth century: those inaugurated by Karl Popper in the anglophone and by Gaston Bachelard in the francophone world. Chapter 4 illustrates the way in which a philosophical system such as positivism can act as an ideology for science and other social institutions, including those of the capitalist economy. Chapter 5 outlines my philosophy of social science, which I call critical naturalism. On it, social objects can be studied scientifically like natural ones – but only on the condition that we accept a realist (non-positivist, non-conventionalist and non-idealist) account of science and respect the specificity of the subject-matter of the social sciences. In Chapter 6, I develop the implications of the transcendental realist and critical naturalist philosophy for projects of human self-emancipation. It is an argument which will recur throughout this book that depth-explanatory human sciences, of the sort that Marx inaugurated but did not complete, are a necessary but insufficient condition for projects such as that of socialist emancipation. Chapter 7 looks at the central themes, traditions and problems of Marxist epistemology, including the highly charged concepts of the dialectic and of materialism. In Chapter 8, I engage in a critique of the work of Richard Rorty, whose *Philosophy and the Mirror of Nature*[3] must be one of the most influential philosophical books of the post-war period. In Chapter 9, I round off the themes of the book and correct some of the emphases of Chapter 1.

All but the first, fourth and last of the chapters have been published before, but these are mostly relatively inaccessible. The chapters may be read in any order, but the neophyte in philosophy should be warned that Chapters 4 and 6 are qualitatively more difficult than the others – so they should be skipped, perhaps, at a first reading. Chapter 9 as a resumé of the argument of the book could usefully be read much earlier. Newcomers to philosophy should try to grasp the flow of the argument, if they become bemused by a particular step. This may involve going on (or back) a paragraph, section or even chapter until things start to 'fall into place'.

This book should be seen as an attempt to start, or rather continue, an argument, not to conclude one. It leaves loose ends and threads. Some, I hope, the reader will pick up and pursue for her- or himself. Others I intend to pursue in a companion volume of essays on recent and contemporary Marxist philosophers and the post-structuralists and post-modernists, provisionally entitled *Philosophical Underlabouring*. The critique of Rorty is expanded and broadened in my forthcoming *Philosophy and the Idea of Freedom*;[4] as the argument of Chapter 7 will be set in its full historical and philosophical context in my book on *Dialectic*.

Chapter 1 is a development of an *Interlink* 7 (June 1988) article for the 2nd Socialist Conference at Chesterfield, which I expanded for the July 1988 Conference of Socialist Economists Annual Conference at Sheffield. I am indebted to my original co-authors, Chris Arthur, Ted Benton, Gregory Elliott, John Lovering, Peter Osborne and Hilary Wainwright; to discussions with many others including Jeremy Beale, Robin Blackburn, Mary Kaldor, Laura Marcus, Doreen Massey, Jenny Taylor and William Outhwaite; and to helpful debates at the two conferences. Chapter 2 comprises an address given to the 6th International Congress of Logic, Methodology and Philosophy of Science at Hanover in August 1979. It is reprinted by kind permission of North-Holland Publishing Company and L.J. Cohen and his fellow editors. Chapter 3 was first published in *New Left Review* 94, 1975. Chapter 4 was originally given as a talk to the British Sociological Association 'Sociology of Science Study Group' at the London School of Economics in February 1976. Chapter 5 was first published in *Journal for the Theory of Social Behaviour* 8 (1), 1978. It is reprinted by kind permission of Basil Blackwell. Chapter 6 was first published in *Radical Philosophy* 26, 1980, and is reprinted by permission of the Radical Philosophy Collective. The three articles which comprise Chapter 7 were first published in *A Dictionary of Marxist Thought*, Ed. T. Bottomore et al., Blackwell 1983. They are reprinted with corrections here by kind permission of Basil Blackwell and Tom Bottomore. Chapter 8 was first published in *Reading Rorty*, Ed. A. Malachowski, Blackwell 1989, and is reprinted here with grateful thanks to Basil Blackwell and Alan Malachowski. Chapter 9 is based on a talk I delivered at the 4th Conference of the Standing Conference on Realism and the Human Sciences in Bristol in September 1988. It has benefited considerably from the stimulating discussions we had there. It covers some of the same ground as my 'Postscript to the Second Edition', *The Possibility of Naturalism*, Harvester Press, 1989.

Acknowledgements of a more personal kind are also in order. Thanks are due to Sue Kelly for secretarial help. I am also extremely grateful to Colin Robinson and all at Verso for their patience and the prompt and efficient production of this book. Above all, I would like to thank Hilary Wainwright for constant encouragement and incessant argument.

Roy Bhaskar
November 1988

1

Critical Realism, Social Relations and Arguing for Socialism

Enlightenment is man's release from self-incurred tutelage. Tutelage is man's inability to make use of his understanding without direction from another. Self-incurred is this tutelage when its cause lies not in lack of reason but in the lack of resolution and courage to use it without direction from another. *Sapere aude!* Have courage to use your own reason! – That is the motto of enlightenment.[1]

1 Philosophical Underlabouring

I take it that whatever our politics, in the narrow party or factional sense, socialists can agree that what we must be about today is the building of a movement for socialism – in which socialism wins a cultural–intellectual hegemony, so that it becomes the enlightened common-sense of our age. My use of the phrase 'enlightened common-sense' is deliberate. In a capitalist world and a bourgeois society, socialism will never be simple sense. But what we can hope to aspire to is the dawning of a new enlightenment, a socialist enlightenment which will stand to some future order of things, as the eighteenth-century bourgeois enlightenment stood to the American Declaration of Independence, the French revolution and the overthrow of colonial slavery for which it helped to prepare the cultural ground. If this is our project as socialist intellectuals – to win the intellectual high-ground for socialism – then it should be clear why we need to take philosophy seriously.

We need to take philosophy seriously because it is the discipline that has traditionally underwritten both what constitutes science or knowledge and which political practices are deemed legitimate. Indeed it could be argued that many of the confusions current on the left, exemplified by the acceptance of a series of false dichotomies, such as between fundamentalism and revisionism, individualism and collectivism, or scientific analysis and moral criticism, stem from unwittingly following utterly

1

inadequate philosophies of science and society. Thus, among radical-chic intellectuals the dominant intellectual 'fashionmeter' has swung from the idealist structuralism and post-structuralism of the seventies and early eighties to the empiricist so-called 'new realism' of the mid and late eighties. Those who have resisted the pull of these fashions have nevertheless lost confidence in the face of them. My aim in this essay is briefly to develop the implications of a more adequate philosophy of science and society for socialism – where philosophy is conceived, in Lockean fashion, as an underlabourer for science and projects of human emancipation and, in Leibnizian mode, as an analyst and potential critic of conceptual systems and the forms of social life in which they are embedded – as part of the longer-term project of capturing the intellectual high-ground. An indication of the extent to which the right – echoed in the labour movement – has managed to seize this ground is that it has not only succeeded in achieving political dominance; it has, under the guise of the 'new realism', even appropriated the very concept of reality and realism for itself!

2 Critical Realism Versus 'New Realism'

The so-called 'new realism' merely reflects and accommodates to the new and rapidly changing surface forms of contemporary capitalist society at home and abroad. Vaunted as a belated adjustment to the facts of political life, the 'new realism' is actually an empiricist or empirical realism. It is a form of realism which fails to recognise that there are enduring structures and generative mechanisms underlying and producing observable phenomena and events. In other words its realism is of the most superficial sort.

It should be appreciated that all philosophies, cognitive discourses and practical activities presuppose a realism – in the sense of some ontology or general account of the world – of one kind or another. The crucial question is: *what kind?*[2] The scientific, transcendental and critical realism which I have expounded conceives the world as being structured, differentiated and changing. It is opposed to empiricism, pragmatism and idealism alike. Critical realists do not deny the reality of events and discourses; on the contrary, they insist upon them. But they hold that we will only be able to understand – and so change – the social world if we identify the structures at work that generate those events or discourses. Such structures are irreducible to the patterns of events and discourses alike. These structures are not spontaneously apparent in the observable pattern of events; they can only be identified through the practical and theoretical work of the social sciences.

Social phenomena (like most natural phenomena) are the product of a plurality of structures. But such structures may be hierarchically ranked in terms of their explanatory importance. Such an approach allows us to avoid the pitfalls of both crude determinism (for example, of an economic reductionist sort) and undifferentiated eclecticism. Thus in order to understand the growth of militarism one must take into account both the dynamics of the international economic order and the political conflicts between nation states (and their blocks) and their interaction. It is worth noting that a hierarchy of explanation prioritizing the economic level need not involve the collapsing of the autonomous organizations of different groups of oppressed people (although it may have implications for their strategic perspectives).

Realism is not, nor does it license, either a set of substantive analyses or a set of practical policies. Rather, it provides a set of perspectives on society (and nature) and on how to understand them. It is not a substitute for, but rather helps to guide, empirically controlled investigations into the structures generating social phenomena. And from this critical realist perspective we can now see the swingometer of intellectual fashion as having lurched from the hyper-structuralist view of people as the mere effects or dupes of structures over which they have neither knowledge nor control to the 'new realist' view which effectively empties the social world of any enduring structural dimension, making, as Raymond Williams put it, 'long-term adjustments to short-term changes'.

3 Understanding Social Relations

Over the last century, popular, academic and political thinking about society has tended to gravitate towards one or other of the poles of a crude polarity between individualism and collectivism. Thus classical social theory has swung between the individualism and voluntarism of utilitarianism and Weberianism on the one hand and the collectivism and reification involved in organicist and Durkheimian social thought on the other. At a political level, the former found expression in liberalism, and the latter in labourism (and Stalinism).

Realists argue for an understanding of the relationship between social structures and human agency that is based on a *transformational* conception of social activity, and which avoids both voluntarism and reification. At the same time they advance an understanding of the social as essentially consisting in or depending upon *relations*. This view is in opposition to both atomistic individualism and undifferentiated collectivism.

According to the transformational understanding of social activity, the existence of social structure is a necessary condition for any human

activity. Society provides the means, media, rules and resources for everything we do. Far from it being the case that, in Mrs Thatcher's dictum,
society doesn't exist, the existence of society is a transcendentally necessary condition for any intentional act at all. It is the unmotivated condition for all our motivated productions. We do not create society – the
error of voluntarism. But these structures which pre-exist us are only
reproduced or transformed in our everyday activities; thus society does
not exist independently of human agency – the error of reification. The
social world is reproduced or transformed in daily life.

All social structures – for instance, the economy, the state, the family,
language – depend upon or presuppose social relations – which may
include the social relations between capital and labour, ministers and civil
servants, parents and children. The relations into which people enter pre-
exist the individuals who enter into them, and whose activity reproduces
or transforms them; so they are themselves structures. And it is to these
structures of social relations that realism directs our attention – both as
the explanatory key to understanding social events and trends and as the
focus of social activity aimed at the self-emancipation of the exploited and
oppressed.

On this transformational and relational conception, society is a skilled
accomplishment of active agents. But the social world may be opaque to
the social agents upon whose activity it depends in four respects, in that
these activities may depend on or involve (a) unacknowledged conditions,
(b) unintended consequences, (c) the exercise of tacit skills, and/or (d)
unconscious motivation. Accordingly, the task of the social sciences is to
describe what social processes (for example, the buying and selling of
labour power, the extraction of surplus value) must be going on for a
Stock Exchange crash or some other manifest phenomenon to be possible.

Society then is the ensemble of positioned practices and networked
interrelationships which individuals never create but in their practical
activity always presuppose, and in so doing everywhere reproduce or
transform.

On this approach, while social structures are dependent upon the
consciousness which the agents who reproduce or transform them have,
they are not reducible to this consciousness. Social practices are concept-
dependent; but, contrary to the hermeneutical tradition in social science,
they are not exhausted by their conceptual aspect. They always have a
material dimension. This is an important consideration, as reflection on
the prevalence and impact of the phenomena of hunger, homelessness and
war upon so much of human history shows. Moreover for critical realism
the social world, being itself a social product, is seen as essentially subject
to the possibility of transformation. Hence it is intrinsically dynamic and
irreducibly geo-historical, a situated and distantiating process. Under-

standing the social world as a (spatial) process should not lead to an exaggerated emphasis on particular fluctuations (for example as in some of the more apocalyptic conclusions drawn by some of the left at the time of the October 1987 Stock Exchange crash – a crash which equally the 'new realist' right could neither foresee nor comprehend).

4 Implications for Socialism

Transforming society towards socialism depends upon knowledge of these underlying structures. The world cannot be rationally changed unless it is adequately interpreted. But there are problems.

First, because social systems are intrinsically open and cannot be artificially closed, our criteria for the empirical testing of social theories cannot be predictive and so must be exclusively explanatory. This means, for instance, that Marxist economic theory cannot be held to have been falsified by the failure of any predictions it might have been used to generate; equally it can only be confirmed or corroborated (and rationally developed) by reference to its explanatory power in illuminating a range of historical and contemporary data. (Of course a powerful explanatory theory will allow us to make conditional predictions about tendencies which may manifest themselves in the future.) Speaking substantively, I think it is vital to conceive Marxism as a research programme, initiated by Marx but no more completed by him than Copernicus completed the revolution in thought which Galileo, Kepler and Newton developed, and Einstein and quantum theory have radically transformed this century.

Second, social theory and social reality are causally interdependent. This is not to say that the social theorist 'constructs' social reality. But it is to say that social theory is practically conditioned by, and potentially has practical consequences in society. Indeed, critical realism suggests that social theory is non-neutral in two ways. It always consists in a practical intervention in social life and sometimes (other things being equal) it logically entails values and actions. In these circumstances, the standard fact/value and theory/practice distinctions break down. Thus if we accept Marx's critique of political economy, which is also a critique of the illusory or false consciousness which capitalist society generates, we may – indeed must – pass immediately to a negative evaluation of those structures and to a positive evaluation of action rationally directed to changing them. (This is of course not to imply that the misleading way capitalism manifests itself is the sole or main reason for being a socialist. This will turn on capitalism's failure to meet human needs and aspirations. It is rather to highlight the way in which a critique of a theory in the social world may often involve an explanation of the reasons why it is believed and a critique of the circumstances in which its belief appears plausible, that is, in which the theory is credible.)

From the critical realist perspective, contrary to the tradition of contemporary social democracy, socialist emancipation depends on the transformation of structures, not the amelioration of states of affairs. Indeed, in present and foreseeable circumstances, the transformation of structures may be a practically necessary condition for more humane states of affairs. But this transformation does not involve a magic transportation into a realm free of determination, as imagined by both utopian and so-called 'scientific' socialists. Rather, it consists in the move or transition from unneeded, unwanted and oppressive to needed, wanted and empowering sources of determination. This might include, for example, a switch from a situation where production is determined by the pursuit of private profit and subject to arbitrary fluctuation, to one where it is subject to democratic negotiation and planning. 'What will the sources and forms of determination be like under socialism?' Socialists need to take such questions seriously; to build, if you like, models of feasible concrete utopias, if socialism is to become the enlightened common-sense of our age.

The structures which agents reproduce or transform in their activity are also structures of power which may involve alienation, domination and oppression. The oppressed, contrary to their oppressors, have a direct material interest in understanding the structural causes of their oppression. The relationship between social knowledge or theory and social (more specifically socialist) practice will take the form of an emancipatory spiral in which deeper understanding make possible new forms of practice, leading to enhanced understanding and so on. (Only if we understand and accomplish the emancipatory spiral at work in history, and the need for structural transformation, will we be able to resolve the old debate between reformists and revolutionaries.)

Philosophies can confuse as well as enlighten. Two crude philosophical distinctions, between mind and body and reasons and causes, have done untold damage here. Thus the social structure is embedded in, conditioned by and in turn efficacious on the rest of nature, the ecosphere. At an epistemological level this means that reasons, and social forms generally, must be causes (as well as effects). Equally, socialists have to break free from the dichotomous opposition between nature and society which found expression in a Promethean view of our relationship to nature, based on the notion of practically infinite resources and geared to ever-expanding technological growth. Instead we have to see the natural and social dimensions of existence as in continuous dynamic causal interaction. Thus not only are many 'natural' ills and disasters *socially* produced, but social production may have absolute *natural* limits and conditions. Socialists must work out a view of socialism, as a social form oriented to human well-being, as an environmentally sustainable form of social life. Related to the crude dichotomy of nature and society is a crude distinction between basic, bodily (physical) or natural needs such as for food or housing, and higher-order psychological (mental) or spiritual needs such as for respect or self-development. These latter needs are not the object of a separate set of practices, but are intrinsic to the way so-called basic needs are met. Thus housing needs can be met in dehumanizing ways or they can be satisfied in ways which, for instance, show respect for individuals, enhance their self-respect and create opportunities for their development. Here again, there is a need for concrete scientific utopianizing by socialist economists, architects and human scientists in general.

5 Arguing for Socialism

It should be emphasized that on this relational conception, I am not denying the existence of individuals and collectivities. I am emphasizing the role that social relations play in determining the course of an individual's life or the possibilities for collective action.

In arguing for socialism we must have a richer understanding of individuality, including the relational preconditions for personal well-being, than that provided by the impoverished, isomorphic, asocial atoms or choice machines of individualist orthodoxy. At the same time, however, we require a differentiated notion of collectivity which, unlike labourist and Stalinist notions of 'the workers' and 'the masses', takes fuller account of the complexity of internal relationships within the group or collective concerned.

On the relational view a person's individuality is primarily constituted by his or her social particularity. In other words, what they are is mainly a product of what they have done or what has been done to them in the particular social relations into which they were born and in which they have lived. What they do or have done to them must be understood in terms of their historically and socially conditioned capacities, powers, liabilities and tendencies.

The task of socialists must be to work for the development and release of our underdeveloped and repressed capacities and for the transformation and dissolution of existing oppressive and repressive tendencies. It must also be to struggle for the social and natural (e.g. environmental) conditions for their fulfilment or transformation. These capacities and tendencies, as the Marxist and socialist tradition has correctly stressed, are inherently social.

In working towards a relational conception of collectivities we need to understand any given collectivity both in terms of its relationships with other collectivities (and in particular those in terms of which it is oppositionally defined or defines itself) and in terms of its internal relationships. Thus in considering the labour movement in a particular country at a particular time, for example, we must take into account not only the relationship of that labour movement to its ruling class, but the role, say, racism and sexism played within that movement.

Foregrounding the internal relations within collectivities focuses attention upon the acute question for the left that has emerged in reaction to the historical débâcles of labourism and Stalinism, of the form and quality of our internal democracy. If it fails to resolve this, and in doing so fails to prefigure in the present something of what it demands for the future, the left will always find itself on the defensive about democracy in any argument for socialism. This itself raises a more general question. Marx said that a new civilization develops in the womb of the old. How do we nourish and grow socialism in our times? This is equivalent to the question of how we switch the social process from a primarily reproductive to a primarily transformative mode.

6 Individualism and Collectivism as Ideologies

Having said something about the concepts of individuality and collectivity that we need to counteract individualism and collectivism, I now want to comment on individualism and collectivism as ideologies. Individualism is a pretty pure ideology of the market, at least as we have it now. But collectivism is a more complex phenomenon. On the one hand, in its right-wing form, it is a *complementary* ideology to the market – it expresses the sum of non-market social institutions, values and interests necessary to make the market work, from the inheritance of property to appeals to national interest. On the other hand, in its left-wing form, it is a *reactive* ideology to the market – it expresses the array of social institutions, values and interests which allow the victims of the market to survive it. The chief collectivist ideologies of these two types in our society today are probably nationalism and labourism respectively. Both are parasitic upon (or at most symbiotic with) individualism as a pure market ideology. Here I want to consider how empiricism, in the form of empirical realism, generates an ideology of the individual which reinforces and resonates with the ideology spontaneously secreted by the market itself.

In the ideology of empiricism the world is regarded as flat, uniform, unstructured and undifferentiated: it consists essentially of atomistic events or states of affairs which are constantly conjoined, so occurring in closed systems. Such events and their constant conjunctions are known by asocial, atomistic individuals who passively sense (or apprehend) these given facts and register their constant conjunctions. Underpinning and necessary for the reified facts and fetishized systems of empiricism are thus dehumanised beings in desocialized relationships. Facts usurp the place of things, conjunctions that of causal laws and automata those of people, as reality is defined in terms of the cosmic contingency of human sense-experience (as conceived by empiricism).

What is the meaning of the fact form? Facts are real, but they are historically specific realities. The mystification attached to them derives from the condition that, in our spontaneous way of thinking and in empiricism, the philosophy which reflects this, the properties possessed by facts as *social objects* are transformed into qualities belonging to them as *natural things*. Fetishism, by naturalizing facts, at once collapses and so destratifies their generative or sustaining social context and the mode of their production, reproduction and transformation in time, ipso facto dehistoricizing and eternalizing them. The fact form thus acts as an ideology of what Kuhn has called 'normal science', obscuring from scientists and non-scientists alike the historically specific structures and relations generating sense-experience in science. It is an objective mystification, partly analogous to the value form, generated by the very nature of the activities in which we engage – a mystification we must achieve distance from if we are to be able to think the possibility of a critique of the very forms in which the social world spontaneously presents itself.

If we turn from the fact to the constant conjunction form, the mystification is not an objective one, like that intrinsic to the value form, but is quite simply false, an illusion properly so-called. If we want a Marxian analogy for it we must turn from the value to the wage form. For just as, according to Marx, wages are not what they appear to be – they are not the value of labour, but of labour power – so causal laws are not the constant conjunctions of events that, when generated under artificially produced and deliberately controlled conditions, comprise their empirical grounds, but the tendencies of mechanisms ontologically irreducible to them. The analogy may be pressed further. For just as, according to Marx, the category mistake in political economy consists in the confusion of powers and their exercise, so the category mistake in philosophy is the confusion of powers or tendencies and their realization. For Marx the social function of the wage form is to conceal the reality of exploitation, unpaid labour, the source of surplus value. What is the social meaning or role of the constant conjunction form? It conceals the reality of structures irreducible to events, and more particularly of social structures to human actions and of societies to individuals. In this way it cuts the ground from under the possibility of the social sciences, and so of any route to human emancipation.

Ontological reductionism transposed to the human zone has particularly damaging consequences. In perfect resonance with the empiricist concept of science as a behavioural response to the stimulus of given facts and their constant conjunctions, society is conceived as composed of individuals, motivated by given desires and conjoined (if at all) by contract. Reason is reduced to the ability to perform an optimizing or satisficing operation and freedom consists in its unimpeded exercise. The constant conjunction form, which lies at the heart of the new realism, which is merely the old superficial empirical realism, is, as Marx said of the wage form, 'as irrational as a yellow logarithm'.[3] In the constant conjunction form history grinds to a halt in the eternalized present. History is what there has been or is elsewhere, but is no longer here now.[4] But, equally, we could say of the constant conjunction form, as Marx said of the wage form, 'if history took a long time to get to the bottom of [its] mystery . . . nothing on the other hand, is easier than to understand the necessity, the raison d'être, of this phenomenon'.[5] It is the ideology of the market place and more generally of the established order of things, of TINA (there is no alternative). But we cannot respond to TINA with TIGMO (this great movement of ours). We need hard intellectual work (informed by critical realism) and dedicated political practice (oriented to the transformation of social relations) to make socialism the reason of our time.

2
Realism in the Natural Sciences

1 Tensions in Recent Philosophy

Recent philosophy of science wears an air of paradox. The fundamental assumptions of the positivist world view, that science is *monistic* in its development and *deductive* in its structure, lie shattered. But the ensuing accounts of science have not found it easy to sustain a coherent notion of the rationality, or even intelligibility, of either scientific change or the non-deductive component of theory. I think that one can trace the source of this difficulty back to the continuance, alongside the new philosophy of science, of an old philosophy of being materially incompatible with it. The result is that philosophy is caught in a cleft stick. With the new epistemology it cannot go back. But without a new ontology it cannot go forward. The effects of this tension are clearly visible along both the anti-monistic and anti-deductivist limbs of the anti-positivist pincer.

Consider first the anti-monistic movement, represented most notably perhaps by the work of Bachelard, Koyré, Popper, Lakatos, Feyerabend and Kuhn. Both Bachelard and Kuhn come very close to the position, whose roots lie in Vico, and which I shall characterise as *super-idealism*, that we create and change the world along with our theories.[1] Neither Kuhn nor Feyerabend have managed to sustain the intelligibility of the concept of a *clash* between incommensurable descriptions, or to say *over* what such descriptions clash. Popper has not shown how the falsification of a conjecture could be rational, *unless* nature were uniform. And he has not furnished any ground for assuming that it is, in the face of Humean and Goodmanesque possibilities. Nor has Lakatos shown how unless nature were uniform, it would be rational to work on progressive rather than degenerating programmes; or, for that matter, pay any attention to the history of science. More generally, the theorists of scientific change have found it difficult to reconcile the phenomenon of discontinuity with the seemingly progressive, cumulative character of scientific development, in which there is growth as well as change.

Parallel problems beset the anti-deductivist movement. Under the initial influence of Wittgenstein, philosophers such as Hanson, Toulmin, Hesse and Harré have sought to show how scientific practice generates cognitive items – be they glossed as paradigms, heuristics, conceptual schemata, models or ideals – irreducible to syntactical operations upon sense-experience, and which are essential for both the intelligibility and the empirical extension of theory. Such items function, as it were, as surrogates for natural necessity.[2] The problem is this: if the surrogate can be empirically described, then its postulation is legitimate, but it now ceases to play any independent role, so that the necessity of the connection, the analogical character of the model, the ideality of the order, or whatever, vanishes. Conversely, if it cannot be empirically described, its cognitive function is retained, but it now (on the ontology of empirical realism) ceases to explain the nature of any real phenomenon.[3] More generally, writers within this tradition have not always succeeded in counterbalancing their stress on the synthesizing activity of the scientific imagination with the messy practicalities of science's causal interaction with nature (the nuts and bolts, so to speak, of scientific life).

Now I think that if the rational insights of both the anti-monistic and anti-deductivist tendencies are to be saved, a new ontology must be constructed for them. Such an ontology involves a Copernican Revolution in the strict sense of an anti-anthropocentric shift in our philosophical conception of the place of humanity in nature. It is my aim in this chapter to show the necessity for the new realist philosophy of natural science which such a shift entails.

2 Types of Realism

Realism is the theory that the ultimate objects of scientific inquiry exist and act (for the most part) quite independently of scientists and their activity. Now, as so defined, it might be thought that the question of whether or not natural science is 'realist' can only be answered empirically, that is, by determining whether or not scientists believe, or act as if they believe, that the theoretical entities and processes they posit are real objects independent of their theorizing.[4] Such questions are clearly legitimate and necessary. But I want to argue the case for a metaphysical realism, consisting in an elaboration of what the world must be like prior to any scientific investigation of it and for any scientific attitudes or behaviour to be possible. Such a realism neither presupposes nor licenses a realistic interpretation of any particular theory.

Clearly, the possibility of such a metaphysical, as distinct from 'internal', realism will depend upon the establishment of the possibility of a *philosophy*, as distinct from sociology (or history) of science. But within philosophy, it will also depend upon the possibility of an *ontology*, as distinct from epistemology. For realism is not a theory of knowledge or of truth, but of *being* (though as such it has of course epistemological implications). Accordingly, a realist position in the philosophy of science will be a theory about the nature of the being, not the knowledge, of the objects investigated by science – roughly to the effect that they exist and act independently of human activity, and hence of both sense-experience and thought. In this way realism is immediately opposed to both empiricism and rationalism; *and* to that opinion of post-Humean philosophy – which I shall call the *epistemic fallacy* – that ontological questions can always be reparsed in epistemological form: that is, that statements about being can always be analysed in terms of statements about our knowledge (of being), that it is sufficient for philosophy to 'treat only the network, and not what the network describes'.[5]

Now it is clear that any theory of the knowledge of objects entails some theory of the objects of knowledge; that every theory of scientific knowledge must logically presuppose a theory of what the world is like for knowledge, under the descriptions given it by the theory, to be possible. Thus, suppose a philosopher analyses scientific laws as, or as dependent upon, constant conjunctions of events, he or she is then committed to the view that there *are* such conjunctions; that, in Mill's words, 'there are such things in nature as parallel cases; that what happens once will, under a sufficient degree of similarity of circumstance, happen again.'[6] In this way, then, as Bachelard recognised, 'all philosophy, explicitly or tacitly, honestly or surreptitiously . . . deposits, projects or presupposes a reality.'[7] So we could say, inverting a famous dictum of Hegel's – every philosophy (at least in as much as it is a philosophy of science)[8] is essentially a realism, or at least has realism for its principle, the only questions being then how far, and *in what form*, this principle is actually carried out.[9] Now the orthodox tradition in the philosophy of science, including both its Humean and Kantian wings, has depended upon an implicit ontology of *empirical realism*, on which the real objects of scientific investigation are the objects of actual or possible experience. More recently, the super-idealist tendency has secreted an implicit ontology of *subjective conceptual realism*, on which the real objects of scientific investigation are the products of scientific theory (that is, of the spontaneous activity of mind, unconstrained by sense-experience). But I want to show that only a realism fully consistent with the principle (or definition) of realism enunciated above, *transcendental realism*, can sustain the intelligibility of the experimental and theoretical work of science.

3 On Method

How then is a philosophy of science possible? What distinguishes
philosophy from science is not its concern with a special field (e.g.
language, culture or man), nor the generality of the questions it asks
(whether this is conceived as a matter of degree, as in Quine, or kind, as in
Lakatos), nor its investigation of (participation in or contribution to) some
autonomous order of being. Rather philosophy distinguishes itself from
science by its *method*, and more generally by the kinds of considerations
and arguments it deploys, which are transcendental in Kant's sense.

Now although if philosophy is to be possible, it must pursue a transcendental procedure, it must reject the idealist and individualist mould into
which Kant pressed his own inquiries. In fact, if the general form of a
philosophical investigation is into the necessary conditions of conceptualized activities, then it must be recognized that both social activity and
philosophical conceptualization may be historically transient; that the
activity may depend upon the powers of people as material objects or
causal agents rather than merely thinkers or perceivers; and that its analysis may yield transcendental realist, not idealist, and epistemically relativist, rather than absolutist (or irrationalist), conclusions. On this
conception, then, both the premisses and conclusions of philosophical
arguments remain contingent facts, the former but not the latter being
necessarily social (and so historical). It is only in this relative or conditional sense that philosophy can establish synthetic a priori truths. For
philosophy gets going always (and only) on the basis of prior conceptualizations of historical practice, that is, of specific ideas of determinate
social forms.

Philosophy, then, does not consider a world apart from that of the
various sciences. Rather it considers just that world, but from the perspective of what can be established about it by *a priori* argument, where it
takes as its premisses scientific activities as conceptualized in experience
(or in a theoretical redescription of it). As such, philosophy is *dependent*
upon the form of scientific practices, but *irreducible* to the content of
scientific beliefs. Thus philosophy can tell us that, if experimental activity
is to be intelligible, the world must be structured and differentiated. But it
cannot tell us what structures the world contains or the ways in which
they are different, which are entirely matters for substantive scientific
investigation. If philosophy does not compete with science, in virtue of its
transcendental nature, it does not exist apart from science, in virtue of its
syncategorematic character. For the terms of a philosophical discourse
denote only on the condition that they are used under particular descriptions in science. Thus whatever is philosophically demonstrable is also in
principle scientifically comprehensible. And hence in the long run rela-

tively autonomous philosophy must be *consistent* with the findings of science.

But how are we to select the premises of our transcendental arguments without already implying an unvalidated commitment to the epistemic significance of the activities described? Recourse to an arbitrary and external criterion of knowledge[10] can be avoided by focusing on those activities which non-realists have historically picked out as most significant in science. Thus considering experimentation, sponsored by empiricists and Kantians, and conceptual transformations, sponsored by super-idealists, I will show (i) how the sponsoring theory cannot sustain the intelligibility of the sponsored activity without metaphysical absurdity, and (ii) how a realist analysis can render the sponsored activity intelligible. I do not claim that my analyses are certain or unique (though they are the only plausible analyses I know of). But they are demonstrably superior to the non-realist alternatives that currently hold the floor in contemporary philosophy. Moreover, the resulting realist account of science provides a clear and consistent alternative to positivism which allows us both to save the cumulative character of science without restoring a monism and to rescue a 'surplus' component in scientific theory without plunging into subjectivism.

4 Experimental Activity and the Vindication of Ontology

For the empiricist experimental activity is necessary, and perhaps sufficient, for the establishment of causal laws and other items of general knowledge; and these causal laws and items are analysed as, or as dependent upon, constant conjunctions of events (or states of affairs) perceived or perceptions. It is not difficult to see that this analysis is faulty.

In an experiment scientists co-determine, or are causally co-responsible for, a pattern of events. There is nothing in itself special about this. For, as causal agents, we are continually co-responsible for events. What is significant about the patterns scientists deliberately produce under conditions which they meticulously control is that it enables them to identify the mode of operation of structures, mechanisms or processes which they do not produce. What distinguishes the phenomena the scientists *actually* produce out of the totality of the phenomena they *could* produce is that, when their experiment is successful, it is an index of what they do *not* produce. A *real* distinction between the objects of experimental investigation, such as causal laws, and patterns of events is thus a condition of the intelligibility of experimental activity. Now as constant conjunctions must in general be artificially produced, if we identify causal laws with them, we are logically committed to the absurdities that scientists, in their experimental activity, cause and even change the laws of nature! Thus the objects of scientific inquiry in an experiment cannot be events and their conjunctions, but are (I suggest) structures, generative mechanisms and the like (forming the real basis of causal laws), which are normally out of phase with them. And it can now be seen that the Humean account depends upon a misidentification of causal laws with their empirical grounds.[11]

But, of course, we not only experimentally establish, we practically *apply* our knowledge – in systems, which may be characterised as *open*, where no constant conjunctions obtain. If this activity is to be rendered intelligible, causal laws must be analysed as tendencies, which may be possessed unexercised and exercised unrealized, just as they may of course be realized unperceived (or undetected) by anyone. Thus in citing a law we are referring to the transfactual activity of mechanisms, that is, to their activity as such, not making a claim about the actual outcome (which will in general be co-determined by the effects of other mechanisms too). And a constant conjunction, or empirical invariance, is no more a necessary, than it is a sufficient condition for the operation of a causal law. Here again, failure to mark the ontological difference between causal laws and patterns of events issues in absurdity. For if causal laws are, or depend upon, constant conjunctions, then we must ask: what governs phenomena in open systems, that is in the vast majority of cases? Empiricists are now impaled on an acute dilemma – for they must either aver that nothing does, so that nature becomes radically indeterministic; or suppose that, as yet, science has discovered no laws![12]

Once made, however, the ontological distinction between causal laws and patterns of events allows us to sustain the universality of the former in the face of the non-invariance of the latter. Moreover the Humean analysis of laws now loses all plausibility. For the non-invariance of conjunctions is a condition of an empirical science and the non-empirical nature of laws a condition of an applied (or pragmatic) one.

Did we not know this all along? Of course, it is in line with our intuitions. Thus we do not suppose that, for instance, Ohm's Law or Prout's Hypothesis hold only in the laboratory – where alone they can be tested. And as every research worker knows: no experiment goes properly the first time. We can *use* our knowledge for the explanation of events and the production of things in open systems, where deductively-justified predictions, and decisive test situations, are impossible. And yet in the reflective consciousness of philosophy, as distinct from the spontaneous practice of science, it has seldom been doubted that the Humean analysis specifies at least necessary conditions for the attribution of laws.

Of course, transcendental idealists and others have long contended that a constant conjunction of events is not a sufficient condition for a causal law. They have seen that no scientist ever fails for a moment to distinguish a necessary from an accidental sequence (even if they are not always sure into which class a given sequence falls). But the problem has always been to ground this intuition in such a way as to sustain a concept of *natural* necessity, that is a necessity in nature quite independent of humans and their activity. More recently, Anscombe, von Wright and some others, have noted that our active *interference* in nature is normally a condition of empirical regularities. But they have not seen that it follows from this that there must be an *ontological* distinction between such regularities and the laws they ground. (We produce not the laws of nature, but their empirical grounds.) On the transcendental realist system, a sequence *A. B* is necessary if and only if there is a natural mechanism *M* such that when stimulated by *A*, *B* tends to be produced. It is a condition of the experimental establishment and practical application of our knowledge that such mechanisms exist and act, as what may be termed the *intransitive* objects of scientific inquiry, independently of their identification by human beings. And it is in their transfactual activity – described in 'normic' statements – that the real ground for the 'surplus-element' in the analysis of laws lies.

The analysis of experimental activity shows that causal laws are ontologically distinct from patterns of events. But experimental activity involves sense-perception (as well as causal agency); and reflection on the necessity for a scientific training (or the possibility of scientific change) shows that events must be ontologically distinct from experiences. The concept of causal laws as, or as dependent upon, empirical regularities thus involves a double reduction: of causal laws to constant conjunctions of events and of such events to experiences. This double reduction involves two category mistakes, expressed most starkly in the concepts of the empirical world and of the actuality of causal laws (which presupposes the ubiquity and spontaneity of closed systems).

Now in a world without human beings there would be no experiences and few, if any, constant conjunctions of events. For both experiences and invariances depend, in general, upon human activity. But causal laws do not. Thus in a world without people, the causal laws that science has now as a matter of fact discovered would continue to prevail, though there would be few sequences of events and no experiences with which they were in correspondence. The analysis of experimental activity shows, then, that the assertion of a causal law entails the possibility of a *non-human world*, that it would operate even if it were unknown, just as it continues to operate when its consequent is unrealized (or if it is unperceived or undetected by human beings), that is, outside the conditions that permit its empirical identification. It follows from this that statements about being cannot be reduced to or analysed in terms of statements about knowledge, that ontological questions cannot always be transposed into epistemological terms. Thus the transcendental analysis of experience, the empiricist's criterion of knowledge, establishes both that a philosophical ontology is possible and some propositions in it (for example that causal laws are distinct from patterns of events, and events from experiences). But the epistemic fallacy in philosophy covers or disguises an *implicit ontology* based on the category of experience, and an *implicit realism* based on the presumed characteristics of the objects of experience, viz. atomistic events, and their relations, constant conjunctions. From Hume onwards philosophers have thus allowed, for the sake of avoiding ontology, a particular concept of our knowledge of reality, which they may wish to explicitly reject, to inform and implicitly define their concept of the reality known by science. The result has been a continuing '*ontological tension*' induced by the conflict between the rational intuitions of philosophers about science and the constraints imposed upon their articulation by their inherited ontology. This has led to a nexus of interminably insoluble problems (such as the problem of induction), the anthropocentric displacement of these intuitions and the opening up of a fissure between the methodological implications of epistemology and the realist practice of science.

Now if the objects of our knowledge exist and act independently of the knowledge of which they are the objects, it is equally the case that such knowledge as we actually possess always consists in historically specific social forms. Thus to think our way clearly in the philosophy of science we need to constitute a *transitive* dimension or epistemology to complement the intransitive dimension or ontology already established. It is evident that, unless we do so, any attempt to establish the irreducibility of knowable being – which is the only kind of being with which science is concerned – to thought must end in failure.

5 On the Epistemology of Scientific Change

Once an intransitive dimension is established, both new and changing knowledge of independently existing and acting objects becomes possible. Now *if* we are to avoid the absurdity of the assumption of the production of such knowledge *ex nihilo* (on which more below), it must depend upon the employment of antecedently existing cognitive materials, which I have called the *transitive* objects, and which function as the material causes, of knowledge. So science must be seen as a social process, irreducible to an individual acquisition, whose aim is the production of the knowledge of the mechanisms of the production of phenomena in nature, the intransitive objects of inquiry.

Now as it is clear that the hypothetical entities and mechanisms imagined for the purposes of theory-construction must initially derive at least part of their meaning from some other source (if they are to be capable of functioning as possible explanations at all) theories must already be understood before correspondence rules are laid down for them. Equally this means that the descriptive terms must initially have possessed a meaning independent of them; so that meaning-change is not only possible, but inevitable in the process of science. Now it clearly could come to pass over some scientific transformation that, as Feyerabend and Kuhn have suggested, no meanings are shared in common between two conflicting scientific theories. Can we then still sustain the notion of a rational choice between such incommensurable theories? Yes. For we can allow quite simply that a theory T_A is preferable to a theory T_B, even if they are incommensurable, provided that T_A can explain *under its descriptions* almost all the phenomena that T_B can explain under its descriptions *plus* some significant phenomena that T_B cannot explain. Now patently the possibility of saying this depends upon the explicit recognition of a philosophical ontology or intransitive dimension, and this is of course just what the super-idealists deny. But such an ontology is already implicit in the very formulation of the problem, or definition of the phenomenon, of incommensurability. For to say of two theories that they conflict, clash or are in competition presupposes that there is something – a domain of real objects or relations existing and acting independently of their (conflicting) descriptions – *over* which they clash. Hence incommensurable theories must share a part world in common. If they do not then no sense can be given to the concept of scientific change, and *a fortiori* to the notion of a clash between the theories (for they are now no longer alternatives). Such a total replacement involves neither transformation nor discursive intelligence, but an archetypal intuitive understanding constructing its world in a single synthetic act;[13] and the inexplicable solipsism it entails is devoid of significance for us.

A rational account of scientific development follows on quickly from the establishment of the transcendental realist ontology of structures and differences. Typically the construction of an explanation for, that is the production of the knowledge of the mechanisms of the production of, some identified phenomenon will involve the building of a model, utilizing antecedently existing cognitive resources (not already employed in the description of the domain in question) and operating under the control of something like a logic of analogy and metaphor,[14] of a mechanism, which *if* it were to exist and act in the postulated way would account for the phenomenon in question (a movement of thought which, following Hanson, may be called 'retroduction'[15]). The reality of the postulated mechanism must then, of course, be subjected to empirical scrutiny.[16] (For in general more than one explanation will be consistent with the phenomenon concerned.) Once this is done, the explanation must then in principle itself be explained. And so we have a three-phase schema of development in which, in a continuing dialectic, science identifies a phenomenon (or range of phenomena), constructs explanations for it and empirically tests its explanations, leading to the identification of the generative mechanism at work, which then becomes the phenomenon to be explained; and so on. If the classical empiricist tradition restricts itself to the first phase, the neo-Kantian tradition sees the need for the second, but it either denies the need for, or does not draw the full implications of, the third. Transcendental realism differentiates itself from empirical realism in interpreting the first phase of the dialectic as the invariance of a *result* rather than a *regularity* and from transcendental idealism in allowing that what is *imagined* at the second need not be *imaginary* but may be (and come to be known as) *real*. Now in this continuing process, as deeper levels or strata of reality are successively unfolded, scientists must construct and test their explanations with the cognitive resources and physical tools at their disposal, which in this process are themselves progressively transformed, modified and refined.

On the transcendental realist view of science, then, its essence lies in the *movement* at any one level from knowledge of manifest phenomena to knowledge, produced by means of antecedent knowledge, of the structures that generate them. Now knowledge of deeper levels may correct, as well as explain, knowledge of more superficial ones. In fact one finds a characteristic pattern of description, explanation and redescription of the phenomena identified at any one level of reality. But only a concept of ontological depth (depending upon the concept of real strata apart from our knowledge of strata) enables us to reconcile the twin aspects of scientific development: growth and change. And hence both to avoid the one-sidedness of the accounts of continuists, such as Nagel, and discontinuists, such as Popper, alike; and to sustain (in opposition for example to Feyerabend and Kuhn) the rationality of scientific transformations. Moreover, only the concept of ontological depth can reveal the actual historical stratification of the sciences as anything other than an accident. For this can now be seen as grounded in the multi-tiered stratification of reality, and the consequent logic – of discovery – *that* stratification imposes on science.

This logic must be located in the movement or transition from the identification of invariances to the classification of the structures or mechanisms that account for them. In this transition, Humean, Lockean and Leibnizian knowledge of the objective world-order is progressively obtained. At the first (Humean) level, we just have the invariance of an experimentally produced result. Given such an invariance, science moves immediately to the construction and testing of possible explanations for it. If there is a correct explanation, located in the nature of the thing or the structure of its system, then there is a reason independent of its actual behaviour for that behaviour. Such a reason may be discovered empirically. And, if we can deduce the thing's normic behaviour from it, then the most stringent possible (or Lockean) criterion for our knowledge of natural necessity is satisfied. For example, we may discover that copper has a certain atomic or electronic structure and then be able to deduce its dispositional properties from a statement of that structure. If we can do so, we may then be said to possess knowledge of natural necessity *a posteriori*. Finally, at the third (or Leibnizian) level, we may seek to express our discovery of its structure in an attempted real definition of the substance, process or thing. (Causal laws then appear as the tendencies of natural kinds, realised under closed conditions.) This is not to put an end to inquiry, but a stepping stone to a new process of discovery in which science seeks to unearth the mechanisms responsible for *that* level of reality.

It is clear that for an adequate account of scientific development both the concepts of a stratified and differentiated reality and of knowledge as a produced means of production must be sustained. A critique of empiricism is achieved by noting how knowledge at the Lockean level, that of real essences, is possible, so resolving the paradoxes and problems (most notoriously, of induction) that stem from the dogmatic postulation or unthinking assumption of empirical realism. But a complementary critique of rationalism is achieved by noting that such knowledge is produced, in the context of a dialectic of explanatory and taxonomic knowledge, *a posteriori* – in the transitive, irreducibly empirical process of science.

6 Philosophies as Ideologies of Science

Now the orthodox tradition in the philosophy of science, including both its empiricist and neo-Kantian wings, has uncritically accepted the doctrine, implicit in the empirical realist dissolution of ontology, of the actuality of causal laws; and it has interpreted these, following Hume, as empirical regularities. In this way, by secreting an ontology based on the category of experience, three domains of reality (the domains of the real, the actual and the empirical) are collapsed to one. Now this double reduction prevents the empirical realist from examining the critical question of the conditions under which experience is *in fact* significant in science. In general this depends upon the transformation of both human beings and nature, so that the percipient is skilled and the system in which the phenomenon occurs is closed. It is only when the distinctiveness of the domains is registered, and the possibility of their disjuncture thereby posed, that we can appreciate the enormous effort – in experimental design and scientific education – required to make human experience epistemically significant in science. (Research and teaching are the two most obvious, yet philosophically underanalysed, *tasks* of scientists, just as the laboratory and the classroom are the two most obvious *sites* of science.)

It is evident that the critical omission from orthodox accounts of science is the notion of scientific activity as *work*. Moreover when, as in transcendental idealism, work is recognised, it is treated only as intellectual, and not also as practical labour, in causal exchange with nature. Accordingly, such accounts cannot see knowledge, or at least the achievement of a closure, as a transient social product. Underlying the undifferentiated ontology of empirical realism is thus an individualistic sociology, in which people are regarded as passively sensing (or else, as conventionally deciding upon) given facts and recording their constant conjunctions, that is to say, as passive spectators of a given world, rather than as active agents in a complex one. In the ensemble of conditions and concerns that constitute empirical realism, it is this model of tacitly gendered man that plays the dominant role. For it is the need felt by the philosophy of science, conceiving its role as the guarantor of justified belief (rather than as the analyst of intelligible activities), for certain foundations for scientific knowledge that determines the atomicity of experiences and hence of their ontological counterparts, which in turn necessitates the constancy of their conjunctions and the closure of the systems within which the events occur.

It can thus be seen that the complement of the anthropocentricity implicit in the empiricist analysis of laws, and necessary for it, is neglect of the conscious human activity required for our knowledge of them. For both experiences, together with the facts they ground, and the conjunctions that, when apprehended in sense-experience, provide the empirical grounds for laws, are social products. But the Humean theory depends upon a view of conjunctions existing quite independently of the human activity necessary for them, and hence upon the *fetishism* of the systems within which the conjoined events occur. And it depends upon a view of what is apprehended in immediate sense-experience as a fact constituting an atomistic event or state-of-affairs, and existing independently of the human activity necessary for it, and hence upon the *reification* of atomized facts, apprehended by autonomized minds. When the conjunctions of such facts are reified and identified with causal laws, science becomes an epiphenomenon of nature. Thus, in the intellectual grid within which philosophical ideas are produced, the human-dependence of knowledge (its social nature) and the human-independence of the world (its transcendentally real character), appear in empirical realism as the human-dependence of the world (its empirical nature) and the activity-independence of knowledge (its asocial character). In this way, a naturalized science is purchased at the price of a humanized nature; and the concept of the empirical world finds its counterpart and condition in a reified account of science.

The effects of these transformations are striking. The positivistic concept of a fact as what is more or less immediately apprehended in sense-perception generates characteristic ideologies *for* and *of* science. The former rationalizes the practice of what Kuhn has called 'normal science'; while the latter secretes mystiques of commonsense and/or expertise. Similarly, descriptivist, instrumentalist and fictionalist interpretations of theory, by reducing the ontological import of theories to a given self-certifying experience, serve to exempt our current claims to theoretical knowledge from criticism. Or again, to consider a more general effect, the Humean theory of causality, presupposing a view of the world as closed and completely described, encourages a conception of the social world as unstructured (hence as 'obvious'), undifferentiated and unchanging, so underpinning certain substantive theories of social life.

If empirical realism involves reification and rationalizes normal science, the super-idealist ontology of subjective conceptual realism involves a *voluntarism*, on which theory is unconstrained by either nature or history, which readily lends itself to the rationalisation of so-called 'revolutionary science'. Of course, both ideologies possess a measure of partial adequacy – in that they accord with aspects of our *spontaneous* consciousness in science. Thus we do tend to read the world *as if* it were constituted by facts, rather than particulars, in 'epistemic perception';[17] and in moments of creativity, we experience ideas as coming 'out of the blue' or, as we say (in defiance of Kant's First Analogy), from nowhere.

7 Some Implications of Realism

In conclusion, I want to indicate briefly some of the implications of the new transcendental realist ontology and account of science.

Transcendental realism explicitly asserts the non-identity of the objects of the transitive and intransitive dimensions, of thought and being. And it relegates the notion of a correspondence between them to the status of a metaphor for the aim of an *adequating practice* (in which cognitive matter is worked into a matching representation of a non-cognitive object). It entails acceptance of (i) the principle of *epistemic relativity*, which states that all beliefs are socially produced, so that all knowledge is transient, and neither truth-values nor criteria of rationality exist outside historical time. But it entails the rejection of (ii) the doctrine of *judgemental rela-tivism*, which maintains that all beliefs are equally valid, in the sense that there can be no rational grounds for preferring one to another. It thus stands opposed to epistemic absolutism and epistemic irrationalism alike. Relativists have wrongly inferred (ii) from (i),[18] while anti-relativists have wrongly taken the unacceptability of (ii) as a *reductio* of (i).[19]

By making the possibility of philosophical discourse contingent upon the actuality of social practices, transcendental realism provides a way of integrating philosophical and sociological (or historical) studies of practices such as science. Moreover, through the resolution of the problems generated by the notion of the contingency of the causal con-nection and the critique of the deductivist (and deterministic) theories generated by the notion of its actuality, the scene is set for a philosophy that will once more act as 'underlabourer',[20] and occasional midwife, to the sciences. On the new world-view that emerges both nature and the sciences are stratified and differentiated; and the possibility arises that the behaviour of higher-order (biological) entitities, such as human beings, might both be explanatorily irreducible to (or emergent from) and yet entirely consistent with, lower-order (physical) laws.

It is clearly in the human sciences that the propaedeutic work of philosophy is likely to be most rewarding – if only by allowing a better contrast to be drawn between the conditions and possibilities of the natural and social sciences. Thus the non-availability of spontaneously occurring and the impossibility of experimentally establishing closed systems means that criteria for the rational assessment and development of theories in the human sciences cannot be predictive and so must be exclusively explanatory. Again, the concept-, activity- and space–time-dependence of social structures means that any social science must incor-porate a historically situated hermeneutics; while the condition that social science is a part of its own field of inquiry means that it must be self-reflexive, critical and totalizing in a way in which natural science is not.[21]

But transcendental realism has implications for the practice of natural science itself. For it follows from my argument that scientists, when they are engaged in experimental and theoretical work, are implicitly acting on transcendental realism. But it does not follow that they *realize* they are. Nor does it follow that transcendental realism is the only, or even (at any moment of time) the dominant, philosophy they are acting on. One is therefore as a philosopher of science fully entitled to criticise the practice of any science for its lack of scientificity. The importance of this should be clear. For example, instrumentalism may be used to impede attempts to build realistic scientific theories, just as empirical realism may be used more generally to suppress alternatives. Of course, the possibility of a realistic description or explanation of any particular level of reality may be bounded in practice by semi-permanent conceptual or technical (or even economic) problems, or by the domain assumptions of the particular science, or by the fact that reality is itself bounded for us there. These possibilities limit internal, but do not refute metaphysical realism. For metaphysical realism says nothing about how much there is to know, or about how much of what there is to know can actually be known by us.

Three main positions characterize the history of philosophical reflection on the natural sciences. For empiricism, the natural order is what is given in experience; for idealism, it is what we make or construct; for realism, it is given as a presupposition of our causal investigations of nature, but our knowledge of it is socially and laboriously constructed – with the cognitive resources at our disposal, on the basis of the effects of those investigations. For realism, it is the nature of objects that determines their cognitive possibilities for us; it is humanity that is the contingent phenomenon in nature and knowledge that is, on a cosmic scale, so to speak, accidental.

In science humans come to know human-independent nature, fallibly and variously. This knowledge-relation is both the theme of philosophical reflection and a topic for scientific investigation. But only transcendental realism, by setting humanity *in* nature, is consistent with the historical emergence, and causal investigation, of science (or philosophy) itself. Now any such investigation will itself already presuppose an intransitive (and so non-human) ontology of transfactually active and potent structures. This ontology is realism. And it is a necessary presupposition of natural science. But it remains an open question how far, and with what results this principle will actually be carried out in the laboratories and classrooms, journals and monographs, colloquia and conference halls of our actual historical sciences.

3

Feyerabend and Bachelard: Two Philosophies of Science

In 1934 when Gaston Bachelard published his *Nouvel Esprit Scientifique*[1] and Karl Popper's *Logik der Forschung*[2] appeared few philosophers would have dissented from the view that science develops in a linear or monistic fashion, so as to leave meaning and truth-value unchanged, on the basis provided by common experience. Meyerson had even undertaken to show that the theory of relativity could be *deduced* from Newtonian principles[3] and it was widely held that, for their part, the concepts of classical physics were just a refinement of the concepts of daily life.[4] Since then Bachelard, in France, and Popper, in England, have been more than any others responsible for the seeping into the general philosophical consciousness (which includes the consciousness of scientists in their reflection upon their work) of the fact, profoundly revolutionary for philosophy, of the phenomenon of scientific discontinuity (with respect to common-sense or experience) and change. In strikingly similar terms Bachelard and Popper attempted to register this phenomenon. Yet neither of them, nor the theoretical traditions they inaugurated, have succeeded in grasping its full significance for philosophy. Dominique Lecourt's *Marxism and Epistemology*[5] and Paul Feyerabend's *Against Method*[6] constitute in a sense extended commentaries on these traditions and their attempts to theorize scientific discontinuity and change – the one, a respectful tribute 'from outside'; the other, a 'wicked' polemic from within.

Why do scientific discontinuity and change have such disturbing consequences for philosophy? Their recognition snaps the privileged relationship between subject and object which, in classical philosophy, uniquely ties thought to things. Thought cannot now be viewed as a mechanical function of given objects (as in empiricism); nor can the activity of creative subjects be regarded as endowing the world with things (as in idealism); nor is any combination of the two possible. In short, it becomes necessary to distinguish clearly between the unchanging real objects that exist outside the scientific process and the changing cognitive

26

objects that are produced within science as a function of scientific practice. Let me call the former *intransitive* and the latter *transitive* objects; the theoretical space in which to talk about them will accordingly become the intransitive and transitive dimensions respectively of the philosophy of science.

I now want to put forward the following theses: Any adequate account of science depends upon the explicit recognition of the necessity for both, and the non-identity of the objects of, the intransitive and transitive dimensions. The history of philosophy is, on the other hand, characterized by persistent attempts to reduce one to the other. These attempts are necessarily unsuccessful so that they result merely in the generation of an implicit or disguised ontology (in the intransitive dimension) or sociology (in the transitive one). But the *attempt* to do so secures the dominance in philosophy of an empiricist ontology and an individualist sociology; and it is in this attempt and its results that the ideological value of classical philosophy lies. An adequate account of science depends, by contrast, upon the development of an explicit non-empiricist ontology and a non-individualist conception of scientific activity (or sociology, in the special sense of the word I am using here).[7]

Now in the operation that structures classical philosophy, empiricist ontology ⇌ individualist sociology, typically, at least, it is knowledge and its subject, man, that plays the leading role. Thus it may be the need expressed for certain foundations for knowledge that results in the establishment of the implicit empiricist ontology – a process covered by the collapse of the concept of an intransitive dimension in the philosophy of science (that is, by the denial of the need for an ontology). Consider, for example, the empiricist variant dominant at the time Bachelard wrote *The New Scientific Mind* and Popper wrote *The Logic of Scientific Discovery*. In response to the question posed by scepticism, knowledge is restricted to what is known for certain; it is then shown, in a phenomenalistic analysis of perception, that what is known in perception is certain; only perception gives knowledge of things (which is a basic principle of empiricism); hence knowledge must be of what is given in perception. Thus on the one hand only items directly given in sense-experience may be said to be known to exist; and, on the other, the world may now, from the point of view of epistemology, be regarded as constituted by facts which are as given as the real objects of perception and certain as a result of the analysis which identifies them with the latter. In this way facts, which are social products, stand in, in philosophy, for the particulars of the world and there is no need to bother with the question of whether things exist independently of them. It should be noted that ontology is denied while being presupposed. For, of course, it must be assumed that the world is such that it could be the object of such a cognitive operation of man. And, in particular, it is presupposed that it consists of discrete atomistic events or states-of-affairs, the ontological surrogates of the knowledge-constituting experiences, revealing an invariant order of coexistence in space and succession over time. As a result of this operation scientific knowledge becomes as certain as what exists and as commonplace as the activity (perception) that establishes it. The question – of scepticism – which initiates the philosophical play must be posed so that philosophy can give the answer its function demands.

The immediate ideological effects, in the transitive dimension, of this operation are clear. Scientific knowledge is *certain*, its development is monistic. At the same time it is *safe*, it does not threaten the spontaneous consciousness of ordinary life (for it is built up out of units available to it). Thus we have both an ideology *for* science and an ideology *of* science: the former constituting beliefs rationalizing the scientific status quo, in Kuhn's terminology, the practice of 'normal science';[8] the latter constituting beliefs *about* science, rationalizing the wider social status quo, bourgeois society as such. But this operation has ideological effects, though less obvious ones, in the *intransitive* dimension too.

Once we break the privileged relationship between subject and object and clearly distinguish between the transitive and intransitive dimensions of the philosophy of science, as we must once we register the discontinuities of scientific knowledge both over time and with respect to common experience, 'scientific knowledge' ceases to be an essential property of either persons or things: it becomes something distinctive, with a site (and worth a study) of its own, bearing relations which are contingent and problematic to both. Now neither Bachelard nor Feyerabend have a concept of the intransitive dimension of the philosophy of science, and they are both still committed to an essentially empiricist ontology. Moreover, in both cases their accounts of the transitive dimension are marred by individualistic deformations (in Bachelard's case, psychologistic, in Feyerabend's, voluntaristic). These are, I intend to show, the fundamental weaknesses of their philosophical positions. It is because of this continuing commitment to an empiricist ontology and an (at least residually) individualist sociology that, though their work marks, in different respects, a great advance on the past, neither of them is capable of providing us with the philosophy that science deserves, and that social science – inescapably – needs.

The most important influence on Feyerabend has been Karl Popper, and to understand the latter's philosophy one must go back to the Vienna of the 1920s where he was a student. As Popper puts it, 'there had been a revolution in Austria: the air was full of revolutionary slogans and ideas, and new and often wild theories' – Einstein's theory of relativity, Marx's

theory of history, Freud's psycho-analysis and Adler's 'individual psychology'.[9] In this context a group of philosophers, whose leading members
were Carnap, Neurath and Schlick, tried to work out a criterion for distinguishing genuinely scientific from non-scientific (or 'metaphysical') propositions. Much influenced by Wittgenstein, they constructed a system,
logical positivism – in essence a restatement of Machian empiricism in a
form made possible by the development of Russellian logic – according to
which our knowledge of the world could be reconstructed from
elementary propositions expressed in sense-experience. Scientific propositions were about the world, known in sense-experience; if a sentence did
not refer directly or indirectly to sense-experience, that is if no possible
observation was relevant to the determination of its truth-value, then it
was unscientific and, according to the logical positivists, meaningless.
Attempting to formulate a criterion which would show propositions
actually accepted in science to be justified, and not unreasonably
assuming that science could know at least some propositions to be true (or
that it possessed some positive knowledge), they formulated their criterion
for the demarcation of scientific from non-scientific propositions in terms
of the *verifiability* (i.e. susceptibility to positive test) of the former.

Such a solution did not satisfy Popper who was much impressed, as
Bachelard was in France, by Einstein's *refutation* of Newtonian mechanics
(which had been the most successful scientific theory ever invented, and
for so long the philosopher's paradigm of knowledge) that presaged the
more or less rapid reorganization of the whole of physics. This showed,
empirically, that no scientific proposition was certain. Moreover there
were also compelling *logical* reasons for rejecting the positivists' criterion.
For its acceptance would in effect rule out just those propositions most
distinctive of science, as it is clear that no finite number of observations can ever verify a universal statement, such as 'all metals conduct
electricity'. But a third consideration was decisive for Popper: the contrast
between the apparent vulnerability of physics and the apparent invulner-
ability of Marxism, psychoanalysis, and so on, (or their theorists) to refutation. It was easy to find confirmations: the hallmark of a critical
scientific *attitude* was to look for refutations. This led Popper to a
question, one might say, of scientific *morality*. What distinguished the
scientist from the non-scientist was that the former was prepared to
specify in advance the conditions under which he would be prepared to
give up his theory. And it was just this that, according to Popper, Marxists
and psychoanalysts, unlike physicists, refused to do. Thus history, logic
and morality all pointed to *falsifiability* as the demarcating criterion of a
science.

Popper soon saw that his work on the demarcation problem enabled a
reconsideration of the traditional problem of induction. No number of

positive instances can ever confirm a universal generalization such as 'all swans are white' or 'all metals conduct electricity'; yet all, or practically all, or the most important part of our scientific knowledge consists of (or depends upon) propositions of this form. A problem, a scandal; indeed 'the scandal of philosophy', Broad had pronounced it in 1926.[10] Popper, rejecting attempts by Carnap and others to give such propositions a probabilistic basis, pointed out that, though they could not be confirmed or made probable (in the sense of the calculus of probability), they could be falsified – by the discovery of a single counter-instance. Scientific propositions and theories, then, though they cannot be confirmed, can be refuted.

This, in turn, led Popper to propose a new general view of science. Induction, he agreed with Hume, cannot be justified. But this does not mean that science is irrational. For induction plays no part at all in science. Science does not proceed inductively, gradually accumulating positive instances until generalizations become probable or, in the terminology of the modern neo-Humean Goodman, entrenched; nor does science depend upon any such processes. Rather generalizations are first proposed as conjectures and then subjected to rigorous test by drawing out their implications; when a theory is refuted, it is replaced by another bolder conjecture, and so on. Science is hypothetico-deductive, not inductive. And it progresses precisely through its mistakes.[11]

Popper's system differed from classical empiricism in yet another respect: refuting observation statements were not regarded as theory-independent reflections of a given world. All statements are theory-impregnated (or theoretical) to a greater or lesser extent: statements are accepted as observational, as being basic or potentially refuting, as a result of methodological decision, by agreement (convention). (Conventionalism may be regarded as an alternative way to phenomenalism of securing a link between human beings and the world – in that instead of the world naturalistically determining our knowledge of it, human beings decide, by convention, what level of their knowledge is to count as knowledge of the empirical world.) Thus Popper completed a remarkable inversion and displacement of the problematic of classical empiricism. His fallibilism enabled him to avoid complete Humean scepticism, though at the price of restricting our knowledge to knowledge of error, of scientific mistakes; while his conventionalism allowed him to sustain the most rationalistic account of science since Kant and Whewell, though at the cost of leaving science with an entirely man-made empirical base. And in the process he worked out a view of science which made revolutionary change of the sort that was occurring in physics its very essence.

Two other philosophers are important for an understanding of the recent development of Feyerabend's work – Popper's successor at LSE, Imre Lakatos, to whom *Against Method* is dedicated; and Thomas Kuhn, whose *Structure of Scientific Revolutions* was the subject of impassioned attack by Popperians, including both Lakatos and initially Feyerabend,[12] who saw it as undermining the idea of the rationality of science (Lakatos) and/or as providing a rationale for scientific conservatism (Feyerabend).[13] Lakatos's fundamental concern in his brilliant development of Popper's philosophy of science was to try and salvage from the historiographical material provided by Kuhn and others the idea that science was a rational enterprise, in which progress was (or could be) made – a proposition to which Kuhn, as a good sociologist, stubbornly refused to subscribe.[14]

Both Lakatos and Kuhn agreed, however, that the Popperian system could not, at least in its original form, stand up to the material provided by history: that, in short, falsificationism was itself refuted by history.[15] (Popper, Lakatos grumbled, 'does not raise, let alone answer the question: "under what conditions would you give up your demarcation criterion?"'[16]) Every theory was always immersed in 'an ocean of anomalies'; so that, strictly speaking, every theory was always falsified. In this context actual scientists had to be much more dogmatic, or tenacious than the Popperian model allowed. Moreover, as Duhem had pointed out,[17] every theory was formulated subject to an implicit *ceteris paribus* clause, so that the hypothesis of an intervening or disturbing influence could always be invoked to explain away apparent counter-instances.[18] Conditions, therefore, could not be specified in advance as to when a theory should be given up, just because of the possibility of the implicit *ceteris paribus* clause breaking down; so that, as Lakatos put it, 'exactly the most admired scientific theories simply fail to forbid any observable state of affairs'.[19] Then again in real history falsifications never issued from a simple dyadic confrontation between a *single* theory and a set of facts; but between *two* (or more) theories and their facts; that is, in real history falsifications were *replacements*.[20] And the replacement, when it came, normally consisted in a refinement and modification of the existing theory, rather than its complete rejection. The original Popperian model had left a mystery: after the refutation – what? Or to put it another way it could not account for the genesis of any new conjecture or research line.[21] In real history scientific theories do not spring from the void – but from the development and reworking of cognitive material that pre-exists them, necessitating the creative employment of ideas from adjacent fields,[22] Bachelard's 'scientific loans'.[23]

In Lakatos's 'methodology of scientific research programmes', a theory T is preferable to theory T′ if it has excess empirical content (i.e. predicts novel facts), some of which is 'corroborated'. (In Popperian terminology a theory is said to be 'corroborated' if it escapes unscathed when subjected to empirical test.) Thus a counter-instance is now not even necessary for a falsification. The subject of normative appraisal ceases to be theories and becomes sequences of theories or *research programmes*, constructed around a hard core, unfalsifiable by methodological fiat.[24] A research programme is *progressive* if it results in some corroborated excess empirical content; that is, as long as its theoretical growth anticipates its empirical growth, i.e. as long as it keeps predicting novel facts with some success; it is *degenerating* when it does not.[25] In this way Lakatos claimed to be able to do justice to the continuity of scientific development, scouted by Popper and stressed by Kuhn, without sacrificing the essential Popperian idea of the rationality of scientific change.[26] It is this claim that Feyerabend disputes in *Against Method*. For 'if it is unwise to reject theories the moment they are born because they might grow and improve, then it is also unwise to reject research programmes on a downward (degenerating) trend because they might recover and attain unforeseen splendour (the butterfly emerges when the caterpillar has reached its lowest stage of degeneration).'[27] Copernicus followed not Ptolemy and Aristotle, but the mad Pythagorean, Philoloas.[28] A sequence $Ta_i \ldots Ta_n$ may stagnate over $t_i \ldots t_j$ but progress after t_j. So the methodology of scientific research programmes, because it cannot anticipate the future development of a science, is powerless to tell it what to do.[29]

Feyerabend, unable to conceive of criteria of rationality that do not satisfy this traditional requirement of philosophy, concludes from this that scientific change must be irrational. But he had already launched an attack on the idea of the rationality of science from another set of considerations, in which not just the possibility of a rational reconstruction by philosophy but the very possibility of objective grounds for a rational choice between conflicting theories *within science* was called into question. Both Feyerabend and Kuhn had pointed out that the history of science is characterized by meaning-change as well as inconsistency (or 'falsification');[30] and had raised the possibility that the conceptual structures of two competing theories might be so radically different that they shared no statements in common, so that they were literally 'incommensurable'.[31] Does it follow, as Feyerabend and Kuhn contend, that there can then be no rational grounds for choosing between them? No. For we can allow that a theory T_a is preferable to a theory T_b, even if they are incommensurable, provided that T_a can explain *under its descriptions* almost all the phenomena $P_1 \ldots P_n$ that T_b can explain under *its* descriptions plus some significant phenomena that T_b cannot explain. This depends of course upon an explicit recognition of the need for a philosophical ontology or intransitive dimension in the philosophy of science. But such an ontology is implicit in the very formulation of the problem. For to say that two theories conflict, clash or are in competition presupposes that there is something – a domain of real objects or relations existing and acting independently of their descriptions – *over* which they clash. (No one bothers to say that the rules of cricket and football are incommensurable.) Of course, it may be that the two theories are only in competition over a very small domain[32] (as may be the case for example with Marxism and psychoanalysis), so that Lakatosian-type decision rules are of very little help in choosing between them,[33] but this is not then the problem of incommensurability.[34]

> *Given any rule, however 'fundamental' or 'necessary' for science, there are always circumstances when it is advisable not only to ignore the rule, but to adopt its opposite.*[35]

Feyerabend's recent intellectual development may be described as, in certain respects, a journey from an ultra-Popperian Popper to an ultra-Kuhnian Kuhn.[36] In 'Problems of Empiricism' he had advanced arguments, which were to be developed by Lakatos, for a *theoretical pluralism* as the basis of every genuine test procedure.[37] And, like Popper and Lakatos, he still believed it was possible to give objective grounds for choosing between theories (even when they were 'incommensurable').[38] In *Against Method*, advocating a *theoretical anarchism* (or 'dadaism' as he prefers to style his philosophy),[39] these positions are abandoned: there are neither criteria for choosing between theories within science nor criteria for choosing between science and other forms of life.[40]

Science, Feyerabend contends, is much more 'sloppy and irrational than its methodological image'.[41] Indeed, 'there is not a single rule, however plausible and firmly grounded in epistemology, that is not violated at some time or another'.[42] 'Progress', according to whatever criterion or standard one chooses to adopt,[43] 'occurred only because some thinkers either decided not to be bound by certain "obvious" methodological rules, or because they *unwittingly broke* them.'[44] This is not just a fact about the history of science but was absolutely necessary for it. The reason: 'history generally, and the history of revolutions in particular, is always richer in content, more varied, more many-sided, more lively and subtle' (Lenin) than even the best methodologists can imagine.[45] The sciences, like nations and governments (Hegel), cannot learn from history but have to act in and out of it.[46] *Decisions* must be made *in* science, which cannot be (derived from history or) anticipated by philosophy.

Moreover rationalistic philosophers of science forget Robespierre's dictum that 'virtue without terror is ineffective'; that in real science as distinct from the philosophers' fantasy of it arguments must have causal efficacy as well as logical force.[47] What rationality cannot achieve must be secured by social or psychological pressures.[48] Creative scientists are ruthless opportunists, disdaining no view, however absurd or immoral; not 'truth-freaks'. Galileo defeated his rivals 'because of his style and his clever techniques of persuasion, because he [wrote] in Italian rather than Latin, and [appealed] to people who were temperamentally opposed to the old ideas and the standards of learning connected with them'.[49] No distinction between 'internal' and 'external' history can save the rationality of science. For a scientific development which appears 'rational' may succeed only because of compensating factors in its external history. Galileo's ignorance of the elementary principles of telescopic vision was bliss.[50] And political interference was a condition for the successful revival of traditional medicine in Communist China.[51] As for the methodology of scientific research programmes, it can only be given practical force, as Lakatos intends that it should,[52] by making it the core of *conservative* institutions.[53] The differing rhetorics of Lakatos and Feyerabend thus reflect fundamentally different attitudes towards freedom of research in science.[54]

For Feyerabend, then, science *is* an essentially anarchistic enterprise. No unique aim or method characterizes it; there can be no *theory* of science. Moreover there can be no criterion distinguishing it from 'any other ideology'. Indeed it is much closer to myth than is generally recognized.[55] A nominalist about science, Feyerabend is a sceptic about its achievements, both cognitive and social. Not only can it not give us any knowledge guarantees,[56] it is not nearly as difficult or as successful as its propagandists would have us believe.[57] Above all it is potentially subversive of a most important liberty: *our freedom to choose what we believe.* Hence 'the separation of state and *church* must be complemented by the separation of state and *science* . . . [as] our only chance to achieve a humanity we are capable of, but have never fully realized.'[58]

Not only is science essentially anarchistic but theoretical anarchism, Feyerabend says, is essential for the progress of science. Yet Feyerabend denies that he is proposing or pre-supposing any criterion of progress.[59] Given this, any anarchistic move which helps progress on one criterion will *impede* it on some other. What, then, is the status of *Against Method* itself? Feyerabend, at least on the face of it, certainly seems to be making the proposal that one should not be bound by explicit rules in science. In Feyerabend's science the policies pursued by individual scientists become 'free', a matter of personal choice (or democratic vote):[60] he, or she, can maintain or change his, or her, aims equally 'as a result of argument, or of boredom, or of a conversion experience or to impress a mistress'.[61] In short, science is an activity in which anything goes. Now if this is good advice according to one criterion or standard S_1, it will be bad advice according to some other S_2. Hence there is as much reason to ignore as to accept the advice of *Against Method*. Feyerabend even seems to accept this. 'To be a true dadaist, one must also be an anti-dadaist.'[62] (If the dadaist 'not only has no programmes, but is against all programmes',[63] then he must also be against the programme of *Against Method* itself.)

What then is the point of *Against Method*? Like an undercover agent who works on both sides of the fence,[64] Feyerabend plays the game of reason in order to undermine the authority of reason.[65] His position is not self-refuting because it is clear that Feyerabend is in fact committed, in *Against Method*, to higher-order values. These may be summed up as: *for freedom* and *against science*. His dadaism is merely a front, a tactical ploy designed to confuse the enemy.

At a first level, then, Feyerabend is arguing that individuals in pursuit of their private aims or essential humanity should be unfettered by any methodological restrictions. For freedom, then; and against method. But it is not just method in general that he wants to cut down to size. His target is more specific: science. 'Is it not possible', he asks, echoing Kierkegaard, 'that my activity as an objective observer of nature will weaken my strength as a human being?'[66] For Feyerabend 'science has no greater authority than any other form of life. Its aims are certainly not more important than those guiding the lives in a religious community or in a tribe united by a myth. At any rate, they have no business restricting the lives, the thoughts, the education of the members of a free society where everyone should have a chance to make up his own mind and to live in accordance with the social beliefs he finds most acceptable.'[67] For freedom, then; and against science. A familiar opposition,[68] which received its quintessential expression in the manichean world of late nineteenth century German thought, posited on the neo-Kantian dichotomy of nature and spirit[69] – an opposition which informed the philosophy of Lukács[70] and of the Frankfurt school and which has now produced out of Vienna in 1919, by a necessary logic set in motion by Popper's simple inversion of positivism, for Berkeley in 1967, a new *Lebensphilosophie*: the philosophy of flower power, dressed up as a dadaism.

Now in all the avatars of this opposition it is never clear if what is being opposed to freedom is:

(1) some particular conception of science, such as empiricism, or of its role in the social totality, such as scientism;

(2) the existing practices and institutions of the sciences; or

(3) scientific knowledge as such.

Lukács, for example, uncritically identifies natural science with the positivist concept of it; and much of what Feyerabend has to say is extremely well taken as a necessary critique of the historical processes of

the production of knowledge in the contemporary world.[71] It is probable
that Feyerabend is attacking, in the name of freedom, all three. Let us see
whether he succeeds in his attack on scientific knowledge and isolate his
concept of it.

Paraphrasing Mill, Feyerabend's hero, we could say that for Feyerabend the only freedom that deserves the name is that of doing one's own
thing in one's own way;[72] specifically, we are to be free to believe what we
choose. But how do we choose? This depends, presumably, upon our aims
and objectives (for which, of course, Feyerabend can give only a purely
voluntaristic explanation, that is, no explanation at all). Human beings are
just subject to certain desires (appetites and aversions, in Hobbes) or feelings
(pleasure and pain, in Hume, Bentham and Mill), which are in the last
instance neurophysiologically given; and we act so as to maximize our
enjoyment (pleasure) or minimize our suffering (pain). Feyerabend's
conception of action thus takes its place in a famous lineage. But how
do they act? For Hume and Mill by the application of their reason, in the
last instance the sole identifying characteristic of human beings, to a
simple maximization problem (or its dual, a minimization one). For Hume
'reason is and ought only to be the slave of the passions'.[73] But in Feyerabend the passions lack their necessary complement: an efficient slave.
Knowledge may not be the most important social activity, but it is the one
upon which the achievement of any human objective depends. Freedom,
in the sense Feyerabend attaches to it, depends upon knowledge (praxis
presupposes theory); we can only be as free as our knowledge is reliable
and complete. We are not free to choose what we believe if we are to
attain the kinds of objectives Feyerabend mentions. Only if belief-in-itself
was the sole end of human action would Feyerabend be warranted in such
an assumption.

In this context it may be useful to refer to Feyerabend's use of Lenin and
Galileo. He makes great play of Lenin's tactical flexibility. But Lenin's
tactical flexibility was subordinated to a specific aim (revolution) and
informed by a specific theory or heuristic (historical materialism). Lukács
remarks that 'Lenin's so-called *realpolitik* was never that of an empirical
pragmatist, but the practical culmination of an essentially theoretical attitude'.[74] And he adds that 'one of Lenin's most characteristic and creative
traits was that he never ceased to learn theoretically from reality, while
remaining ever equally ready for action. This determines one of the most
striking and apparently paradoxical attributes of his theoretical style: he
never saw his lessons from reality as closed, but what he had learned from
it was so organized and directed in him that action was possible at any
given moment'.[75]

Feyerabend is at his most convincing in his case-study of Galileo's successful defence and development of the Copernican Revolution in astronomy, which forms the main empirical ground for his conclusions in philosophy. He describes the way in which, in order to 'defuse' Aristotelian objections to the Copernican hypothesis, Galileo first identified the 'natural (or spontaneous) interpretations' of experience that the Aristotelians made use of in their objections; and then, surreptitiously, using the Platonic method of anamnesis, replaced them with others, in turn inimical to Aristotelianism. Thus Galileo drew the attention of his contemporaries away from the old paradigm of the motion of compact objects in stable surroundings (deer in a forest) towards cases of relative motion in moving systems such as boats and coaches, insinuating that they already implicitly possessed, but incompletely applied, the Copernican conceptual system (and smoothing over difficulties arising from the substitution in an ad hoc way). But this substitution presupposed of course precisely what was to be proved, that is, the relativity of all motion. Moreover Galileo set out to change not just the natural interpretations of experience but its 'sensory core' as well – in particular through his use of the telescope. Ignoring both those telescopic phenomena that did not support Copernicanism and those phenomena that did not support the telescope (i.e. the theory that telescopic phenomena provide an accurate picture of the sky), Galileo nevertheless seized on the few telescopic phenomena that did indicate Copernicanism as a triumphant vindication of it. And Galileo succeeded in all this, according to Feyerabend, only because of factors, such as his ignorance of optics and the changing class structure of Italian society, on any criterion extrinsic to the internal history of his science.

Galileo's procedures are clearly irrational by the standards of orthodox philosophy of science. But is Feyerabend correct to conclude from this that they are *per se* irrational? His own continuing commitment to an essentially empiricist ontology prevents him from seeing in Galileo's procedures an alternative rationale. He quotes Galileo's 'astonishment' at the way in which 'Aristarchus and Copernicus were able to make reason so conquer sense that, in defiance of the latter, the former became mistress of their belief'[76] and tells us some of the ways in which Galileo set out to change sense. But why? For Galileo, human sense-experience depends upon the contingencies of our sense-organs, the aids to them and the beliefs associated with them. There is thus no necessary correspondence between reality and sense-experience. However sense-experience so impresses itself upon our consciousness that it takes an effort to appreciate the possibility of a disjuncture between it and reality. Copernicus made this leap, Galileo praises him for it, and begins the arduous task of bringing the empirical basis of science into line with what reason (theory) has shown must be so. At the same time because both science and scientists are social products

Galileo, on this interpretation, has few illusions (and might have even fewer had he been able to read *Against Method*) about the tactics that must be employed in this project.

In Feyerabend the voluntaristic[77] and sceptical[78] elements already present in Popper's philosophy are taken to their limit; and *Against Method* ends in a relativism far more complete than anything to be found in Kuhn.[79] Feyerabend's intentions are *humanistic*; his method *empiricist*. Empiricism was a *theory* of the production of knowledge; in denying the very possibility of a theory of the production of knowledge (the prescription '*anything goes*' is based on the idea (theory) that '*anything has gone*' in the history of science), Feyerabend produces not a philosophy of science which is empiricist but an empiricist philosophy of science. (Or we could say that Feyerabend is an empiricist in the philosophy of the philosophy of science.) Let us see how this transformation occurs.

The starting point is the Humean problem of induction. This is the problem of:

(A)   what warrant have we for supposing that the course of nature will not change.

This, as stated, is an *ontological* problem. If nature is non-uniform then established generalizations may break down. (A) demands some guarantee of, or for, nature that this will not be the case. But because Hume was an *empirical realist* (that is, identified the world with our experience of it, the domains of the real and the empirical),[80] (A) became equivalent of the problem of:

(AB)   what warrant have we for supposing the regularities in our experience will continue.

Two operations riveted Hume's philosophy of science: a *fusion* of the world and experience (a conflation of the ontological and epistemic orders, and paralleling this of the intransitive and transitive dimensions in the philosophy of science); and a *reduction* of our knowledge to the level of experience (which was, as constitutive of the very nature of reality itself, held to be certain). Reductionism was gradually seen to be untenable. But the conflation of the epistemic and ontological orders introduced by Hume led to the generalization of problem (AB) in the following direction:

(B)   what warrant have we for supposing some general proposition, statement or theory is true.

This, as stated, is an *epistemological* problem. It demands some guarantee of, or for, our knowledge. Popper restated (B) as:

(B)′   what warrant have we for supposing some general proposition, statement or theory is true or false.

And Lakatos further generalized it in the following way:

(B)″   what grounds have we for rationally choosing between theories, deciding how to proportion research time, distribute research funds, and so on.

It is of course vital to keep (B) and its derivatives clearly distinct from (A). (B) seems particularly apposite once we are faced with the phenomena of scientific change, or change in knowledge of objects; whereas (A) raises the spectre of change in the (intransitive) objects of knowledge.

Now Hume's answer to (A) was a sceptical one; we have no warrant: *anything might happen* (in the world). Feyerabend's answer to (B)-(B)″ is similarly sceptical; we have no warrant or grounds: *anything goes* (in science). Feyerabend's position is thus, in the transitive dimension, directly analogous to that of Hume in the intransitive dimension. It is an empiricist answer to a displacement onto the plane of epistemology of the Humean ontological problem of induction. And as such it represents a significant limit in philosophy. Of course whereas Hume presupposed ontological regularity, Feyerabend argues for epistemological irregularity. (The opposition between freedom and science, which was for Kant and Dilthey an ontological one, differentiating objects of possible knowledge, now appears, in Feyerabend, on the plane of epistemology, differentiating possible forms of the knowledge process.) And because of this their ideological effects differ (through Hume science becomes certain and safe; in Feyerabend it is dangerous and illusory). But just as Hume's rejection of theory (in science) led, formally, to the impossibility of knowledge, so Feyerabend's rejection of any theory of science leads to the impossibility of any theory of knowledge, and hence of any criteria of rationality for its production.

Any theory of science as rational depends upon a resolution of the (ontological) problem of induction and any resolution of the problem of induction depends upon a rejection of the ontology that informs it, and in particular the empirical realist doctrine that laws are, or depend upon, empirical regularities.[81]

Now a distinction between causal laws and empirical invariances (patterns of events) is implied by experimental activity. For in an experiment scientists produce (as a result of certain human operations) a sequence of events, but they do not produce the causal law their activity

enables them to identify. Causal laws must thus persist and act independently of empirical invariances and the activity of human beings alike.
The philosophy of science must thus draw a distinction between the *real*
structures, mechanisms and systems of relations at work in nature (and
society), providing the ontological basis of causal laws, and the manifest
(or *actual*) patterns of events they generate, whether humans are causal
agents in their production or not.

But experimental activity also implies that empirical invariances are not
in general available, being restricted to only a few effectively *closed*
contexts. Once we realize that they occur only under very special conditions and that in general, outside astronomy, they have to be laboriously
worked for in the laboratories of science, the very grounds for the problem
of induction collapse. Nature is *not* uniform, but its *stratification*, which
must be assumed to be in principle open-ended, provides each science
with its own inductive warrant.[82]

Once we constitute a non-empiricist ontology that pitches invariance in
nature at the level of *structure*, not *event* (and distinguish clearly between
structure, event and experience), it becomes possible to discern in the
historical development of the sciences a certain characteristic pattern or
dialectic of discovery. In the schema that emerges *ontological depth*
appears as a condition of the development of the sciences, so that knowledge *grows* (as well as changes) as new and deeper layers of reality are
progressively identified, described and explained. In this dialectic, which I
have elaborated elsewhere, the rationality of the experimental and theoretical procedures of the sciences becomes manifest. Within this schema,
the methodology of scientific research programmes, if developed in a more
'rationalistic'[83] and materialist direction and if supplemented by a more
adequate concept of the external history of a science (whose weakness
Feyerabend clearly demonstrates), provides some useful rules for the
appraisal of historical situations. But only if science has returned to it its
most precious possession, its *aim*: the attempt to discover the reasons, for
all we know necessarily opaque to humankind, for the phenomena of
nature; to fathom the intransitive structure of the world.

Against Method is an important sceptical work, which should serve to
rouse dogmatic rationalists and materialists from their slumbers. It is a
provocative and challenging book, full of interesting material; well worth
reading. 'Always remember', Feyerabend cautions his readers, 'the
demonstrations and rhetorics used do not express any "deep convictions"
of mine'.[84] The serious student should not be misled by this disclaimer.
Much of the time Feyerabend *is* joking.

Science no longer raises up a world by a magical force immanent in reality, but rather by a rational force immanent to the mind.[85]

Gaston Bachelard is perhaps best (or even only?) known to English readers as a result of Louis Althusser's systematic use of the concept of an 'epistemological break' in his attempt to register the radical discontinuity between Marx's science of history and the ideologies that preceded it.[86] It is fitting therefore that the first full-length study of his work to be published in English should be by a pupil of Althusser, Dominique Lecourt; and that *Marxism and Epistemology* should not only attempt a 'materialist' reading of Bachelard, but specifically take up the subject of the relationship between materialism and his work. This useful introduction to Bachelard also contains essays on Canguilhem, Bachelard's successor at the University of Paris, and Foucault.

Bachelard's neglect by the so-called 'analytic' (largely Anglo-Saxon) tradition in philosophy is difficult to explain. It certainly cannot be ascribed to cultural chauvinism alone: both Bergson and Meyerson received considerable attention in their time. Duhem was a major influence on Popper; Poincaré, the founder of conventionalism, had an important influence on the Vienna Circle; and Koyré has been the most important influence on Kuhn. Whatever the causes of this neglect, the superficial similarities between Popper and Bachelard are striking. If Popper's philosophy could be described as a 'negativism'[87] Bachelard specifically characterized his as a 'philosophie du non',[88] both in resonance with the revolutionary upheavals occurring across the whole spectrum of scientific knowledge and in defiance of the ideologies that threatened to emasculate them (by reabsorbing them into a continuist schema or by some procedure of reduction to the categories of everyday life). For both, scientific *error* played a positive function, constituting an (or the) essential moment in the production of scientific knowledge.[89] Both, moreover, lived in constant regard for the sciences of their time, and inaugurated traditions characterized by a detailed concern for their histories.

But whereas Popper stressed scientific change, Bachelard stressed the rupture involved between scientific work and ordinary experience. Popper's excessive tolerance of common-sense[90] is paralleled by Bachelard's ambivalence about the nature of the reorganizations that take place within knowledge once a science has been constituted. It is absolutely vital to insist upon the reality both of scientific change and of the break between scientific and ordinary experience.

Bachelard wrote two sets of books: one on the philosophy of science; and the other on art and poetics. And in many ways the pivotal point of his work lies in his contrast between science and *reverie*. Scientific work requires a break from reverie, the dreamlike character of everyday experience that forms the stuff of art and poetry. Science is the domain of reason; art that of imagination; their independence is total, though both have an equal right to exist. As Dagognet says 'Bachelard never ceased to deepen the opposition between the two worlds . . . so much so that they came to correspond negatively to each other'.[91] Thus Bachelard contrasts the torture that the imagination undergoes in scientific abstraction with the delights that reason finds in it and the happiness that it recovers in reverie. Yet despite this contrast, there is a unity in Bachelard's thought: art and science have a common origin, accessible only to psychoanalysis, in the projective or creative activity of mind. Thus in art 'the subject projects his dream upon things'; whereas in science 'above the subject, beyond the immediate object . . . is the project'[92] – an objectivication (or inter-subjectivication) of reason. Reason and imagination constitute, then, the two aspects of mind.

In *The Psycho-analysis of Fire*[93] Bachelard rejects the common account of the discovery of fire as the chance outcome of the rubbing together of two sticks, seeing it instead as the necessary outcome of the symbolic representation of sexual intercourse. Thus fire is as much metaphorical passion as passion is metaphorical fire. Now fire which, because of this psychic connection, had been the subject of incessant pre-scientific speculation, was destroyed as a concept by Lavoisier's theory of combustion. And yet it retained its psychic power and fascination in reverie. The natural tendencies of the mind are anti-scientific and science is a constant struggle against these tendencies. This struggle requires of the subject a tremendous effort which 'splits him and demands of him, often to the point of his being existentially torn, that he make a *break* with the "spontaneous" interests of life':[94] this effort is the formation of the scientific mind (its socialization into reason), a process never completed, because of the continuing power exercised upon it by reverie, around which obstacles to science (the 'epistemological obstacles') are continually threatening to form by resorbing scientific concepts into spontaneous modes of thought.

Sciences are born by breaking with these modes of thought and they progress discontinuously by further breaks, or recastings (*refonte*) of knowledge, in which the epistemological obstacles secreted by those modes of thought must be overcome. In this recurring struggle philosophy inevitably appears on the side of the obstacles – against science. Epistemological obstacles always function to the same effect: to close the rupture between scientific and ordinary thought by resorbing the former in the images and preoccupations of the latter, thus feigning a continuity between them, and *a fortiori* giving to science itself the image of a continuous development. Philosophy oversees, and rationalizes, in a variety of ways, this spontaneous play of mind. The scientific character of science is guaranteed not by its foundations in reality, as in classical empiricism, but by the social character of its institutions, the cohesion and effectivity of what Bachelard calls 'the scientific city'. Socialization into this city requires the censorship of the id, a complete break, by the subject, from the world of reverie that forms the substance of everyday experience.[95]

Science itself proceeds by a dialectic of 'applied rationalism' and 'technical materialism': a historical process of mutual adjustment between theory and experiment. The sciences must incorporate a phenomeno-technics: a technique for the production of phenomena, as well as concepts. (Indeed 'a concept has become scientific only in so far as it has become technical, is accompanied by a realization technique.'[96]) Thus the category of experimentation must replace the traditional philosophical category of experience. Conversely, and in opposition to the thesis that theories are instruments for describing and predicting experience, Bachelard advances the thesis that instruments are materialized theories.

Two types of moment are crucial in the history of the sciences: the moment at which scientificity is installed, the moment of rupture; and the moments of recasting, when a science reorganizes its bases. Each decisive event opens upon a new field of possibilities, whose development cannot be predicted in advance. It is only *after* the rupture that the 'tissue of tenacious errors' from which a science breaks can be described. And after each break or recasting of knowledge the past history of the science has to be rewritten, by what Bachelard calls 'recurrence', thus creating a double history: a history of error (*histoire périmée*), a lapsed history; and a history of the positive development of the science since the moment of rupture (*histoire sanctionnée*), a ratified history.[97] It should be clear schematically that these two histories correspond respectively to the history of the obstacles and the history of the sciences. It is at the moment of *refonte* that the threat from the obstacles is greatest, for it is then that the fate of a new concept or theory, marked by its discontinuity from what precedes it, is at stake.

Meyerson had argued that the discontinuities (such as between Newtonian and Einsteinian mechanics) then being registered across the whole field of scientific knowledge were mere illusions attributable to the philosophical ignorance of scientists. For Bachelard, on the other hand, it was philosophical theses such as Meyersonian continuism and realism that were illusory and had to be explained by the scientific ignorance of philosophers (who thus had 'to go to school with the sciences'). His polemic with Meyerson led Bachelard to propound a general theory of the function of philosophy as a support for the obstacles that were continually threatening to form as the sciences progressively reorganized (or sought to establish) themselves: it imports extra-scientific values into science.[98] Thus

Bachelard contrasts the 'diurnal philosophy' of the sciences with the 'nocturnal philosophy' of the philosophers, to which scientists inevitably return when they reflect upon their practice. The scientist lives an imaginary relationship to his actual practice; and the different philosophies may be defined by the degree of their displacement from this practice.[99] Philosophy is thus conceived purely negatively, as having no positive role to play vis-à-vis the sciences; it functions instead, necessarily, as an unwitting agent of reverie, of the idle chatter of the id, humus of the epistemological obstacles.

In a moment we shall have to assess the adequacy of Bachelard's conception of philosophy and of his account of the diurnal philosophy of the sciences, that is, of their actual practice as described in the theses of applied rationalism and technical materialism. I want, however, at the outset to note the two main weaknesses of Bachelardian epistemology. The first, which should be obvious, is his *psychologism*; his conception of the scientific enterprise as mind. The second is his commitment to empirical realism. Lecourt identifies Bachelard's psychologism[100] but fails to identify his empirical realism which leads him in places and despite certain Althusserian qualifications to endorse an essentially Bachelardian conception of philosophy. Science is spontaneously 'dialectical materialist';[101] conversely, where Bachelard errs, in his psychologism, (which Lecourt sees as sustaining his poetics as a 'point of retreat'), this is conceived as a 'return of philosophy'.[102] Bachelard is right to stress that realism is a function but fails to conceive the possibility, implied by the progressive character of science, of a realism which does not identify the real with the field of experience. He is thus forced to fight on the ontological ground of the enemy. There is no concept in his epistemology of *depth* – of the multitiered stratification of reality and the consequent stratification this imposes on scientific knowledge. The result is that science becomes, for Bachelard, a progressive series of reorganizations or recastings of knowledge, a continuing linear series rather than a progressive deepening of knowledge.[103]

The scientific mind which, in Bachelardian epistemology, stands in for the reason of the philosophers is materialized in the form of institutions, meetings, colloquia – the scientific city. It is 'the city's *cohesion* that makes it possible to eliminate every abberation related to the subjective character of any particular research',[104] freeing science from the encumbrance of reverie and making it more difficult for epistemological obstacles to form. It is the scientific city which holds the criteria of objectivity and truth. The objectivity of scientific knowledge is thus grounded in inter-subjectivity, the classical stance of Kantian philosophical idealism (a stance shared by both Popper and Kuhn).

For Bachelard 'science has no object outside its own activity'.[105] Writing in 1936 he says 'we have reached a level of knowledge at which the scientific objects are what we make of them, no more and no less . . . We are realizing by degrees our theoretical thought'.[106] He designates objects posited in scientific theory as 'secondary objects'. Considering the tetrahedral structure of carbon, he writes: 'as we shall see, the debate definitely turns on an object without a direct realistic value in ordinary experience, on an object which has to be designated as a *secondary object*, on an object preceded by theories', adding 'I repeat these philosophical observations again and again because I venture to uphold the thesis of a rupture between scientific and ordinary knowledge'.[107]

Now I am going to propose the following: Bachelard confuses here transitive and intransitive objects (in the sense in which I earlier defined these terms); his inability to think the irreducibility of being and thought and the necessity for both leads him to neglect the intransitive dimension (a mistake characteristic of Kantian idealism); which is to be explained in terms of his incapacity to think anything other than an empirical realist form of realism. First, let us consider the realist problematic he is up against. Meyerson had defined realism as 'every doctrine that maintains the organization of impressions at the level of the impressions themselves, that places the general after the particular, that believes, consequently, in the prolix richness of individual sensation and the systematic impoverishment of the thought which abstracts'.[108] Now, although towards the end of his career Bachelard came to see that 'all philosophy, explicitly or tacitly, honestly, or surreptitiously . . . deposits, projects or presupposes a reality',[109] meaning that realism is necessary (even for the most idealist philosophies of science), he never engaged in the necessary critique of empirical realism. He continued to attack empirical realism, without constructing an alternative realist function.

Of course the tetrahedral structure of carbon has no direct realistic value in experience, though it may come to possess such in the ongoing process of science, as science's phenomeno-technics is developed and refined. But the tetrahedral structure of carbon is not preceded by theories, though the *concept* of it is. The concept 'dog' cannot bark but real dogs do . . . and would do without their concept. Failing to distinguish between the transitive and intransitive dimensions of science, it becomes clear why Bachelard feels that this theory (of secondary objects) is necessitated by his discovery of a rupture between scientific and ordinary knowledge. For as empirical realism identifies experience and the world in as much as an object posited in scientific investigation does not correspond to anything in experience, change can only be conceived as a construction in thought and not as a work in thought (on thought objects) with an (intransitive) object outside thought. Or if the latter concept is sustained then it can only be thought as a simple correction of experience and not as a movement (in thought) to an object unavailable to experience (a movement which may of course and generally will involve a 'rectification' of ordinary experience).

The point may be further developed by considering the inadequacies of his concept of experimentation. Bachelard stresses that science is a material as well as a theoretical labour.[110] 'Science', he says, '*realizes* its objects without ever finding them already in existence. Phenomeno-technics *extends* phenomenology.'[111] A phenomeno-technics is necessary to produce *scientifically significant* phenomena. 'The true scientific phenomenology is essentially a phenomeno-technics. It instructs itself by what it constructs . . . Science raises up a world no longer by a magical force immanent in reality [rejection of classical empiricism], but rather by a rational force immanent to the mind [acceptance of transcendental idealism]'.[112]

Exactly the same absolutely crucial ambiguity is involved here: for what science produces are phenomena which are significant only on the condition that they are an index of phenomena that science does not produce. Science could produce a vast array of phenomena, most of no conceivable significance. What distinguishes the phenomena actually produced in the laboratories of science is the fact that they consist in effects of mechanisms, structures and systems of relations that persist and act independently of science but which can only be 'caught' in a form which renders them accessible to *human beings*, as the contingent phenomenon of nature, under conditions which are experimentally produced and controlled. Science does not produce its intransitive objects of investigation; it produces the conditions for their identification. Bachelard is thus quite wrong to say 'experimental conditions are the same as preconditions of experimentation'.[113] The conditions of the possibility of experience are not, to make Bachelard's relationship to Kant explicit, the same as the conditions of the possibility of the objects of experience. For the latter takes in (includes) the possibility of a world without humanity; and, as I have argued elsewhere, *that* is a condition of the possibility of science.

Again, Bachelard refers to the way in which purification processes in chemistry reveal the social character of science;[114] yet misses their rationale: the fact that chemical reactions always occur in pure form. Purification is important because it is a necessary means to the discovery (isolation) of processes that occur quite independently of men and women and the social character of science.

Bachelard's concept of the transitive dimension of science is flawed by operationism and an unrelenting hostility to the role of the imagination in science.[115] The requirement that all scientific concepts be accompanied by a realization technique is far too stringent: it would effectively make conceptual change impossible. As Engels astutely observed of 'modern socialism': 'Like every new theory, it had first to link itself onto the intellectual material which lay ready to its hands, however deep its roots lay in economic facts.'[116] Every new theory is the result of (theoretical) work on cognitive material that pre-exists it – theoretical work must have a degree of autonomy from the operational procedures of science, even if the latter are held to be in the last instance epistemically decisive. And within theory, a science that excludes the imagination totally is a science that is necessarily incapable of growth.

Bachelard's psychologism is particularly telling in the absence of any theory of the intervention of non-scientific elements in scientific practice, and so of any theory of *ideology*. Nowhere is the necessity for epistemological obstacles to form and reform explained. Lacking is the kind of demonstration of the necessity for (and limits of) the epistemological obstacles that Marx undertook for political economy in his theory of fetishism. Instead the epistemological obstacles are conceived, in a way unrelated to the constitution of any scientific object, as natural products of the human mind and explained, in an undifferentiated way, in terms of the libido of the individual scientists. The result is, as Lecourt notes, a lopsided history,[117] in which *histoire périmée* cannot be written, for in it there is nothing to say.

Obstacles, errors and mistakes are all manifestations of the individual psyche; conversely, socialization into the scientific city is a sufficient guarantee against these manifestations, and hence of scientific truth. (One could therefore say that Bachelard produces a psychology of error and a sociology of truth.) And with this guarantee a teleology re-emerges, in which the advance of scientific knowledge is accounted for by the social conditions of its existence. In Bachelard the problem of knowledge is solved by a *cogitamus*, constructed on the censorship of the id. Mind as materialized in the scientific city appears as the central category of Bachelardian epistemology; opposed to the scientific mind is reverie. Opposed to reason is imagination; to the scientific city, individual error; to *histoire sanctionnée, histoire périmée*; to science itself, the obstacles. Thus Bachelard's philosophy, which would be an anti-philosophy, abounds with couples homologous to those of the traditional philosophy he assails. Instead of the subject we have the *project*, inscribed in the scientific city, and instead of the object of empirical realism, the *secondary object* of scientific thought. Trapped in the philosophical problematic of empirical realism, and despite his psychologism, Bachelard produces a philosophy as 'close' to the diurnal philosophy of the sciences as it is possible to get and it is important to read him for this. But in the end we have an idealism in which the couple the individual subject/the empirical world is rejected in favour of the scientific city and its products; in which science can have knowledge of objects only because the objects concerned are its products. Bachelard's cogitamus is, in the final instance, posited on a *facimus* – an idea as old as Vico.

What, finally, are we to make of Bachelard's conception of the possibility of a non-philosophical philosophy, the diurnal philosophy of the sciences? To argue for a non-philosophical philosophy is like arguing for a non-theoretical science. Empiricism, at whatever level, always leads to the tacit acceptance of an implicit theory (in Bachelard's case, empirical realism). There is no alternative but to construct a philosophical philosophy of the sciences, constituting an analysis of their necessary conditions, as part of the *Kampfplatz* between ideology and science.[118] The ontology and sociology that, I have suggested, emerges from such an analysis is to be in no way opposed to science (any more than the philosophical and scientific concepts of matter can be opposed).[119] For example, that the world is structured and differentiated can, I suggest, be established by philosophical argument; but the particular structures it contains and the way in which it is differentiated are entirely matters for substantive scientific investigation. Althusser is thus correct to assert that philosophy has no object,[120] in that it is its task to analyse concepts which can only be used syncategorematically, that is, under some particular description, in science. But if philosophy is the last line of defence of all ideology and it is, as I have argued, irreducible then it must be, by the very reason for its existence, an essential moment in the constitution of the science of history, what ideology would deny by the title 'social science'.

4

Philosophies as Ideologies of Science: A Contribution to the Critique of Positivism

1 Introduction

It is my aim in this chapter to describe the way in which a philosophical system, such as positivism, can function as an ideology for science and other social practices. I want to focus on positivism both because of its intrinsic historical importance and because it represents a *limit* with respect to which other philosophies can be defined.

Positivism is, in the first instance, a theory of the nature, limits and unity of knowledge. Particular knowledge is of events sensed in perception; general knowledge is of the patterns such events show in space and over time which, if it is to be possible, must be *constant* (the Humean theory of causal laws). Sense-perception exhausts the possible objects of knowledge. Conversely any object of sense-perception constitutes a possible object of knowledge. Thus the cognitive claims of theory, metaphysics, morality, aesthetics and politics alike are rejected; and (tacitly gendered) man is located within the system of objects on which he acts. Positivism is a limit form of empiricism.

Positivism is a theory of *knowledge*. But any theory of knowledge presupposes an *ontology* – for it must be assumed, implicitly if not explicitly, that the world is such that it could be the object of knowledge of the specified type. Thus the Humean theory, which forms the lynchpin of the positivist system, presupposes an ontology of closed systems and atomistic events, constituting the objects of actual or possible experiences.[1] Moreover any theory of knowledge presupposes a *sociology* in the sense that it must be assumed, implicitly if not explicitly, that the nature of human beings and the institutions they reproduce or transform is such that such knowledge could be produced. Thus the Humean theory presupposes a conception of people as passive sensors of given facts and recorders of their given constant conjunctions, which has the corollary

49

that knowledge can always be analysed in a purely individualistic way.

A theory of knowledge, such as positivism, thus *automatically* constitutes two dimensions in the philosophy of science: an *intransitive* dimension or ontology; and a *transitive* one or sociology. But in exactly the same way it presupposes some philosophical method, that is a method by which its characteristic results are produced, and hence explicitly or implicitly some theory of philosophy, just as its results constitute a metaphysics. Positivist philosophy, notoriously, denies this. Positivism presupposes, then, as necessary conditions of its results: an ontology of empirical realism; a sociology defined by that model of human beings; and a philosophy that lacks a concept of itself, and of these three transcendental necessities to which any theory of knowledge is subject.

It will transpire that some of the most interesting and significant ideological effects of positivism are generated by the requirement that that system satisfies, if it is to be any use at all, what it formally denies. In such cases the mechanism of ideology-production is necessarily *covert* or disguised. Now it is in the inconsistent system so resulting that positivism's tremendous versatility and flexibility as an ideology lies. As contradictory conclusions can be derived from an inconsistent system, the particular conclusions actually derived can only be explained by factors *external* to the system – by, I shall suggest in the case of positivism, the characteristic functions they are required to satisfy. However, there are other ideological effects of positivism which are *overt* in the sense that they are generated as straightforward consequences of positivist assumptions (whether they are recognized as such or not); and which need not, at least in as much as the generative system is not itself inconsistent or overdetermined, give rise to permutable results, and which can thus be explained as immanent necessities of the system itself (however the latter is explained). Positivism accumulates an ideological value in our society in both ways – but if overt effects are more important in the intransitive dimension, covert ones hold sway in the transitive dimension, over science itself.

Positivism is, or purports to be, a theory, even if only by default, of much else besides science. But in this chapter I can deal with its ideological effects only in as much as they turn on its characteristic theory of science. However, even in this limited respect, positivism functions, as we shall see, as an ideology for social practices other than science. It does this partly by generating an ideology *of* science (to complement the one it generates *for* it); and partly by encouraging, by injunction or resonance, certain substantive conceptions of the nature of nature, society, persons and their interconnections. In the former case, *injunction*, it generates a set of methodological norms; whereas in *resonance* it reflect the interests, preoccupations and assumptions of substantive social science, so constituting the inverse of what Buchdahl has called a philosophy of science's 'analogical grammar'.[2]

Now if positivism is an ideology we must attempt to ascertain its necessity. That is to say, we must ask: *to what extent does science necessarily appear to its agents* (or to members of other groups in society) *in positivist guise*, i.e. as something other than it really is? I hold of course that positivism is not a necessary philosophical position: but this does not mean that it is not a necessary scientific position, or that it does not have a degree of necessity as a scientific one.

2 Positivism

I have said that positivism presupposes an ontology of closed systems and atomistic events constituting the objects of actual or possible experiences and a conception of people as passive sensors of given facts and recorders of their given constant conjunctions. Now I have argued elsewhere[3] that constant conjunctions are not in general spontaneously available in nature but rather have to be worked for in the laboratories of science, so that causal laws and the other objects of experimental investigation must, if that activity is to be rendered intelligible, be regarded as ontologically independent of the patterns of events and the activities of human beings alike; and that, conversely, the concepts and descriptions under which we bring them must, if *inter alia* scientific development is to be possible, be seen as part of the irreducibly social process of science. Thus experiences (and the facts they ground), and the constant conjunctions of events that form the empirical grounds for causal laws, are social products. But the objects to which they afford us access, such as causal laws, exist and act quite independently of us.

Now positivism can sustain neither the idea of an independent reality nor the idea of a socially produced science. Rather what happens is in a way quite extraordinary – for, as in the interests of a particular conception of philosophy, it allows a particular conception of our knowledge of reality to inform and implicitly define the concept of the reality known by science, these ideas (absolutely minimally necessary conditions for an adequate account of science) become crossed, so that we have a *naturalized science* purchased at the expense of a *humanized nature*. And it is in this exchange (or transference), or rather in the philosophical crucible in which it occurs, that the most fateful ideological consequences of positivism are formed.

Let us examine the mechanism of this peculiar chemistry in more detail. For positivism our knowledge of the world consists only of atomistic events or states of affairs sensed in perception. If the world consists only of such events then of course any connection between them must be the product or contribution of mind (so that no concept of natural necessity can be sustained). Moreover if particular knowledge consists only of knowledge of atomistic events, then general knowledge can only consist of a knowledge of their relationships, more particularly of co-existence in space and succession over time, which must be assumed to be constant. And so the Humean theory depends upon a view of conjunctions existing independently of the human activity in general necessary for them, and hence upon a *fetishism* of the systems within which the conjoined events occur. But in similar manner it depends upon a view of what is apprehended in immediate sense-experience as a fact constituting an atomistic event or state of affairs, existing independently of the human activity necessary for *it*, and hence upon a *reification* of facts. When the conjunctions of such facts are reified and identified with causal laws, science becomes an epiphenomenon of nature. The condition of positivism's *reduction* of causal laws to sequences of events and events to experiences is thus a denial of the social character of science, and more particularly of its character as *work* involving the transformation of antecedent objects, both material and ideational. Thus the concept of an empirical world has its counterpart and condition, in positivism, in a reified account of science.

In positivist philosophy, then, facts usurp the place of things and constant conjunctions of events that of causal laws. But the price of the reification of facts and the fetishism of the systems within which the events they describe occur is positivism's incapacity to sustain, or when as in practice it *must* to sustain in anything other than an ambivalent (or equivocal) way, the ideas of the *existence* of things independently of our perceiving them and (as I have shown in detail elsewhere) of the *applicability* of laws in open systems, that is, systems where no constant conjunctions of events prevail.[4] And this results in positivism's inability to sustain, unequivocally, the universality of law or the independent efficacy of things.

The structure of the positivist account of science is represented in Diagrams 1 and 2 below. There are two key moments in the theory of particular knowledge. In the first, the real content of science is reduced to or reconstructed from atomistic facts apprehended – or stated – in sense-experience. And in the second, these facts are treated as being identical to, or in one-to-one correspondence with, the objects to which the referring expression, in the sentence with which they are stated, refers. Such things may be physical objects, sensations or operations. Now whether the facts are identified with the statements or the features the vital correspondence between them is ensured by the apprehension of the features in autonomized sense-experience; that is, in a moment of subjectivity which is free from the effects of all pre-formed or extraneous, including theoretical,

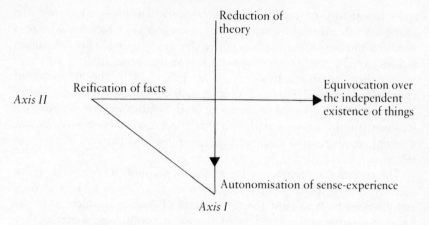

Diagram 1 The Core Structure of Positivism: The Production of Particular Knowledge

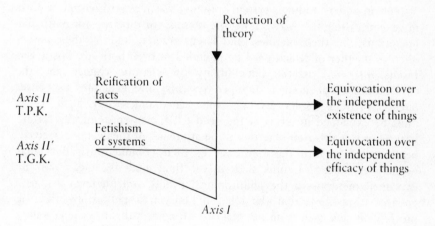

Note: T.P.K. = theory of particular knowledge
      T.G.K. = theory of general knowledge

Diagram 2 Generalisation of the Core Structure: The Production of General Knowledge

content (so that in it we become, as it were, pure sense-objects of the world). For any such content would affect the completeness, and if it is variable, the uniqueness of the correspondence; which must be secured by a theory of ostensive or operational definition. In this way the ontology of our world consists not (or not simply) of things to which we refer but of facts of which we are aware, which are also meanings we cannot help but intend.

In the theory of the production of particular knowledge then the *autonomized sense-experience* constitutes the *form* in which knowledge is acquired and the *reified fact* the *content* that is expressed. This determines a theory of the production of general knowledge isomorphic in structure with it. For the atomicity of the events generated by the autonomized character of sense-experience necessitates, as a condition of the possibility of general knowledge, the constancy of their conjunctions, presupposing a fetishism of the systems within which the events they conjoin occur, resulting in a parallel equivocation, over the independent efficacy of things.

The central co-ordinates of the positivist account of science are given then by the *reification* and *atomization* of facts. Such facts and their conjunctions both exhaust the real content of science and determine the knowable nature of the world, or fix science in its ontology. Together they establish the development of science as *monistic* and its structure as *deductive*.

Now in understanding a system of thought such as positivism one must in general distinguish between (a) the *reasons* (or motives) for particular operations; (b) their manifest and latent *results*; and (c) their *consequences* (neither of which need be intended or even noticed). Positivism results *inter alia* in the impossibility of scientific change and the explanation of phenomena in open systems; and generates as consequences of these results ideologies for science and society. Such results must be explained in terms of the need felt for an epistemically certain base. (For it is this that determines the atomicity of the events perceived, necessitating in turn the constancy of their conjunctions.) But what explains this need? I think that, in the final analysis, it can only be explained in terms of the philosophical results and ideological consequences it justifies; that the relation between a philosophy and the problems it sets itself is an *internal* one. (If correct this has the corollary that philosophical problems can only be rendered intelligible in relation to the solutions they engender.)

Now positivism's problem-field, which determines the formal constitution of its results, is that of 'the problem of knowledge'. As Lukács explained it: 'acknowledging as given and necessary the results and achievements of the special sciences philosophy's task is to exhibit and justify the grounds for regarding the concepts they construct as valid';[5] that is, philosophy's task is the certification of our knowledge to the title of 'knowledge' in response to the possibility of sceptical doubts. Now empirical realism is *made* for this problem-field. For it perfectly satisfies its requirements: (a) it attaches our knowledge, analytically, to the world (so demonstrating that it is knowledge of what it claims to be); and (b) it renders it insusceptible, by nature or convention, of further justification (so showing that it is naturally or practically certain). Empirical realism is, it should be noted, susceptible of both empiricist (including conventionalist as well as positivist) and transcendental idealist interpretations; and is consistent with non-reductionist forms of empiricism in which the uniqueness, and even the unilinearity, of the relationship between facts and theory is snapped. It presupposes an individualist sociology, but not necessarily a reifying one.

An immediate caveat is necessary concerning my use of the term 'reification'. In saying that an account of facts is 'reified' I am not simply saying that in it facts are regarded as things. For indeed facts *are* things, but they are social not natural things, belonging to the transitive world of science, not the intransitive world of nature. Moreover merely to possess a non-reified view of facts is insufficient for an adequate concept of them. For in conventionalism they are conceived as being constituted by human agreement and hence as dependent upon human activity. But there they are conceived as being *created*, rather than merely *sustained* or *transformed* by humans; so that in this way their independent social reality, and characteristic coercive power, is denied.

Two operations, then, structure the positivist account of science: a *fusion* of the world and experience, crystallized in the doctrine of empirical realism; and, a *reduction* of our knowledge to the level of experience which is, as constitutive of the nature of reality itself, held to be certain.

3 The Grid of Phenomenalism

Positivism, we have seen, involves the idea of a statement/feature conformity. Two general forms of such conformity may be defined: correspondence and identity. Phenomenalism involves the latter; what I am going to call 'material object empiricism' the former. According to phenomenalism things just are, or must be analysed as, clusters of actual or possible experience; whereas material object empiricism attempts to preserve the idea that the objects apprehended in sense-perception exist independently of it. It is clear that the language of science is, or at least depends upon, a material object language. Only material object empiricism can satisfy what I am going to call the realist and social functions,[6] which may be expressed as the imperatives to satisfy, however minimally, the ideas of an independent reality and the irreducibly social nature of science.

Now we have seen that positivism's problem is to show that our actual knowledge, which is or depends upon a knowledge of material things, is justified. But merely to assert a correspondence between knowledge and the world leaves the former still vulnerable to sceptical attack. For we have not as yet furnished any guarantee that our statements, which would be true if they were in perfect correspondence with the given facts, are indeed true. Only with such a guarantee can we be sure that we have indeed come right up against the world, that we have found the base of our knowledge or made this base of knowledge ours. And it is the task of phenomenalism, at what I am going to call Level 2 of analysis, to arm material object empiricism with this missing guarantee, so incorrigibly grounding our present claims to knowledge.

The objective of the phenomenalist exercise is thus:

(a) the generation of a class of incorrigible sense-datum propositions; and

(b) the transference, through programmes of reconstruction (normative phenomenalism) or analysis (descriptive phenomenalism), of the incorrigibility of sense-datum propositions to material object propositions.

The critique of phenomenalism, which is by now quite well-known, has turned on step (a); and I am not going to repeat it here. Our concern is with the mode of generation of ideological effects and here step (b) is the crucial one. Now it is clear that if sense-datum propositions are to be capable of doing the job they are designed to do, they must stand in a relation of entailment or equivalence to the propositions they are held to ground or analyse. But such relations cannot hold in *all* cases, as is shown by consideration of the very examples – illusions, hallucinations, and so on – that phenomenalists invoke in support of their project. Hence either the inference is never legitimate or we can only allow it if we have made a *prior* decision in favour of the truth of the corresponding material object proposition. So that it is now our material object knowledge that is required to justify or analyse its alleged sense-foundations! To put it another way, if an inference beyond a subjective state of mind is possible, there is no need for the introduction of sense-datum propositions in the first place. And if it is not possible, sense-datum propositions cannot ground or analyse our public knowledge. Either way, phenomenalism is devoid of *cognitive* point. Phenomenologically, this is reflected in the fact that it is my consciousness of a material object that is required to define sense-data as the objects of my consciousness. Hence though phenomenalism *claims* a direction of analysis:

$$r_{sd} \to m_{sd} \to m_{mo} \to r_{mo}$$

(where r = reference, m = meaning, $_{sd}$ = sense-datum proposition, $_{mo}$ = material object proposition)

it actually depends, in epistemological reality, upon a precise reversal, viz.

$$r_{mo} \rightarrow m_{mo} \rightarrow m_{sd} \rightarrow r_{sd}$$

(In saying this I am concerned only with the direction, and am not of course committed to the validity of the links.)

But is step (b) of the phenomenalist programme really necessary? That is to say, is not a consistent phenomenalism without any material object commitments possible? Not if the philosophy is to satisfy the realist function, and so be of any use to science; not, that is, more generally, if it is to have any *practical* import. As Hume said long ago in his *Dialogues Concerning Natural Religion*: 'Whether your scepticism be as absolute and sincere as you pretend, we shall learn by and by, when the company breaks up; we shall then see whether you go out at the door or the window, and whether you doubt if your body has gravity or can be injured by its fall, according to popular opinion derived from our fallacious senses and more fallacious experience'.[7] And as Hegel put it in his more extravagant way: '[scepticism] pronounces absolute disappearance, and the pronouncement exists . . .; it pronounces the nullity of seeing, hearing, etc., and it itself sees and hears, etc.; it pronounces the nullity of ethical realities and acts according to them'.[8]

To generalize, provisionally, if it is to be of any use at all positivism depends upon the satisfaction of what it formally denies. Thus we have either a philosophy which is consistent with its epistemology but of no use to science; or one which is relevant to science but more or less inconsistent with its epistemology.[9] Formally this disjunction is manifest in various antinomies or internally destructive dilemmas which cannot be discussed here. Practically, it is in the contradictions yielded by the necessity to hold both of two incompatible positions, as conditions for each other, that the most fertile ground of ideology lies. The transformational possibilities of such a system are limited only by the number of terms that can be introduced; and, in practice, by the number of non-equivalent (non-vacuous) functions that must be uniquely satisfied.

The result of the phenomenalist exercise is thus a redefinition of the world in which the genuine incorrigibility of spurious propositions is transubstantiated into the spurious incorrigibility of genuine propositions. But the supposition of the incorrigibility of the latter is the effective precondition, as well as the real meaning, of this transition. In the same way the subjective certainty expressed in a state of intuitive awareness finds its objective counterpart in the fact that the material object proposition states. Thus underlying the solipsism of Level 2 is a theory of the absence of inconsistency; and underpinning scepticism, certainty.

The structure of what might be termed 'the grid of phenomenalism' is set out in Diagrams 3 and 4. Material object empiricism is necessary to

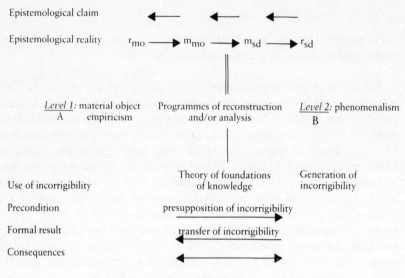

Diagram 3   The Grid of Phenomenalism

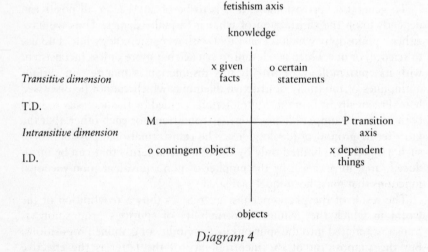

Diagram 4

satisfy the realist imperatives of science; phenomenalism to satisfy the demands of the philosophical (problem-of-knowledge) problem-field. The conditions of the transition from Level 2 of analysis establish a series of equivalences between the material and the sensuous, the public and the private, the contingent (or doubtful) and the necessary (or certain) and so on. The combination of the equivalences established by the transition with the results of the fetishism already presupposed at Level 1, establishing an isomorphism between knowledge and the world, result in the constitution of certain statements in the transitive dimension, satisfying the epistemic function, at the price of contingent (or doubtful) objects in the intransitive dimension; and of given facts in the transitive dimension, satisfying the realist function, at the price of dependent things in the intransitive one.

Let us analyse the micro-logic of these operations in more detail. Any position in A (at Level 1) necessitates as its condition a position in B (at Level 2) and vice-versa. But any position in the transitive dimension (T) automatically constitutes a position in the intransitive dimension (I). Hence TA has a unique image IB and TB a unique image IA in the opposite quadrant of Diagram 4. The condition of the possibility of reified facts is dependent things: that is, given facts are only possible in practice if we have dependent things in theory. Conversely the condition of certain statements in philosophy is contingent objects in science. But both realist and epistemic functions must be satisfied. And so we have the characteristic equivocation (or ambivalence) referred to in Diagrams 1 and 2. But if things can be viewed alternatively as given or dependent according to which operation is applied, so too can alternate operations be performed on the properties ascribed to statements. For if certainty is distributive, doubt, which is its condition, is too. Hence one could with equal facility argue *to* the doubtfulness of our public knowledge as a condition of the possibility of the phenomenalist programme. This duality of structure, enabling a corresponding duplicity of use, is a most convenient property of ideological systems. The realist and epistemic vectors specified in Diagram 4 fix only the *dominant* tendencies of the system (explicable in terms of the results and consequences they justify); they are always subject to transformation in any given case.

The principal ideological consequences of the grid should be clear. The transference of certainty to scientific knowledge establishes its development as monistic and rationalises the scientific status quo, in Kuhn's terminology the practice of 'normal science';[10] while the identification of what is immediately apprehended in sense-perception as certain (and the reduction of scientific knowledge to that level) encourages a set of beliefs about science generally comforting to the common-sense of mankind. The condition of the satisfaction of the epistemic function in the intransitive dimension, that is, the idea of the contingency of objects, plays a key role in the generation of ideological effects in that dimension as we shall see below.

There is a parallel to the grid of phenomenalism at the level of the theory of the production of general knowledge. Here, analogously, deductive–nomological and inductive–falsificationist concepts of law prove to be necessary for each other (the former to satisfy the realist, the latter the epistemic function); universal generalizations are purchased at the price of restricted laws; and the explanation of phenomena in open systems becomes impossible, a consequence that renders impossible a methodology of social science. Hence we can already begin to see how positivism in the very move in which it seeks to vest its products with certainty, comes to *understate* the scope of application and critical significance of science.

I turn now to a more detailed investigation of the ideological effects of positivism in the transitive and intransitive dimensions respectively.

4 Ideology in the Transitive Dimension: The Concept of a Fact

Without doubt the concept most pregnant with ideological connotations in the transitive dimension is that of a fact. It is to its analysis that I now turn.

One might take 'a fact' as a synonym for a 'true assertion' or alternatively, to consider Strawson's well-known formula, to attempt to explicate it as what a true statement states.[11] But this will not do – for we make statements, but we do not make facts (rather it is as if they were made for us); and it is unclear, to say the least, how statements can *do* anything. Why do we not make facts? The answer is because, as the etymology of the word suggests, they are *already made*. In stating facts we are acknowledging results already achieved, the results being achieved (in the domain of empirical discourse) by *readings*,[12] of which the varieties of sense-experience constitute special kinds of skill. But of course we discover as well as state results: the facts pre-exist their discovery as results to be achieved (just as they pre-exist their statement as achievements). They must thus be conceived as *potentialities* of the conceptual schemes or paradigms that govern our enquiries, which when *actualized* constitute discoveries. A fact, then, is a potentiality actualized in discovery, sustained in practice (both discursive and non-discursive) and objectified in sense-perception.

Facts are paradigm social institutions: they are possibilities inherent in the cognitive structures that human agents reproduce and transform but do not create (with reification, committed by positivism, and voluntarism, committed by conventionalism, constituting two opposed errors). If the criterion of *externality* establishes the *social* nature of facts, the criterion of *constraint* establishes their independent *reality* as social forms.[13] If, to be is in the last instance just to be able to do,[14] the facts exist in as much as but for them certain determinate states of the physical world, for which our intentional action is a necessary condition, would not be realized; but, to stress, their existence is social, not natural.

The facts, then, are not what we apprehend in sense-perception, but results of the theories in terms of which our apprehension of things is organized. Now we have learnt from Wittgenstein[15] and Hanson[16] that we tend to see things under concepts and descriptions, such that it is as if, at least in the case of so-called 'epistemic perception',[17] we (to use Rom Harré's apt expression) 'read propositions off the world',[18] that is, we tend to read the world *as if* it were constituted by facts. What is involved in the categories in terms of which positivistic philosophical consciousness understands the concept of a fact is not therefore so much a crass mistake or straightforward error, as a superficiality which merely reflects this spontaneous consciousness of science. Now to stop at this spontaneous consciousness is not only a mistake in philosophy but ultimately damaging to science. For it is only if, through their capacity to be conscious of that spontaneous consciousness of theirs, they are able to achieve distance from it and see it as a social product that scientists can conceive the possibility of a rational criticism (or development) of that fact-constituting consciousness, i.e. of their readings of the world.

Facts, then, are real; but they are historically specific social realities. The mystification attached to them derives from the fact that in our spontaneous mode of thought and the philosophy of positivism that reflects it, the properties possessed by facts *qua social objects* are transformed into qualities belonging to them as *things*. Fetishism by *naturalizing* facts, *de-historicizes* them. Its social function is thus to conceal the historically specific structures and relations constituting sense-experience in science. And we could say of positivism, as Marx said of 'vulgar economy', that it is content to 'stick to appearances in opposition to the law which regulates and explains them'.[19]

A degree of necessity attaches, then, to positivism in the transitive dimension: its concept of a fact reflects our *spontaneous* consciousness in perception. Nevertheless it is an ideological category that scientists in their *reflective* consciousness must transcend. It is as Marx said of the process of circulation merely 'the phenomenon of a process [viz. production] taking place behind it'.[20] Diagram 5 is an attempt to schematize this process.[21] Theory generates the phenomenal forms in terms of which we

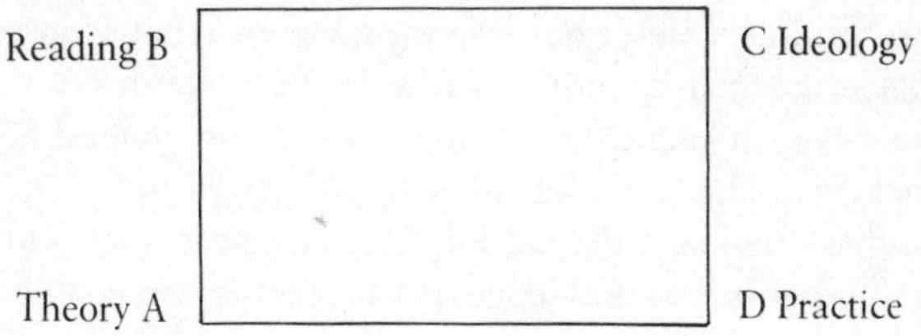

Reading B   C Ideology

Theory A   D Practice

Diagram 5

read the world, which are reflected in the ideological categories of positivism, which in turn sustain the normal practice of science, reproducing
theory. Rejecting the positivist concept of a fact, or reification, at C,
would not destroy our spontaneous concept of a fact,[22] i.e. objectivication,
at B, but would, by situating the possibility of a plurality of possible readings of the world, allow greater rationality in the choice of theory[23] and
hence enhance our scientific literacy.

5 Ideology in the Intransitive Dimension: Causal Laws, Methodological Individualism and Social Science

Geras, in a perspicacious article,[24] points out that Marx employed two
concepts of mystification: one, exemplified by his treatment of value
relations, in which the mystification pertained as it were to reality itself;
and the other, exemplified by his treatment of the wage form, in which the
mystification consisted of a proposition that was quite simply false, an
illusion properly so called.

Now when we turn to the intransitive dimension, it is immediately
apparent that the mystification is of the latter type. Just as, according to
Marx, wages are not what they appear to be (they are not the value of
labour but of labour power); so causal laws are not the constant conjunctions of events that, when generated under conditions that are artificially produced and controlled, constitute their empirical grounds, but
the tendencies of mechanisms ontologically irreducible to them.[25] (Moreover the analogy may be pressed further. For just as, according to Marx,
the category mistake in political economy consists in confusing powers
with their exercise, so that in philosophy consists in confusing the exercise
of powers with their realization.) For Marx the social function of the
wage-form is to conceal the reality of exploitation, unpaid labour, the
source of surplus value. What is the social function of the constant
conjunction form? It is, I suggest, to conceal the reality of structures irreducible to events (and of societies to individuals).

It is of course true that the constant conjunction analysis has a domain
of plausibility in that it describes one moment of what is in effect a dialectic in science,[26] but it cannot describe its own conditions: it must, of
necessity, pass over in silence the human activity in general necessary for
such conjunctions. The consciousness it reflects is not that of science,
which everywhere makes a distinction between necessary and accidental
sequences and regards its knowledge as universally applicable. Hence the
explanation for the constant conjunction form must lie outside science –
in the ensemble of practices (including philosophy) constituting the rest of
society.

As a result of the Humean analysis reality becomes unstructured, uniform and unchanging. The world contains no hidden mechanisms, no powers of which we are unaware; it consists merely in the passing flux of experience, as described by common-sense. The space denied to science can then of course be used to make room for, for example, religion – as Duhem, for instance, tried to do in *The Physics of a Believer*,[27] in a move already sanctified by Kant. Such reductionism transposed to the domain of social science has particularly damaging consequences. In perfect resonance with the conception of science as a behavioural response to the stimulus of given facts and their conjunctions, society is conceived as being constituted by individuals, motivated by given desires and conjoined, if at all, by contract.[28] When it is necessary to conceive the components of such a society, the atomized individuals, as *agents*, a form of consistency is preserved by the simple expedient of the separation of reason from desire. A person's freedom then consists in their ability to calculate their own best interests in relation to their given desires (that is, to perform an optimizing calculation). Utilitarianism is the natural hand-maiden of positivism.

Hume expressed the corollary of this conception of social science well when he averred 'mankind is much the same in all times and all places'.[29] Of course when and where the implicit assumptions of this model break down, then history or its spatial analogue, anthropology, are invoked. But in general we can say with Marx of this conception of social science that 'history [and we could add, diversity] . . . does not exist anymore'.[30] This is particularly ironic in view of the fact that positivism originated in its modern form, with Comte, as a theory of history.[31]

The anti-historical impetus of modern positivism is however explicit in its deductive–nomological conception of explanation.[32] Now given the essential openness of social systems this conception is totally inapplicable. But such is the prestige that it derives from its identification with the natural sciences that the lines of demarcation between natural and social science become quite misleadingly drawn.[33] Thus it seems clear, for example, that any future defence of naturalism in social science must respect the insights of the *verstehende* tradition.[34]

A theoretical individualism is both a consequence and a condition of positivism. But it cannot be over-stressed that while the properties and powers of individuals and societies are *necessary* for one another, they are *irreducible* to one another. Can it be seriously maintained that wars are determined by soldiers or speech acts by grammar? Now both the psycho-logical and social sciences must start their haul to scientificity without that priceless asset available to the experimental sciences of sometimes being able to observe or detect in undisturbed fashion the workings of the latent structures of the world. Owing to its assumption of an unstructured and undifferentiated reality, positivism cannot think this specific difference and so pose for the human sciences the central task for their methodology: that of devising (or reconstructing) analogues for the process of controlled experimentation that enables the rational confirmation and rejection of theory in the experimental sciences of nature. On the other hand this same inability enables positivism to afford to a system once it has got off the ground all the privileges, such as resistance to pseudo-falsification, properly accorded to sciences, when such systems may, for all we know, have no claim to that title at all; they may rate as substantive ideology. If one believes that a society tends to generate the kind of social science it needs (or perhaps deserves), then one has here a most powerful reinforcement mechanism for the defence of the social status quo, whatever and wherever that is.

6 Conclusion

In conclusion, then, it must be said that while positivism has a degree of necessity in the transitive dimension in that it reflects the spontaneous consciousness of science, in the intransitive dimension it constitutes sheer mystification. While the raison d'être for the properties it ascribes to knowledge can be seen to lie in their functionality for science, those it ascribes to the world must be seen as constituting more general social ideologies.

Positivism is a theory of the nature, limits and unity of knowledge. But it is not a theory of its *possibility*. Knowledge is, for positivism, quite *unproblematic* – a given fact, it never inquires for a moment into its conditions or conceives that it might not be. (In this it is irredeemably pre-critical.) But knowledge is a transient historical phenomenon, whose conditions are subject to both philosophical analysis and scientific investigation. Foremost among the conditions that can be established by a priori argument are:

(1) the independent existence and transfactual activity of the objects of knowledge;

(2) the social production of knowledge by means of knowledge; and

(3) the irreducibility of the discourse (philosophy) in which such propositions and their contraries are expressed.

Now any system such as positivism that fails to satisfy (1)–(3) is susceptible, I suggest, to transcendental refutation. But if (1)–(3) are necessary conditions for scientific activity then any system that does not satisfy it will *in practice* have to contain it as a proper sub-set; so generating a contradiction and constituting itself as a candidate for the generation of covert ideology effects, as well as the overt ones that flow directly from its misrepresentation of the nature of the world, science and philosophy.

I have thought it better to deal with a specific case in some detail rather than range widely over the topic that forms the first half of the title of this chapter. Even so I think that I have established something like a general conclusion. In any event I make only a muted apology for dealing at such length with positivism: for it is still, despite Popper (and Kuhn), the most influential philosophy of science. Positivism has always co-existed in symbiosis with anti-scientific romantic reaction,[35] a reaction which, now that science itself has come to be seen as a social activity, has penetrated into its citadel in the philosophy of science.[36] A more adequate account of science should help us to steer our way to a fairer assessment of its value in our culture.

5

On the Possibility of Social Scientific Knowledge and the Limits of Naturalism

1 Introduction

In this chapter I want to discuss an old question that refuses to lie down. It is a question that continually resurfaces in philosophical discussions on the social sciences and reappears, in one guise or another, in methodological discussions within them: *to what extent can society be studied in the same way as nature?* Without exaggerating, I think one could call this question the primal problem of the philosophy of the social sciences. For the history of that subject has been dominated by a dispute between two traditions. The first – a naturalistic tradition – has typically seen science as (actually or ideally) unified in its concordance with *positivist* principles, based in the last instance on the Humean notion of law. The second – a rival anti-naturalist tradition, of *hermeneutics* – has posited, by contrast, a radical distinction in method between the natural and social sciences, flowing from and grounded in the idea of a radical distinction in their subject matters. The philosophical lineage of this tradition is traceable back through Weber and Dilthey to the transcendental idealism of Kant. Within the Marxist camp an exactly parallel dispute has occurred, with the so-called 'dialectical materialists' on one side and Lukács, the Frankfurt school and Sartre on the other.

Now, with the possible exception of the 'dialectical materialists' (whose specificity I do not want to discuss here), the great error that unites these disputants is their acceptance of an essentially positivist account of natural science, and more generally of an empiricist ontology. This is very evident if one looks at Peter Winch's *The Idea of a Social Science*, perhaps the most influential tract written within the so-called 'analytical' school. Winch, it will be remembered, wants to argue that there is an essential identity between philosophy and social science, on the one hand, and a fundamental contrast between the latter and the natural sciences, on the

66

other. When we turn to his arguments for such a contrast we find that they boil down to two. The first is an argument to the effect that constant conjunctions of events are neither sufficient nor (contrary to Weber, for instance) even necessary for social scientific explanation, which is achieved instead by the discovery of intelligible connections in its subject matter.[1] This may be granted. But the required contrast is only generated if we assume that the discovery of intelligible connections in *its* subject matter is not equally the goal of natural scientific explanation. The second is an argument to the effect that social things have no existence, other than a purely physical existence, i.e. as social things, apart from the concepts that agents possess of them.[2] Besides leaving the ontological status of concepts unclear, once more the assumed contrast only gets off the ground if we tacitly assume that, with the privileged exception of thought itself, only material objects can properly be said to be 'real', that in natural science *esse est percipi*. Winch's anti-naturalism thus depends entirely on empiricist theories of existence and causality. By in effect ceding natural science to positivism, Winch precludes himself from locating the true differences between the natural and the social sciences. Lukács in the Marxist tradition makes an exactly parallel mistake.

Now I think that recent developments in the philosophy of science allow,[3] as the current crisis in the social sciences necessitates, a reconsideration of the problem of naturalism. *Naturalism* may be defined as the thesis that there is (or can be) an essential unity of method between the natural and the social sciences. It must be straightaway distinguished from two species of it: *reductionism*, which posits an actual identity of subject matter as well; and *scientism*, which denies that there are any important differences in the methods appropriate to studying societies and nature, whether or not they are actually (as in reductionism) identified. In contrast to both these forms of naturalism I want to argue for a qualified anti-positivist naturalism. Such a naturalism holds that it is possible to give an account of science under which the proper and more or less specific methods of both the natural and social sciences can fall. But it does not deny that there are important differences in these methods, grounded in the real differences that exist in their subject matters. In particular we shall see that *ontological*, *epistemological* and *relational* considerations reveal differences that place limits on the possibility of naturalism, or rather qualify the form it must take in the social sciences. Moreover these differences all carry methodological import. However, it will transpire that it is not in spite of, but rather just in *virtue of*, the real differences that distinguish the subject matter of the social from the natural sciences that social science is possible; that here, as elsewhere, it is the nature of the object that determines the form of its science. So that to investigate the limits of naturalism is *ipso facto* to investigate the conditions which make social science, whether or not it is actualized in practice, possible.

I want first to sketch the elements of an adequate account of natural science, in relation to which the possibility of social scientific knowledge can be re-appraised.

2 Transcendental Realism and the Problem of Naturalism

I have argued elsewhere that it is a condition of the intelligibility of the experimental establishment and the practical application of our knowledge that its objects are real structures which exist and act independently of the patterns of events they generate.[4] It follows from this that causal laws must be analysed as tendencies, which are only necessarily manifest in empirical invariances under relatively special closed conditions.[5] Thus, contrary to the specific claims of Popper and Hempel and the tacit presupposition of Winch, deducibility from empirical invariances, depending upon the availability of constant conjunctions of events, can be neither necessary nor sufficient for a natural scientific explanation. There is an ontological gap between causal laws and their empirical grounds, which both parties to the naturalist debate have hitherto ignored. This not only renders standard positivist methodological injunctions patently inapplicable, it also vitiates the most familiar hermeneutical contrasts. Thus just as a rule can be broken without being changed, so a natural mechanism may continue to endure, and the law it grounds be both applicable and true (that is, not falsified), though its effect, the consequent, be unrealized.[6]

Knowledge, then, has 'intransitive' objects which exist and act independently of it. But it is itself a social process, whose aim is the production of the knowledge of such objects, that is, of the mechanisms of the production of phenomena in nature. Now if we are to avoid the absurdity of the assumption of the production of such knowledge *ex nihilo* it must depend on the utilization of antecedently existing cognitive materials (which I have called the 'transitive' objects of knowledge). Typically, then, the construction of an explanation for some identified phenomenon will involve the building of a model, making use of such cognitive materials and operating under the control of something like a logic of analogy and metaphor,[7] of a mechanism, which *if* it were to exist and act in the postulated way would account for the phenomenon in question.[8] The reality of the posited explanation must then, of course, be subjected to empirical scrutiny (for in general more than one explanation will be consistent with the phenomenon concerned). Once done, it must then itself in principle be explained. And so we have in science a three-phase schema of development, in which in a continuing dialectic, science identifies a phenomenon (or range of phenomena), constructs explanations for it and empirically tests its explanations, leading to the identification of the generative mechanism at work, which now becomes the phenomenon to be explained, and so on. On this view of science its essence lies in the move at any one level from manifest phenomena to the structures that generate them. The question of naturalism can thus be posed as follows: to what extent is it possible to suppose that a comparable move can be made in the domain of the social sciences?

Now our analysis of science immediately pinpoints an internal difficulty in this project. For the objects of scientific inquiry are neither empirically given nor even actually determinate chunks of the world, but rather real structures, whose actual presence and appropriate concept have to be produced by the experimental and theoretical work of science. Thus it would seem that we must first know what kinds of things societies are before we can consider whether it is possible to study them scientifically. Indeed without some prior specification of an object of inquiry, any discourse on method is bound to be more or less arbitrary. The question to which this chapter aspires to make a contribution may therefore be set as follows: what properties do societies possess that might make them possible objects of knowledge for us?

In considering this question it is essential to establish that these properties, and *a fortiori* their bearers, societies, are real. For unless this is done our analysis of science entails that the possibility of a non-reductionist naturalism must straightaway collapse. Now, in this respect, it is important to note that science employs two criteria for the ascription of reality to a posited object: a perceptual and a causal one. The latter turns on the capacity of the entity whose existence is in doubt to bring about changes in material things. It should be noticed that a magnetic or gravitational field satisfies this criterion, but not a criterion of perceivability. On this criterion to be is not to be perceived, but (in the last instance) just to be able to do.[9] The standard hermeneutical fork, turning on a conceptual/perceptible dichotomy, which we have already seen invoked by Winch, ignores of course just the possibilities opened up by a causal criterion for ascribing reality.

My strategy in this chapter will be based on a pincer movement. First I will concentrate mainly on the ontological question of the properties that societies possess. Then I will shift to the epistemological question of how this might make them objects of knowledge for us. In considering the former I want to argue that society is irreducible to persons and to attempt a sketch of their relationship. For our purposes merely to argue against methodological individualism, though necessary, is not sufficient. For we must show not only that in explanations in the field of the human sciences social predicates are irreducible, but that a realistic interpretation of social scientific explanations is in principle acceptable; we must show that some possible objects designated by social scientific theory are real.

3 Against Methodological Individualism

Methodological individualism asserts that facts about society and social phenomena are to be explained solely in terms of facts about individuals. For Popper, for example, 'all social phenomena, and especially the functioning of social institutions, should be understood as resulting from the decisions etc. of human individuals . . . we should never be satisfied by explanations in terms of so-called "collectives".'[10] Social institutions are merely 'abstract models' designed to interpret the facts of individual experience. As Jarvie has put it: '"army" is just the plural of "soldier" and all statements about the army can be reduced to statements about the particular soldiers comprising it'.[11] Watkins concedes that 'there may be unfinished or half-way explanations of large-scale phenomena in terms of other large-scale phenomena (such as of inflation in terms of full employment)',[12] but contends that we will not have arrived at so-called 'rock-bottom' (ultimate?) explanations of such phenomena until we have deduced them from statements about the dispositions, beliefs, resources and inter-relations of individuals.[13] Specifically, social events are to be explained by deducing them from the principles governing the behaviour of the 'participating' individuals,[14] together with statements of their situations. In this way, methodological individualism stipulates the *material* conditions for adequate explanation in the social sciences to complement the *formal* ones laid down by the deductive–nomological model.

Now when we consider the range of predicates applicable to individuals and individual behaviour – from those that designate properties, such as shape and texture, that people possess in common with other material objects, through those that pick out states, such as hunger and pain, that they share with other higher animals, to those that designate actions that are, as far as we know, uniquely characteristic of them – the real problem appears to be not so much that of how we could give an individualistic explanation of social behaviour, but that of how we could give a non-social (or strictly individualistic) explanation of individual, at least characteristically human, behaviour![15] For the predicates designating properties special to persons all presuppose a social context for their employment. A tribesman implies a tribe, the cashing of a cheque a banking system. Explanation, whether by subsumption under general laws, advertion to motives and rules, or by redescription (identification), always seems to involve irreducibly social predicates.

Moreover it is not difficult to show that the arguments adduced in support of methodological individualism will not bear the weight placed upon them. For example, a comparison of the motives of a criminal with the procedures of a court is sufficient to show that facts about individuals are neither necessarily more observable nor necessarily easier to understand than social phenomena. Again, a comparison of the concepts of love and war shows that concepts applicable to individuals are not necessarily either clearer or easier to define than those that designate social phenomena.

Significantly, the qualifications and refinements proposed by the advocates of methodological individualism weaken rather than strengthen the case for it. Thus the admission of ideal types for instance weakens the force of the ontological considerations in favour of it, while allowing 'halfway' and statistical explanations undermines the epistemological ones. Moreover the examples cited of supposedly genuinely 'holistic' behaviour, such as riots and the biological union of mating couples,[16] merely reveal the poverty of their implicit conception of the social. For, upon analysis of their writing, it is clear that most methodological individualists regard 'the social' as a synonym for 'the group'. The issue for them, then, becomes that of whether society, the whole, is greater than the sum of its constituent parts, individual people. Social behaviour, on this view, then becomes explicable as the behaviour of groups of individuals or of individuals in groups.

Now I think that this definition of the social is radically misconceived: sociology is not concerned, as such, with large-scale, mass or group behaviour, conceived as the behaviour of large numbers, masses or groups of individuals, but (paradigmatically) with the persistent *relations* between individuals (and groups), and with the relations between these relations. Relations such as between capitalist and worker, MP and constituent, student and teacher, husband and wife. Now such relations are general and relatively enduring but they do not involve collective or mass behaviour as such in the way in which a strike or a demonstration does (though of course they may help to explain the latter). Mass behaviour is an interesting social psychological phenomenon, but it is not the subject matter of sociology.

Now what makes this situation particularly ironical is that the more sophisticated methodological individualists formally concede that relations must play some role in explanation. What then accounts for the polemics and the passion? I think that it can only be explained in terms of their desire to defend a particular form of substantive social scientific explanation, which they mistakenly hold to be uniquely consistent with political liberalism. As Watkins himself has put it: 'Since Mandeville's *Fable of the Bees* was published in 1714, individualistic social science with its emphasis on unintended consequences has largely been a sophisticated elaboration on the simple theme that, in certain situations, selfish private motives [i.e. capitalism] may have good social consequences and good political intentions [i.e. socialism] bad social consequences'.[17] There is in fact one body of social doctrine, whose avatars are utilitarianism, liberal political theory, pre-Ricardian classical and neo-classical economic theory, that does conform to individualistic prescriptions, on the assumption that what is in effect a generalized aggregation problem can be solved. According to this model reason is the efficient slave of the passions[18] and social behaviour can be seen as the outcome of a simple maximization problem or its dual, a minimization one: the application of reason, the sole identifying characteristic of man, to desires (appetites and aversions, in Hobbes) or feelings (pleasure and pain, in Hume, Bentham and Mill) that may be regarded as neurophysiologically given. Relations play no part in this model; and this model, if it applies at all, applies as much to Crusoe as to socialized man, and to men whatever (i.e. wherever and whenever) their socialisation – with the corollary expressed by Hume that 'mankind is much the same at all times and places'.[19]

The limitations of this approach to social science should by now be well known. To say that human beings are rational does not explain *what* they do, but only at best (that is, supposing that an objective function could be reconstructed for their behaviour and empirically tested independently of it) *how* they do it. Rationality, purporting to explain everything, ends up explaining nothing. To explain a human action by reference to its rationality is like explaining some natural event by reference to its being caused. Rationality is, in this sense, a presupposition of investigation. As for neo-classical economic theory, the most developed form of this tendency in social thought, it may best be regarded as a normative theory of efficient action, generating a set of techniques for achieving given ends, rather than as an explanatory theory capable of casting light on actual empirical episodes. That is, as a praxiology,[20] not a sociology.

Aside from its championship of a particular explanation form, methodological individualism derives plausibility from the fact that it seems to touch on an important truth, awareness of which accounts for its apparent necessity: namely the idea that society is made up of or consists of and only of people. In what sense is this true? In the sense that the material presence of social effects consists only of changes in people and changes brought about by people on other material things – objects of nature, such as land, and artefacts produced by work on objects of nature. We could express this truth as follows: *the material presence of society = persons and the (material) results of their actions*. It is this truth that the methodological individualists have glimpsed, only to shroud it with their apologetic shifts.

It is clear that there is, in methodological individualism, a sociological reductionism and a psycho-(or praxio-) logical atomism at work, exactly paralleling with respect to the content of explanation, the theoretical reductionism and ontological atomism determining its form. In the philosophy of social science the sociology of individualism plays as important a role in defining the object of investigation as the ontology of empiricism does in defining its method. Together I think that they must be held largely responsible (or rather, they theoretically reflect whatever is responsible) for the social scientific malaise.

The *relational* conception of the subject matter of sociology advocated here may be contrasted not only with the *individualist* conception, exemplified by utilitarian social theory, but with what I shall call the *collectivist* conception, best exemplified perhaps by the work of Durkheim, with its heavy emphasis on the concept of the group. Durkheim's group is not of course the same as Popper's. It is to use a Sartrean analogy more of the nature of a fused group than a series.[21] In particular, as definitive of the social, it is characterized by the possession of certain emergent powers, whose justification I will consider below. Nevertheless the key concepts of the Durkheimian corpus, such as conscience collective, organic *vs.* mechanical solidarity, anomie and so on, all derive their meaning from their relationship to the concept of the collective nature of social phenomena. Thus, for Durkheim, to the extent at least that he is to remain committed to positivism, enduring relationships must be reconstructed from collective phenomena; whereas on the realist and relational view advanced here, collective phenomena are seen primarily as the expressions of enduring relationships. Note that on this conception sociology is not only not essentially concerned with the group, it is not even essentially concerned with behaviour.

If Durkheim combined a collectivist conception of sociology with a positivist methodology, Weber combined a neo-Kantian methodology with a still essentially individualist conception of sociology. His break from utilitarianism is primarily at the level of the forms of action or types of behaviour he is prepared to recognize, not at the level of the unit of study. It is significant that just as the thrust contained in Durkheim's isolation of the emergent properties of the group is constrained by his continuing commitment to an empiricist methodology, so the possibilities opened up by Weber's isolation of the ideal type are constrained by his continuing commitment to an empiricist ontology.[22] In both cases a residual empiricism holds back, and ultimately annuls, a real scientific advance. For it is as futile to attempt to sustain a concept of the social on the basis of the category of the group, as it is to attempt to sustain a concept of natural necessity on the basis of the category of experience. Marx, I think, did make the attempt to combine a realist ontology and a

relational sociology.[23] One can thus schematize four tendencies in social
thought as in Table 1.

Table 1

	Method	*Object*
Utilitarianism	empiricist	individualist
Weber	neo-Kantian	individualist
Durkheim	empiricist	collectivist
Marx	realist	relational

Note: concepts of method (social epistemology) underpinned by general ontology; concepts
of object (social ontology) underpinned by general epistemology.

It should be noted that as the relations between the relations that
constitute the proper subject matter of sociology may themselves be
internally related only the category of *totality* can express this. Some
problems that this gives rise to will be considered below. But now I want
to consider the nature of the connection between society and people.

4 Four Models of the Society/Person Relationship

It is customary to draw a divide between two camps in sociological
theory: one, represented above all by Weber, in which social objects are
seen as the results of (or as constituted by) intentional or meaningful
human behaviour; and the other, represented by Durkheim, in which they
are seen as possessing a life of their own, external to and coercing the individual. With some stretching the various schools of social thought –
phenomenology, existentialism, structuralism, etc. – can then be seen as
instances of one or other of these positions. And various brands of
Marxism can then also be neatly classified. These two stereotypes can be
represented as in the diagrams below.

Society	Society
↑	↓
Individual	Individual

Model I   The Weberian Stereotype   *Model II*   The Durkheimian
   'Voluntarism'   Stereotype 'Reification'

Now it is tempting to try to develop a general model capable of synthesizing these conflicting perspectives, on the assumption of a dialectical inter-relationship between society and individuals. I want to discuss a plausible variant of such a model, advocated most convincingly by Peter Berger and his associates.[24] Its weaknesses will, I think, enable us to work our way to a more adequate conception of the relationship between society and people, as well as to better display the errors of the conventional stereotypes.

According to the Berger model, which I shall call Model III, society forms the individuals who create society; society, that is, produces people, who produce society, in a continuous dialectic. Model III can be represented by the diagram below.

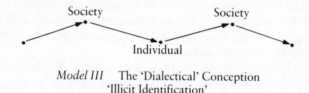

Model III   The 'Dialectical' Conception
'Illicit Identification'

According to the proponents of this model 'social structure is not characterisable as a thing able to stand on its own, apart from the human activity that produced it'.[25] But equally, once created, 'it is encountered by the individual [both] as an alien facticity [and] . . . as a coercive instrumentality'.[26] 'It is *there*, impervious to his wishes, . . . other than [and resistant to] himself.'[27] This schema thus seems able to do justice both to the subjective and intentional aspects of social life and to the externality and coercive power of social facts. In this way any voluntaristic implications of the Weberian tradition and any reification associated with the Durkheimian one are simultaneously avoided; for a radical distinction is now drawn between natural and social facts, in that the latter but not the former do not exist independently of human activity.

Thus while agreeing with Durkheim that 'the system of signs I use to express my thoughts, the system of currency I employ to pay my debts, the instruments of credit I utilise in my commercial relations, the practices followed in my profession etc. function independently of my use of them,'[28] advocates of this model regard such systems, instruments and practices as *objectivations* that, under certain conditions, take on an alienated form. According to them objectivation is 'the process whereby human subjectivity embodies itself in products that are available to oneself and one's fellow men as elements of a common world'[29] and 'alienation is the process whereby the unity of the producing and the product is broken.'[30] Thus languages, forms of economic and political organization, cultural and ethical norms are all ultimately embodiments of human subjectivity. And any consciousness which does not see them as such is necessarily reified. Reification must, however, be distinguished from *objectivication*. This is necessary for any conceivable social life and is defined as 'the moment in the process of objectivation in which man establishes distance from his producing and its product, such that he can take cognizance of it and make of it an object of his consciousness'.[31]

On Model III, then, society is an objectivation or externalization of people. And people, for their part, are the internalization or re-appropriation in consciousness of society. Now I think that this model is seriously misleading. For it encourages, on the one hand, a voluntaristic idealism with respect to our understanding of social structure and, on the other, a mechanistic determinism with respect to our understanding of people. People and society are not, I shall argue, related 'dialectically'. They do not constitute two moments of the same process. Rather they refer to radically different kinds of thing.

Let us consider society. To return for a moment to Durkheim. It will be remembered that, reminding us that the church-member, or let us say the language-user, finds the beliefs and practices of his religious life, or the structure of his language, ready-made at birth, he argues that it is their existence *prior* to his own that implies their existence *outside* himself, and from which their coercive power is ultimately derived.[32] Now if this is the case and the social structure, and the natural world in so far as it is appro-priated by human agents, is always *already made*, then Model III must be corrected in a fundamental way. It is still true to say that society would not exist without human activity, so that reification remains an error. And it is still true to say that such activity would not occur unless the agents engaging in it had a conception of what they were doing.[33] But it is no longer true to say that human agents *create* it. Rather we must say: they *reproduce* or *transform* it. That is to say, if society is already made, then any concrete human praxis or, if you like, act of objectivation, can only modify it; and the totality of such acts sustain or change it. It is not the product of their activity (any more than their actions are completely determined by it). Society stands to individuals, then, as something that they never make, but that exists only in virtue of their activity.

The alternative model I propose, Model IV, may thus be expressed as follows: people do not create society. For it always pre-exists them. Rather it is an ensemble of structures, practices and conventions that individuals reproduce or transform. But which would not exist unless they did so. Society does not exist independently of conscious human activity (the error of reification). But it is not the product of the latter (the error of voluntarism). This model may be represented diagrammatically as below.

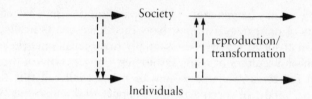

Model IV   The Transformational Model of Social Activity

What is the counterpart, represented by the downward vertical lines, to the relationship of reproduction/transformation in which individuals stand to society? Society provides the necessary conditions for intentional human activity (as well as, in any given case, to a greater or lesser extent circumscribing its form). The processes whereby the stock of skills and competences appropriate to given social contexts are acquired could be generically referred to as 'socialization'. Notice that on Model I there are actions, but no conditions; on Model II conditions but no actions; on Model III no distinction between the two. Thus in Durkheim subjectivity tends to appear only in the guise of the interiorized form of social constraint. But a moment's reflection shows equally that real subjectivity requires conditions under which, and materials (such as language) with which, the subject can act.

It should be noted that Model IV, as a result of its emphasis on material continuity, can sustain a genuine concept of *change*, and hence of *history*[34] – something that neither Model III nor the methodological stereotypes it attempts to situate as special cases can do. Thus Model III appears to involve continuous recreation with genuine novelty, seemingly entailing incomplete social formation, something of a mystery. On the Weberian methodological stereotype change reduces to contrast, and on the Durkheimian one it can only be explained by advertion to exogenous variables. Model IV, moreover, generates a clear criterion of historically significant events, namely those that initiate or constitute ruptures, mutations or more generally transformations in social forms (such as Dalton's training as a meteorologist or the French Revolution).

5 Some Emergent Properties of Social Systems

Now if society pre-exists the individual, objectivation takes on a very different significance. For it, conscious human activity, consists of work on *given* objects, and cannot be conceived as taking place in their absence.

These objects may be material or ideational. And they may be regarded as the results of prior objectivations. Now this suggests a radically different conception of social activity, an essentially Aristotelian one: the paradigm being that of a sculptor at work, fashioning a product out of the material and with the tools available to him or her. I shall call this the transformational model of social activity. It applies to discursive as well as to non-discursive practices; to science and politics, as much as to economics. Thus in science the raw materials used in the construction of new theories are established results, half-forgotten ideas, the stock of available paradigms and models, methods and techniques of inquiry; so that the scientific innovator comes to appear in retrospect as a kind of cognitive *bricoleur*.[35] To use the Aristotelian terms, then, in every process of productive activity a material as well as an efficient cause is necessary. And social activity consists, then, at least paradigmatically in work on and the transformation of given materials.

If such work constitutes the analogue of natural events, then we need an analogue for the mechanisms that generate them. If social structures constitute the appropriate mechanism-analogue then we must at once register an important difference – in that, unlike natural mechanisms, they exist only in virtue of the activities they govern and cannot be empirically identified independently of them. Because of this they must be social products themselves. Thus people in their social activity must perform a double function: they must not only make social products but make the conditions of their making, that is, reproduce (or to a greater or lesser extent transform) the structures governing their substantive activities of production. Because social structures are themselves social products, they are themselves possible objects of transformation and so may be only relatively enduring. And because social activities are interdependent, social structures may be only relatively autonomous. Society may thus be conceived as an articulated ensemble of such relatively independent and enduring structures; that is, as a complex totality subject to change both in its components and their interrelations. Moreover it is important to note that because social structures exist only in virtue of the activities they govern, they do not exist independently of the conceptions that the agents possess of what they are doing in their activity; that is, of some theory of these activities. Finally, because social structures are themselves social products, social activity must be given a social explanation, and cannot be explained by reference to non-social parameters (though the latter may impose constraints on the possible forms of social activity).

Some ontological limitations on a possible naturalism in the domain of the social sciences can be immediately derived from these emergent social properties, on the assumption (to be vindicated in the next section) that society is *sui generis* real:

(i) social structures, unlike natural structures, do not exist independently of the activities they govern;

(ii) social structures, unlike natural structures, do not exist independently of the agents' conceptions of what they are doing in their activity;

(iii) social structures, unlike natural structures, may be only relatively enduring (so that the tendencies they ground may not be universal in the sense of space–time invariant).[36]

These all indicate real differences in the possible objects of knowledge in the case of the natural and social sciences. They are not of course unconnected. Though one should be wary of drawing conclusions of the sort: 'Society exists only in virtue of human activity. Human activity is conscious. Therefore consciousness brings about change.' For (a) social changes need not be consciously intended and (b) if there are social conditions for consciousness, changes in it can in principle be socially explained. Society, then, is an articulated ensemble of tendencies and powers which, unlike natural ones, exist only as long as they (or at least some of them) are being exercised; are exercised in the last instance via the intentional activity of human beings; and are not necessarily space–time invariant.

To turn now to people. Human action is characterized by the striking phenomenon of intentionality. This seems to stem from the fact that persons are material things with a degree of neurophysiological complexity which enables them not just, like the higher animals, to initiate changes in a purposeful way, to monitor and control their performances, but to monitor the monitoring of these performances and to be capable of a commentary upon them.[37] This capacity for second-order monitoring also makes possible a restrospective commentary upon actions, which gives a person's own account of his or her behaviour a special status, which is acknowledged in the best practice of all the psychological sciences.

The importance of distinguishing, in the most categorical way, between human action and the social structure will now be apparent. For the properties possessed by social forms may be very different from those possessed by the individuals upon whose activity they depend. For instance we can suppose without paradox or tension that purposefulness, intentionality and sometimes self-consciousness characterize human action, but not changes in the social structure. I want to distinguish sharply then between the genesis of human actions, lying in the reasons, intentions and plans of human beings, on the one hand; and the structures governing the reproduction and transformation of social activities, on the other; and hence between the domains of the psychological and the social sciences. The problem of how people reproduce any particular society belongs to a linking science of social psychology. It should be noted that engagement in a social activity is itself a conscious human action which may, in general, be described either in terms of the agent's reasons for engaging in it or in terms of its social function or role.

Now the autonomy of the social and the psychological does justice to our intuitions. Thus we do not suppose that the reason why garbage is collected is necessarily the garbage collector's reason for collecting it (though it depends upon the latter). And we can allow that our speech is governed by the rules of grammar without supposing either that these rules exist independently of our speech habits (reification) or that they determine what we say. The rules of grammar, like natural structures, impose *limits* upon the speech acts that we can perform, but they do not *determine* our performances. One great advantage of this conception of social science is thus that it preserves the status of human agency, while doing away with the myth of creation (logical or historical), which depends upon the possibility of an individualist reduction. And in so doing it allows us to see that necessity in social life operates in the last instance via the intentional activity of agents. Looked at in this way, then, we may regard it as the task of the various social sciences to lay out the structural conditions for various forms of conscious action – for example, what economic processes must take place for Christmas shopping to be possible – but they do not describe the latter.

To return once again to the relationship between society and people. The conception I am proposing is that people, in their conscious human activity, for the most part unconsciously reproduce (or occasionally, transform) the structures that govern their substantive activities of production. Thus people do not marry to reproduce the nuclear family, or work to reproduce the capitalist economy. But it is nevertheless the unintended consequence (and inexorable result) of, as it is also the necessary condition for, their activity.

6 On the Reality of Society and the Subject Matter of Sociology

I now want to return to the question of the ontological status of societies. I have argued elsewhere that living things determine the conditions of applicability of the physical laws to which they are subject, so that their properties cannot be reduced to the latter; and hence that emergence characterizes both the natural and the human worlds.[38] (And that this is consistent with what may be termed a 'diachronic explanatory reduction', that is, a reconstruction of the historical processes of their formation out of 'simpler' things.) If intentional action is a necessary condition for certain determinate states of the physical world, then the properties and powers that persons possess in virtue of which intentionality is correctly attributed to them are real. Similarly, if it can be shown that but for society, certain physical actions would not be performed, then, employing the causal criterion set out at the beginning, we are justified in asserting that it is real.

Now I think that Durkheim, having established the autonomy of social facts using the criterion of externality, in effect employed just such a criterion to establish their reality, in invoking his other criterion of constraint: 'I am not obliged to speak French with my fellow-countrymen nor to use the legal currency, but I cannot possibly do otherwise. If I tried to escape this necessity, my attempts would fail miserably. As an industrialist, I am free to apply the technical methods of former centuries; but by doing so I should invite certain ruin. Even when I free myself from these rules and violate them successfully, I am always compelled to struggle with them. When finally overcome, they make their constraining power felt by the resistance they offer.'[39] Durkheim is saying in effect that, but for the range of social facts, particular sequences of sounds, movements of bodies etc. would not occur. Of course we must insist, against Durkheim, that the range of social facts depends upon the intentional activity of human beings. The individualist truth that people are the only moving forces in history – in the sense that nothing happens behind their backs, that is, everything that happens, happens in and through their actions – must be retained. Moreover we must conceive social structures as in principle enabling, and not just coercive. Nevertheless, in employing a causal criterion to establish the reality of social facts, Durkheim observed perfectly proper scientific practice.[40] It must be noticed, however, that we are here dealing with a most peculiar kind of entity: a structure irreducible to, but present only, in its effects.

What is the connection between the transformational model of social activity developed in §5 and the relational conception of the subject matter of sociology advanced in §3? The relational conception does not of course deny that factories and books are social forms. But it maintains that their being *social*, as distinct from (or rather in addition to) material, objects, consists only in the relationships between persons or between such relationships and nature that such objects causally presuppose or entail. The *social* conditions for the structures that govern the substantive activities of transformation in which human beings engage (and which constitute the immediate explanation of these activities) can thus only be relations of various kinds: between people and each other, their products, their activities, nature and themselves. If social activity is to be given a social explanation it is in this nexus that it must be found. It is thus in the enduring relations presupposed by, rather than the actual complex motley of, particular social forms, that on this conception, sociology's distinctive theoretical interest lies.

Marx combined a relational conception of social science and a transformational model of social activities with the additional premiss – of historical materialism – that it is material production that is ultimately determining of the rest of social life.[41] Now, as is well known, although it can be established a priori that material production is a necessary condition for social life, it cannot be established a priori that it is the ultimately determining one. And so like any other fundamental metaphysical blueprint or paradigm in science, historical materialism can only be justified by its fruitfulness in generating research programmes capable of yielding sequences of theories, progressively richer in explanatory power. Not the least of the problems facing historical materialism is that, although progress has been made in particular areas of explanation, the blueprint itself still awaits adequate articulation. (One has only to think of the problem of reconciling the thesis of the relative autonomy of the superstructures with that of their determination in the last instance by the base[42] to be reminded of this.)

7 The Limits of Naturalism

How, given that societies exist, and have the kinds of properties that they do, might they become possible objects of knowledge for us?

The major ontological limits on the possibility of naturalism, turning on the activity-, concept-, and space–time-dependence of social structures, have already been isolated. Before considering how social scientific knowledge is possible, despite or as I shall try to show because of these features, I want to consider two other kinds of limits on naturalism, which I shall characterize as epistemological and relational respectively.

Society, as an object of inquiry, is necessarily 'theoretical' in the sense that, like a magnetic field, it is necessarily unperceivable; so that it cannot be empirically identified independently of its effects. It can only be known, not shown, to exist. However in this respect it is no different from many objects of natural scientific inquiry. What does differentiate it is that society not only cannot be empirically identified independently of its effects, but it does not *exist* independently of them either. But, however strange this is from an ontological point of view,[43] it raises no special epistemological difficulties.

The chief epistemological limit on naturalism is not raised by the necessarily unperceivable character of the objects of social scientific investigation, but by the fact that they only manifest themselves in 'open systems'; that is, in systems where invariant empirical regularities do not obtain. Now the real methodological import of this point must be distinguished most carefully from its significance for the doctrines of received philosophy of science. It is as easy to exaggerate the former, as to underestimate the latter. For, as I have shown in detail elsewhere,[44] practically all the theories of orthodox philosophy of science, and the methodological directives they secrete presuppose closed systems. Because of this, they are totally inapplicable to the social sciences – which is not of course to say that the attempt cannot be made to apply them, with disastrous results. Humean theories of causality and law, deductive–nomological and statistical models of explanation, inductivist theories of scientific development and criteria of confirmation, and Popperian theories of scientific rationality and criteria of falsification, together with the hermeneutical contrasts parasitic upon them, must all be totally discarded. The only concern of social science with them is as objects of substantive explanation.

The real methodological import of the absence of spontaneously occurring, and the impossibility of artificially creating, closed systems is strictly limited: it is that the social sciences are denied, in principle, decisive test situations for their theories. This means that the criteria for the rational confirmation and rejection of theories in social science *cannot be predictive*, and so must be *exclusively explanatory*. Particularly important here will be the capacity of a theory to be developed in a non-*ad hoc* way so as to situate, and preferably explain, without strain, a possibility, once (and perhaps even before) it is realized, when it could never, given the openness of the social world, have predicted it. It should be stressed that this difference has in itself no ontological significance whatsoever. It does not affect the form of laws, which in natural science too must be analysed as tendencies; only the form of our knowledge of them. Because the mode of application of laws is the same in open and closed systems alike,[45] the mode of application of laws is the same in society as in nature. And although the necessity to rely exclusively on explanatory criteria *may* affect the subjective confidence with which we hold social scientific theories, if we have *independently* validated claims to social scientific knowledge (on explanatory criteria) then we are just as warranted in applying our knowledge as in natural science. Or rather, given that the problem is not typically whether or not to apply some theory, T, to the world, but rather *which* out of two or more theories, T, T′ ... etc. to apply, the degree of our preference for one theory over another will not be affected by a limitation on the grounds with which that preference must be justified.

In addition to allowing (relatively)[46] decisive test situations, experimental activity in the natural sciences, in enabling access to the otherwise latent structures of nature, may provide an invaluable component of the process of scientific discovery that the social sciences, in this respect, will be denied. However, our discussion of the relational and ontological limits will generate an analogue and a compensator respectively for this role in discovery.

The chief relational difference is that the social sciences are part of their own field of inquiry, in principle susceptible to explanation in terms of the concepts and laws of the explanatory theories they employ; so that they are *internal* with respect to their subject matter in a way in which natural science is not. This qualifies the sense in which the objects of social scientific investigation can be said to be intransitive, or exist and act independently of it. For it is possible and indeed likely, given the internal complexity and interdependence of social activities, that its objects do not exist independently of, and may be causally affected by, social science; just as one might expect that social science is affected or conditioned by developments in, as it patently cannot exist independently of, the rest of society. So far the argument has turned merely on the possibility of a relatively undifferentiated society/social science link. But the case for such a link may be strengthened by noting that just as a social science without a society is impossible, so a society without some kind of scientific, proto-scientific, or ideological theory of itself is inconceivable (even if it consists merely in the conceptions that the agents have of what they are doing in their activity). Now if we denote the proto-scientific set of ideas P, then the transformational model of social activity applied to the activity of knowledge-production would suggest that social scientific theory, T, requiring cognitive resources is produced, at least in part, by the transformation of P. The hypothesis under consideration is that this transformation will be vitally affected by developments in the rest of society, S.

It might be conjectured that in periods of transition or crisis generative structures, formerly opaque, become more visible to men and women.[47] And that this, though it never yields the epistemic possibilities of a closure, does provide a partial analogue to the role that experimental activity plays in natural science. The social conditions for the production and emergence of a social scientific theory must of course be distinguished from the conditions for its subsequent development and (though there are evident connections between the two) from the conditions for its wider societal influence or assent.[48] Thus it is surely no accident that Marxism was born in the 1840s or stunted in the East under Stalin and in the West during the Cold War and post-war boom. Or that sociology, in the narrow sense, was the fruit of the two decades before the First World War.[49]

It should be noted that because social systems are open historicism (in the sense of deductively justified prediction) is untenable. Moreover, because of the historical (transformational) character of social systems, qualitatively new developments in society will be occurring which social scientific theory cannot be expected to anticipate. Hence for ontological, as distinct from purely epistemological, reasons, social scientific, unlike natural scientific, theory is *necessarily* incomplete. Moreover, as the possibilities inherent in a new social development will often only become apparent long after the development itself, and as each new development is, in a sense, a product of a previous one, we can see why it is that history must be continually rewritten. There is a relational tie between the development of the object of knowledge and the development of know-ledge that any adequate theory of social science, and methodology of social scientific research programmes, must take account of. In particular, Lakatosian judgements about the progressive or degenerating nature of research programmes[50] in the social sciences cannot be made in isolation from judgements about factors in the rest of society, S, conditioning work in particular programmes.

Once a hypothesis of a causal mechanism has been produced in social science it can then be tested quite *empirically*, though exclusively by refer-ence to its explanatory power. But I have so far said nothing about how the hypothesis of the generative mechanism is produced, or indeed about what its status is. It is to these questions that I now turn.

In considering theory construction in the social sciences it should be borne in mind that the putative social scientist would, in the absence of some prior theory, be faced with an inchoate mass of social phenomena, which he or she would somehow have to sort out and define. In systems, like social ones, which are necessarily open, the problem of constituting an appropriate (i.e. explanatorily significant) object of inquiry becomes par-ticularly acute. Fortunately most of the phenomena with which the social scientist has to deal will already be identified, thanks to the *concept-dependent* nature of social activities, under certain descriptions. In prin-ciple the descriptions or nominal definitions of social activities that form the transitive objects of social scientific theory may be those of the agents concerned or theoretical redescriptions of them. The first step in the trans-formation P → T will thus be an attempt at a real definition of a form of social life that has already been identified under a particular description. Note that in the absence of such a definition, and failing a closure, any hypothesis of a causal mechanism is bound to be more or less arbitrary. Thus in social science attempts at real definitions will in general precede rather than follow successful causal hypotheses – though in both cases they can only be justified empirically, that is, by the revealed explanatory power of the hypotheses that can be derived from them.

The problem, then, is shifted from that of how to establish a non-arbitrary procedure for generating causal hypotheses to that of how to establish a non-arbitrary procedure for generating real definitions. And here a second differentiating feature of the subject-matter of the social

sciences should be recalled – the *activity-dependent* nature of social structures, such that the mechanisms at work in society exist only in virtue of
their effects. In this respect society is quite distinct from other objects of
scientific knowledge. But note that, in this, it is analogous to the objects of
philosophical knowledge. For just as the objects of philosophical knowledge do not exist as objects of a world apart from the objects of scientific
knowledge, so social structures do not exist apart from their effects. So I
suggest that in principle as philosophical discourse stands to scientific
discourse, so a discourse about society stands to a discourse about its
effects. Moreover, in both cases we are dealing with conceptualized
activities, whose conditions of possibility or presuppositions the second-
order discourse seeks to explicate. However, there are also important
differences. For in social scientific discourse we are concerned not to isolate the general conditions of knowledge as such, but the particular
mechanisms and relations at work in some identified sphere of social life.
Moreover, its conclusions will be historical, not formal; and subject to
empirical test, as well as to various a priori controls.[51]

It is here that the hermeneutical tradition, in highlighting what may be
called the conceptual moment in social scientific work, has made a real
contribution. But it makes two mistakes. Its continuing commitment to
the ontology of empirical realism prevents it from seeing (1) that the
conditions for the phenomena, namely social activities as conceptualized
in experience, may be *real*; and (2) that the phenomena themselves may
be *false* or in an important sense inadequate.

Thus what has been established, by conceptual analysis, as necessary
for the phenomena may consist precisely in that extra-conceptual reality
which consists of the real relations and processes in which people stand to
each other and nature, of which they may or may not be aware; which is
really generative of social life and yet unavailable to direct inspection by
the senses. Moreover, such a transcendental analysis in social science in
showing the historical conditions under which a set of categories may be
validly applied *ipso facto* shows the conditions under which they may not
be applied. This makes possible a second-order critique of consciousness,
best exemplified perhaps by Marx's analysis of commodity fetishism.[52]
Value relations, it will be remembered, for Marx, are real but they are
historically specific social realities. And fetishism consists of their transformation in thought into the natural, and so ahistorical, qualities of
things. But, as Norman Geras has pointed out,[53] Marx employed another
concept of mystification. This is best exemplified by his treatment of the
wage form, in which the value of labour power is transformed into the
value of labour. This Marx declares to be an expression 'as imaginary as
the value of the earth', 'as irrational as a yellow logarithm'.[54] Here he
engages in what we may call a first-order critique of consciousness – in

which, to put it bluntly, he identifies the phenomena themselves as false; or, more formally, shows that a certain set of categories are not properly applicable to experience at all. Thus, contrary to what is implied in the transcendental idealist tradition, the transformation P → T both (1) isolates real but non-empirical conditions and (2) consists essentially, as critique, in two types of conceptual criticism and change.

Now the appellation 'ideology' to the set of ideas P is only justified if their *necessity* can be demonstrated; that is, if they can be explained, as well as criticized.[55] This involves something more than just being able to say that the beliefs concerned are false (or superficial) and being able to say why they are false or superficial, which normally entails of course having a superior explanation for the phenomenon in question. It involves, in addition, being able to give an account of the *reasons* why the false or superficial beliefs are *held* – a mode of explanation clearly without parallel in the natural sciences. For beliefs, whether about society or nature, are clearly social objects.

Once this step is taken then conceptual criticism and change passes over into social criticism and change. For, in a possibility unique to social science, the object that renders illusory beliefs necessary comes, at least in the absence of any overriding considerations, to be criticized in being explained. So that the point now becomes, *ceteris paribus*, to change it. In the full development of the concept of ideology, theory fuses into practice, as facts about values, mediated by theories about facts, are transformed into values about facts.[56] The rule of value-neutrality, the last shibboleth of the philosophy of social science, collapses, when we come to see that values themselves can be false.

To sum up, then, society is not given in, but presupposed by, experience. But it is precisely its peculiar ontological status, its transcendentally real character, that makes it a possible object of knowledge for us. Such knowledge is non-natural but still scientific.

As for the law-like statements of the social sciences, they designate tendencies operating at a single level of the social structure only. Because they are defined only for one relatively autonomous component of the social structure and because they act in systems that are always open, they designate tendencies (such as for the rates of profit on capitalist enterprises to be equalized) which may never be manifested. But they are nevertheless essential to the understanding and the changing of, just because they are really productive of, the different forms of social life.

As for society itself it is not, as the positivists would have it, a mass of separable events and sequences. Nor is it constituted, as a rival school would have it, by the momentary meanings that we attach to our physiological states. Rather it is a complex and causally efficacious whole – a totality, whose concept must be constructed in theory, and which is being continually transformed in practice. As an object of study, it cannot be read straight off the empirical world. But neither can it be reconstructed from our subjective experiences. But, though positivism would have had us forget it, that much at least is the case with the objects of study in natural science too.

6

Scientific Explanation and Human Emancipation

1 Introduction

What connections, if any, exist between explanations in the human sciences and the project of human emancipation?[1] I want to address this issue in the light of the transcendental realist reconstruction of science[2] and the critical naturalism which that reconstruction enables.[3]

My main target will be *positivism*, and the doctrine of the *value-neutrality* of social science. But I will also be attacking a rationalistic *intellectualism*, which sees social theory as (actually or potentially) immediately efficacious in practice.

In opposition to positivism, and its historicist/hermeneuticist displacements, I want to argue that the human sciences are intrinsically critical and self-critical; that accounts of social objects are not only value-impregnated, but *value-impregnating*; and that the possibility of a scientific *critique* of lay (and proto-scientific) ideas, grounded in explanatory practices based on respect for the authenticity and epistemic significance of those ideas, affords to the human sciences an essential emancipatory impulse, in virtue of which, subject to the operation of various *ceteris paribus* clauses, we pass securely from statements of fact to value.

However, in opposition to the idealist (theoreticist) notion of the unmediated efficacy of social science, I want to insist that it always occurs in the context of a situation co-determined by non-cognitive features too. Social theory appears, then, as *conditioned critique*: as subject, in its genesis and effect, to non-theoretical, as well as theoretical, determinations (whose critical understanding is itself part of the task of theory). This is of course an implication of historical *materialism*. To conceive critique as conditioned by factors outside itself is not to impugn its normative power, merely to be realistic about its practical impact.

On the view advocated here, knowledge, though necessary, is insufficient, for freedom. For to be free is (i) to know, (ii) to possess the opportunity and (iii) to be disposed to act in (or towards) one's real interests. Freedom can thus be no more the simple recognition of, than it is escape from, necessity. Hegel (and Engels) and Sartre (and perhaps Marx, at least in his more chiliastic proclamations) are equally wrong – on the condition that circumstances or wants contain any non-cognitive components. It is salutary to remember that there is a logical gap between 'knowing' and 'doing', which can only be bridged by 'wanting in suitable circumstances'. It is the argument of this chapter that the special qualitative kind of becoming free, or liberation, which is *emancipation*, and which consists in the *transformation*, in 'self-emancipation' by the agent or agents concerned, *from an unwanted to a wanted source of determination*, is both *causally presaged* and *logically entailed* by explanatory theory, but that it can only be effected in *practice*.

2 Explanatory Schemata and Transcendental Realism

To explain something is to resolve some agent's perplexity about it: it is to render the unintelligible intelligible – by the elucidation, extension, modification or replacement of that agent's existing conceptual field.[4] In particular, scientific explanations do not resolve problems by subsuming some particular problem under a more general one, but by locating such (normally already generalized) problems in the context of a new cognitive setting; it is (new) *concepts*, not (universal) *quantifiers* which accomplish explanatory problem-resolution in science. But the empirical adequacy of any such resolution must be tested by devising or finding conditions under which the referent of the (conceptual) object posited in the explanans operates free from extraneous influences. Now the enduring and transfactually active nature of such referents is a condition of the intelligibility of this experimental/exploratory activity; and so the philosophy of science must draw ontological distinctions between structures and events (the domains of the real and the actual) and open systems and closed, indexing the stratification and differentiation of reality.[5]

Typically, then, to *explain* an event or a regularity is to bring it under a new scheme of concepts, designating the structures, generative mechanisms or agents producing it. But, in line with their undifferentiated ontology, the dominant traditions in the philosophy of science have not clearly distinguished *theoretical* from *practical* (concrete, 'historical' or applied) explanations, neither of which is either deductive or inductive in form. Theoretical explanations are iteratively analogical and retroductive; that is, antecedently available cognitive resources are used to construct plausible models of the mechanisms producing identified patterns of phenomena, which are then empirically checked out, and, if deemed adequate, in turn explained, in a continuingly unfolding dialectic of taxonomic and explanatory knowledge.[6] Practical explanations involve the RRRE schema. This consists in the resolution of complexes ('conjunctures' or 'compounds'); the redescription of their components; the retrodiction to possible antecedents of these components; and the elimination of alternative possible causes.[7] Thus if theory assumes the form of the abduction of the abstract from the concrete, applied work characteristically depends upon the reverse movement, leading to the recovery from the abstract of the concrete, now reconstructed as the product of a multiplicity of abstractly apprehended determinants. Knowledge of structures and of their contingent modes of articulation in time thus appear as distinct moments of scientific activity. Between abstract sciences and the reconstructed concepts of concrete objects lie the concrete sciences (like biography) which study the ensemble of significant truths about a given thing and the intermediate sciences (like ecology) which study the confluence of two or more orders of determination. Of course inasmuch as these types of explanation succeed in identifying *real*, but hitherto *unrecognized*, conditions and patterns of determination they immediately augment our knowledge, and hence (on the definition enlisted above), *ceteris paribus*, our freedom.

On the metaphysics implied by the new analysis of science, ontology is vindicated as a study of the presuppositions of scientific practice, and the error of its reduction to epistemology is isolated. Moreover the world, *as we actually know it* (under the descriptions currently available to science), is now revealed as characterized by situations of dual and multiple control and by the phenomenon of emergence.

But transcendental realism does not license the simple-minded application of results derived from reflection on the conditions of the natural sciences to the social sphere. Rather, it is only in virtue of an independent analysis, that we are in a position to see that there is a *paramorphic* relationship between the natural and the human sciences, such that there are knowable structures at work in the human domain partially analogous, but irreducible, to those identified in nature. Thus the material causality of social forms appears as a condition of intentional agency, and the efficient causality of beliefs as a condition of discursive thought. But a realist interpretation of non-physical (*sui generis* sociological, psychological) explanations of human phenomena is only justified if it can be shown that there are properties instantiated in the human world inexplicable in terms of different sets of conditions of purely natural laws. In concrete terms, the emergence of society is manifest in the causal irreducibility of social forms in the genesis of human action (or being), and the emergence of mind in the causal irreducibility of beliefs in the explanation of those changes in the states of the physical world which are the result of intentional agency. (Of course the relations are two-way. But the human effects of natural causes are normally mediated as cultural products, and the social effects of human actions in institutions.)

The resulting critical naturalism has nothing in common with either positivism or scientism, because clear differences transpire between positivism and science, on the one hand, and the human and natural sciences, on the other. Nor is it 'objectivist' in either method or result: for it is predicated on the analysis of (existing conceptualizations of) historical practices, and it situates these analyses within the framework of the same historical processes which social science describes and philosophy explicates. But positivism's anti-scientific hermeneutical foil is shown to be equally untenable – for the very features it picks upon (such as *Verstehen*) themselves require for their intelligibility crucial aspects of the categorial framework of natural science (existential intransitivity, causality and so on). Nor do neo-Kantian syntheses of dual criteria or multiple interests fare any better. This is not only because the components of the attempted syntheses are faulty (for example, in being based on a positivistic misconception of natural science), but because the very project of rendering ontological mediations as epistemological divisions is fundamentally mistaken. Thus conceptuality is a condition of generality in the historical domain; and there too an emancipatory conatus is initiated as an effect of explanatory power, in circumstances where it cannot be a universal or constitutive condition for it. (The critical cutting edge that Habermas's work retains despite this is achieved only by the effective noumenalization of discourse as a counter-factual counterpoint to the realm of historical agency.[8])

3 Social Structure and Human Agency

On the transformational model of social activity (TMSA), entailed by the new critical naturalism, the ontological structure of human activity or praxis is conceived, after Aristotle, as consisting in the transformation by efficient (intentional) agency of pre-given material (natural and social) causes. A criterion for differentiating the *social* from the purely *natural* material causes is given by their property that, though necessarily pre-given to any particular agent, and a condition for every intentional act, they exist and persist only in virtue of human agency. On this model, then, social structure and human agency are seen as existentially interdependent but essentially distinct.[9] Society is both ever-present *condition* and continually reproduced *outcome* of human agency: this is the duality of structure.[10] And human agency is both work (generically conceived), that is, (normally conscious) *production*, and (normally unconscious) *reproduction* of the conditions of production, including society: this is the duality of praxis. Thus agents reproduce, *non-teleologically* and *recursively*, in their substantive motivated productions, the unmotivated conditions necessary for – as means of – those productions; and society is both the medium and result of this activity. From this model flow a series of limits on naturalism, which may be summarized as the activity-, concept-, and space–time-dependence of social forms, in virtue of which (as I have attempted to argue elsewhere)[11] a *sui generis* social science is possible. Of course the holistic, hermeneutical and historical character of social objects necessitates differences in the structure of social scientific explanations; so that, paradigmatically, social complexes must be understood as partially conceptually articulated totalities in continual transformation. Similarly, the impossibility of artificially producing, and the unavailability of spontaneously occurring, closed systems requires reliance on purely explanatory (non-predictive) criteria of confirmation and falsification, and more generally theory-development and theory-assessment. However, in relation to the specificity of social objects, (non-scientistic) scientific knowledge of them is *possible*.

The TMSA allows us to pinpoint a double set of paired mistakes: the ontological errors of reification and voluntarism, and the epistemological ones of (social) determinism and (methodological) individualism. (Both may be combined to produce various pseudo-dialectical hybrids.) And it allows us to isolate the closely affiliated weaknesses of the substantive traditions of structuralism and functionalism, on the one hand, and action-oriented and interpretative sociologies, on the other. For its part, the TMSA respects a methodological distinction between the *social sciences*, which abstract from human agency, studying the structure of reproduced outcomes; and the *social psychological sciences*, which abstract from reproduced outcomes, studying the rules governing the mobilization of resources by agents in their everyday interaction with one another and nature. If the object of the former is *social structure*, that of the latter is *social interaction*. They may be linked by the study of *society* as such, identified as the system of *relations* between the positions and practices agents reproduce and transform, which is the subject matter of the social science of sociology. The TMSA can allow that the form of psychology, the study of mental processes, *may* be species-general, but its content will always be historically specific.

The transformational model and the structures/praxis connection are represented as in diagrams 1 and 2 below. On the TMSA unintended consequences and unacknowledged conditions (see 1 and 2 in diagram 2) limit the actor's understanding of her social world, while unacknowledged (unconscious) motivation and tacit skills (see 3 and 4 in diagram 2) limit her understanding of herself. Corresponding to each of these limits, knowledge has a distinct emancipatory role – at 2 and 3 via the conditions and at 1 and 4 via the effects and form of praxis.

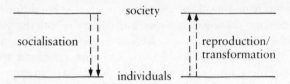

Diagram 1   The Transformational Model of Society Activity

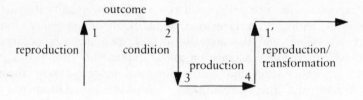

Note: 1, 1' = unintended consequences; 2 = unacknowledged conditions;
3 = unacknowledged motivation; 4 = tacit skills

Diagram 2   Structure and Praxis

Now the continuity, depth and reflexivity of human agency suggest the model of it represented in diagram 3, based on a model proposed by Anthony Giddens.[12] Discursivity presupposes a distinction between real and possible (including ratiocinated) reasons, grounded in the causal efficacy of the former. Ratiocination, R_m, is a property of the reflexive monitoring of conduct. Where $R_m \neq R_r$ there is the possibility of rationalization. Real reasons are the wants that prompt motivation and *ceteris paribus* issue in action.[13] As such they may be regarded as efficacious beliefs, which may be conscious or unconscious, trained on objects of desire. And as such they consist in a cognitive–conative vector or ensemble (see diagram 4).

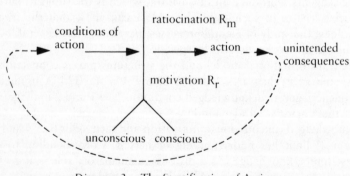

Diagram 3   The Stratification of Action

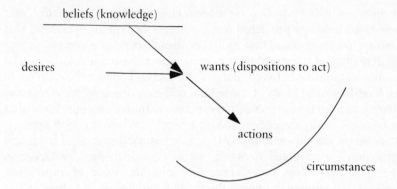

Diagram 4   Beliefs, Desires and Actions

The error of 'theoreticism' (see Section 1) is now clear: it involves the attempted elimination of the conative and/or affective components, no doubt as rooted in our 'inner nature' as the cognitive component, from the generative matrix of action.

In social phenomenology unintended consequences may take the well-known forms of counterfinality and suboptimality (as in a prisoner's dilemma).[14] The conditions figuring on the left-hand side of Diagram 3 include the rules and resources agents command in such games. Like all such conditions they may be unmotivated and unacknowledged. These are features that a general social phenomenology, whether rational or empirical, cannot itself, without vicious circularity, explain. For such rules and resources are at once historical deposits, and so always subject to a potentially unrecognized possibility of supersession. The games of the life-world (*Lebenswelt*) are always initiated, conditioned and closed outside the life-world itself.

4 On the Critique of Interpretative Fundamentalism

The TMSA shows what may escape (and so be misconstrued by) consciousness in our conscious activity. But are there perhaps elements in our experience or aspects of our consciousness of which we must be certain, and which (perhaps in virtue of this) are not subject to the possibility of historical supersession?

The history of post-Cartesian philosophy is largely the history of the attempt to establish just such an Archimedean point for knowledge, free from the possibility of error and impervious to every form of doubt. Thus in a recent empiricist incarnation, scientific knowledge was conceived as incorrigibly grounded in (or even exhausted by) sense-data or operations.

Of course we now know that there are no foundations of knowledge, that there is no uniquely privileged level, moment or type of operation, that there are no *brute data*; that the facts already contain a certain 'sedimented' reading of the world (that natural facts are social institutions), and that the relationship between theories and facts is between the contents of two interdependent kinds of conceptual schemes, one of which is taken as referring to objects apprehended in experience. In short we now know that the facts are theory-dependent and changeable; and science itself appears, as one might anticipate on the TMSA, as a historical process of levels and connections, a weighted network, without foundations, developing in time. This view does not dispute the epistemic value of experience. However, it interprets this not as the absolute privilege of a *content*, but as dependent upon the ontological and social *contexts* within which the significant experience occurs.[15]

Now in as much as there has been a 'coupure' in the recent philosophy of the human sciences, it lies in recognition of the significance of the condition that human beings are self-interpreting and self-motivating animals, whose language and beliefs are in some manner necessary for and productive of their life; so that human reality faces the scientific neophyte as already *pre-interpreted*, as (as it were) linguistically and cognitively 'done', prior to any scientific investigation of it. These pre-interpretations are *not* externally related and contingently conjoined to what happens in the human sphere, but internally related to and constitutive of it.[16] It was natural, then, in the wake of this understanding, to suppose that these interpretations (or beliefs) would constitute the base or foundations of social knowledge; to regard them as consisting, so to speak, in *brute interpretations* (or beliefs), whether such data-analogues were conceived positivistically as immediately available to the investigator or dialogically as dependent upon work within her own culture. Thus one had a transposition of the familiar thematics of classical philosophy in a hermeneutical key – more plausible than in the original perhaps, because nature is not self-interpreting, but little different in logical form or epistemological effect. For both the reductionist thesis that social knowledge is *exhausted* by, and the milder position that it is *rooted* in (and so must be *consistent* with), self-interpretations lead inexorably to a displaced hermeneuticized scientism and a consequent 'disavowal of reflection'.[17] In either variant the doctrine of the incorrigible (because ontologically constitutive), foundations of social knowledge, secretes, like its positivist prototype, as an inevitable corollary the doctrine of the *neutrality* of social science.

Of course Hegel, demonstrated long ago[18] that the fundamentalist programme is both radically incomplete and viciously circular, in that it not only cannot establish its own legitimacy, but must (implicitly or explicitly) presuppose some unvalidated 'knowledge'. And it is clear that, in these respects, any Vichian *facimus* must share the same limitations as the Cartesian *cogito*. For just as Descartes must assume some content to initiate his axiomatics; so, for Vico, God or human beings must already possess some matter for their constructions, that is to make their worlds, and what any agent does not make (what it must take to make) it possesses no privileged understanding of (just as what an ego cannot demonstrate it must remain uncertain about). It should be noted that on the transformational model we do not make the conditions or consequences, skills or motives of our intentional making (see Diagram 2 above); so that our beliefs about, or interpretations of, our actions cannot be constitutive in the requisite sense.

In considering the social-incorrigibilist position in slightly more detail, it is convenient to distinguish two sub-arguments for it: one Vichian, the other hermeneutical in inspiration.

The more strictly Vichian argument contends that one and the same knowledge is used to generate as to explain behaviour; so, as it were, superimposing a transcendental unity of agency on that of consciousness. But agency may consist in the exercise of *tacit skills*.[19] Moreover, the consciousness involved, and knowledge exploited, in action may be *practical* and so cannot immediately ground, even if it is held to be the ultimate empirical touchstone of, a supposedly discursive theoretical science. Thus we need not be able to *say* how we do what we know very well how to *do* (or vice versa), even when, as Chomsky has made abundantly clear, the first-order skills are themselves verbal, discursive ones. Secondly, while it is surely the case that communication (and interaction generally) would be impossible unless we were normally able to identify agents' immediate reasons for acting, it does not follow (a) that we must be always able to do so, or (more fundamentally) (b) that we must be able to identify the underlying reasons for (or causes of) those reasons. For example, we may know *that* a person is washing her hands or polishing an icon, but not *why* she is doing so. And so the possibility arises of the systematic misdescription of reasons in rationalization or ideological mystification, that is, in the self-misunderstanding of agents or forms of life.

The hermeneutical argument for social foundations maintains that it is *interpretations* that uniquely and completely differentiate the social world from mere assemblages of physical happenings, so that it is only and sufficiently by reference to them that its *sui generis* character can be sustained. Elsewhere I have attempted to show that the social world is not exhausted by its conceptual aspects, and that such aspects are in any event not necessarily immediately available to consciousness.[20] Thus although the immediate intentions of agents and meanings of acts cannot normally be misdescribed for mutual understanding or functioning language-games to be possible, both intentions and meanings may be opaque to agents (a) occasionally, at the level of everyday interaction and (b) systematically, at the level of the underlying explanations and descriptions of the reasons motivating their behaviour in such interaction. Particularly significant here is the possibility of a contingent generalization of Gödel's theorem in the direction of what I shall call '*metacritique*'. This consists of a critique of a language on the grounds of its incapacity to adequately express ideas or institutions which are customarily described by means of them. Such a critique aims to pinpoint precisely what cannot be said *in* a particular language about what is said or done *by means of* it.

In general, then, the *generative* role of agents' skills and wants, and of agents' (and other social) beliefs and meanings must be recognized without lapsing into an interpretative fundamentalism by conferring discursive and/or incorrigible status upon them. But how are beliefs and meanings in particular to be identified in the face of the corrigibility of statements of them? Now agents' accounts are more than just evidence; they are an internally related aspect of what they are about. Thus any resolution of this problem must be two-way: the social investigator must avoid both the extremes of arrogant dismissal of and of fawning assent to first-person accounts.[21] But agreement between agent and investigator hardly seems either a necessary or sufficient criterion for an adequate interpretation. Rather, it would seem that the adequacy of any interpretation (or of any act of self-understanding) can only be shown in relation to the point of the interpretation (or understanding) in the always more or less contingently circumscribed context of the agents' self-formation, that is, total developing life-activity.[22]

If judgements about belief cannot be separated from judgements about activity, judgements of meaning, again presupposing a dialogical fusion of horizons,[23] cannot be separated from judgements of explanatory adequacy (presupposing a degree of causal interaction). Thus the so-called 'problem of the indeterminacy of translation' is resolved in practice by selecting that translation which is *explanatorily most adequate* (whether or not it is the most 'charitable') in the context of what is already known about the organization of the particular society in question (and societies in general). The most adequate explanation will save the maximum of significant phenomena in the subject matter at stake, showing in that subject matter precisely the degree and type of 'irrationality' that does so.

5 Facts and Values: Hume's Law and Helices

I now want to show that the human sciences are necessarily non-neutral; that they are intrinsically critical (both of beliefs, and of the objects of beliefs), self-critical and value-impregnating; and in particular that they both causally motivate and logically entail value-judgements *ceteris paribus* (CP). I will not be concerned to argue against the scientistic misconception that factual judgements are value-free, partly because this connection has been, if not always adequately theorized, widely recognized (inside as well as outside the analytic tradition),[24] but mainly because I want to address myself more to an aspiration than what is characteristically misconstrued as a 'difficulty': the hope that the human sciences might yet come to be in a position to cast some light on what we ought to do and say, feel and think.

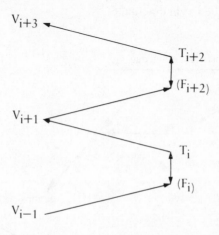

Diagram 5   Fact/Value Helix

In fact of course one is dealing with a fact-value helix here (see diagram 5). And it is clear that the scientistic denial of the value-impregnation of factual discourse, involving the *reification* of propositional contents, shares with the positivist denial of its converse, as a common condition of their plausibility, a naive extensionalist theory of meaning (whether in physicalist, sensationalist or Platonist guise). Moreover it shares with the theoreticist (rationalist) conception of the unmediated efficacy of theoretical discourse a neglect of the conative and affective bases of action, involving a *voluntarism* of theoretical praxis. The converse 'practicalist' error – of anti-intellectualist irrationalism – ignores of course the cognitive bases of action. These four errors can be represented as in table 1 below. Theoreticism, as defined here, leads naturally to the denial that practice (to the extent that it is not merely a redescription of 'theory') possesses any efficacy in the generation of theory.

Table 1

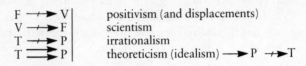

F ⟶ V	positivism (and displacements)
V ⟶ F	scientism
T ⟶ P	irrationalism
T ⟹ P	theoreticism (idealism) ⟶ P ⟶ T

Note: F stands for facts and theories
P stands for practice

Once the value-implications of theory, and the rational assessability of wants (in virtue of their grounding in beliefs), are accepted, then diagram 4 can be modified as in diagram 6.

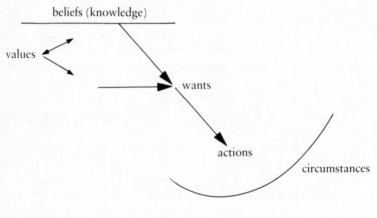

Diagram 6

Of course there is a feedback between values and actions, mediated by practices, including scientific (knowledge-producing) ones, so that they should be understood as connected by a loop as in diagram 3.

There is an important asymmetry between the F → V and T → P relationships, on the one hand, and the V → F and P → T relationships, on the other. Factual and theoretical considerations not only predispose and motivate but, in favourable circumstances (and subject to the operation of CP clauses), logically *entail* value and practical judgements. On the other hand, value and practical considerations, while they may (and in general will) predispose and sometimes motivate, do not (non-trivially) entail factual and theoretical judgements.[25] It is just *this* asymmetry which makes the helices in Diagram 5 (and in its theory/practice analogue) potentially rational ones: that is, progressive, or developing, spirals, rather than viciously self-confirming, and so self-destroying, more or less rapidly vanishing, circles.

My core argument is relatively simple. It turns on the condition that the subject matter of the human sciences includes both social objects (including beliefs) and beliefs about those objects. Philosophers have characteristically overlooked, or concealed, the internal relations connecting these aspects: empiricists by objectivizing ·beliefs, idealists by bracketing away objects. Now these relations, which may or may not be intra-discursive (depending upon whether the first-order object is itself a belief), are *both* causal and cognitive – in the ontological or intransitive dimension we are concerned with relations of *generation*; in the epistemological or transitive dimension of *critique*. But it is the causal relation of generation that grounds the epistemological programme of critique.

Now I am going to contend that if we possess (i) adequate grounds for supposing that a belief P (about some object O) is *false* and (ii) adequate grounds for supposing that S *explains* P, then we may, and must, pass immediately to (iii) a negative evaluation of S (CP) and (iv) a positive evaluation of action rationally directed at the removal of S (CP). To elaborate: inasmuch as we can explain, that is show the (perhaps contingent) necessity for some determinate false consciousness, or perhaps just some determinate consciousness under the determinable 'false', then the inferences to a negative evaluation of its source(s) and a positive evaluation of action oriented towards their dissolution are *ceteris paribus* mandatory.

It should be stressed straightaway that such action can only be rationally justified CP to the extent that there are grounds for supposing the source to be dissoluble; and that the TMSA does not in itself license the supposition of a society without some false consciousness. The notion of false consciousness here involves simply in the first instance the notion of disjuncture, mismatch or lack of correspondence between belief and object. But, as I shall presently show, this general pattern of argument may be readily extended to accommodate both the cases of more interestingly specific forms of false consciousness and that of other types of inadequate consciousness (and, indeed, more generally, defective being).

In principle this pattern of inference applies equally to beliefs *about* natural, as well as social, objects, on the condition (and to the extent) that the relevant *source* of false consciousness S, is itself a social object. But in this case S cannot be the same as, or internally related to, O, and neither S nor P can be causal conditions for the genesis or persistence of O, as in the cases of psychological rationalisation and ideological mystification, where S, P and O are typically causally interrelated. Only in the case of beliefs about social objects can the illusory (or more generally defective) character

of consciousness be a condition of what it is about. However, given that
beliefs about nature are social objects *all* the modalities of false consciousness may clearly apply to our beliefs about our beliefs about nature: that
is, to our understanding *of* – as distinct from *in* – science.

I shall call (i) the critical and (ii) the explanatory condition. Of course
even if the critical condition alone is satisfied, then we also pass immediately to a negative evaluation of P (CP), and of action based on or
informed by P (CP). But I want to distinguish this kind of '*criticism*'
which, although it formally violates and so refutes 'Hume's Law',[26]
remains silent on the causes of error, from an *explanatory critique*. Criticism, in Marx's words, 'knows how to judge and condemn the present,
but not how to comprehend it'.[27] The essence of Marx's objection to
criticism may, I think, be stated thus: it employs value (and particularly,
although contingently, moral) terms in the absence of any kind of causal
grounding. At its best, if displayed in naturalistic (i.e. non-intuitionist or
-emotivist) form, it can furnish grounds for belief and action which, if true,
a fortiori increase our freedom. But criticism says nothing *about*, although
it may of course (intentionally or unintentionally) causally affect, the
(causal) conditions of actions, the springs (so to speak) of belief and
behaviour, the sources of determination. And so criticism cannot con-
tribute to the discursive elucidation of the topic of the transformation of
the sources of an agent's determination from unwanted to wanted
ones: that is, of emancipation. Only a discourse in which the explanatory,
as well as the critical, condition is satisfied can be intrinsically
emancipatory.

As the concept of a 'critique' is better known I shall not discuss it here.
The structures of the various types of 'depth-explanation', which may be
undertaken at several different levels (including the psychoanalytical,
phenomenological and ideological), is considerably more complicated
than that depicted in the bare form of an explanatory critique, but the
transition from fact to value is effected in essentially the same way. The
possibility of an explanatory critique constitutes the kernel of the emancipatory potential of the human sciences. But to illustrate the possibilities
here fully, I want to develop the argument on a series of levels, which may
be regarded as so many ratchets of reason.

6 Instrumental vs. Critical Rationality

At the first two levels, no attempt is made to question the logical hetero-
geneity (and impenetrability) of facts and values. Despite this, the human
sciences may still have emancipatory implications (contingently, so to
speak) in virtue of (i) their use as sheer technique and (ii) their effects in

the context of the existence of relations of domination, exploitation and oppression.

Level I: Technical rationality

Patently, the human sciences may be used, like any other sciences, to achieve (more or less consciously formulated, and justified) ends, which may of course be adjudged equally good or bad. In particular, explanatory theories may be used, in conjunction with statements of particular initial conditions, to generate technical imperatives akin to 'put anti-freeze in the radiator (if you want to avoid it bursting in winter) CP'. If such imperatives ever appear to depart from the ends–means schema, it is only because they already presuppose a context of human purposes in the domain of their intended applications.

Level II: Contextually-situated instrumental rationality

The human sciences, even at the level of instrumental rationality, are not symmetrically beneficial to the parties involved in relations of domination. For, in the first place, explanatory knowledge increases the range of real (non-utopian) human possibilities, which may mean of course decreasing the range of assumed or fancied ones. But CP this will tilt the 'balance of – in a broad sense – political argument' against the status quo. This is quite consistent with the existence of only a simple external connection between knowledge and politics.

Secondly, even on an instrumental interpretation, explanatory knowledge appears as a necessary condition for rational self-emancipation (whether from the oppression of individuals, groups, classes, organizations, systems of relations, structures of interaction and so on, or from the oppression of conscious or unconscious systems of ideas, in which the agent is entrapped). Hence the dominated, exploited, oppressed, repressed, or whoever, have an *interest* in knowledge (in the straightforward sense that it facilitates the achievement of their wants). And the dominating, in as much as their interests are antagonistic to those they dominate, possess an interest in the ignorance of the dominated (and perhaps even in their own ignorance of the nature, or even the fact, of their dominance). Thus the human sciences, and at a remove philosophy, cannot be regarded as *equally* 'a potential instrument of domination' as of 'the expansion of the rational autonomy of action'.[28] The human sciences are not neutral in their consequences.

Level III: Intra-discursive (non-explanatory) critical rationality

The point has been made, particularly effectively by Roy Edgley,[29] that any science involves intra-discursive criticism, that is, criticism of other actually or possibly believed (and therefore potentially efficacious) theories, hypotheses, and so on. Acceptance of some theory T entails, CP, a series of negative evaluations: on theories etc. which are incompatible with it, on beliefs such theories underpin, on actions they sustain or inform. Granted that 'X is false' does not just *mean* 'Don't believe (act on) X' it certainly CP entails it. It is only if one denied any ontological connection between beliefs and action, or theory and practice, that one might have grounds for supposing that a change in theoretical does not entail a change in practical judgements (CP). But denying such a connection makes practical discourse practically otiose. Again, this point is consistent with a contingent relationship between a science and its subject matter; and it applies, quite indifferently, at the level of intra-discursive critical rationality, to all sciences alike. All the sciences, then, irrespective of subject matter, are intrinsically critical, and so evaluative.

Level IV: Explanatory critical rationality

All the sciences make judgements of truth or falsity on beliefs about their object domain. But the human sciences, in virtue of the distinguishing feature of their object-domain that it includes beliefs about inter alia social objects, also make (or at least entail) judgements of truth or falsity on (aspects of) that domain. And such belief/object correspondence, or lack of it, appears immediately as a legitimate object of social scientific explanation. However, inasmuch as the natural sciences are also concerned in their own substantive critical discourse not just to isolate and criticize, but to comprehend and causally explain, illusory or inadequate beliefs about the natural world, then they too, assuming the second-order standpoint of the intermediate science (in the terminology of Section 2) of the natural sociology (or natural psychology) of belief – in which natural science is seen as a resultant of natural and cultural determinants[30] – may come to explain false consciousness of nature at least partially in terms of human causes (for example, faulty instruments, inadequate funds, superstition, the power of the church, state or corporations). In virtue of their explanatory charter, and inasmuch as they are in a position to give well-grounded explanations of false consciousness, then, the human sciences *must*, and the natural sciences *may* (mediately, via the natural sociology of belief), arrive at value judgements on the causes, as well as the contents, of consciousness.

To recapitulate the central argument, then, if we have a consistent set of theories T which (i) shows some belief P to be false, and (ii) explains why that, or perhaps some such false (illusory, inadequate, misleading), belief is believed; then the inferences to (iii) a negative evaluation of the object S (for example, a system of social relations) accounting for the falsity of the belief (amounting to a mismatch in reality between the belief P and what it is about O) and (iv) a positive evaluation of action rationally directed at removing (disconnecting or transforming) that object, or the source of false consciousness, appear mandatory CP. This could be represented, schematically, in the inference scheme below as:

I.S.1.   (i) $T > P$. (ii) $T \exp I(P)$ → (iii) $- V(S → I(P))$ → (iv) $V\phi_{-s}$[31]

and we certainly seem to have derived value conclusions (CP) from purely factual premisses.

Now for some possible objections.

1.   It might be objected that 'P is false' is not value-neutral. But if it is not value-neutral, then the value-judgement 'P is false' can be derived from premisses concerning the lack of correspondence, or mismatch, of objects and beliefs (in the object domain). Moreover as, assuming that such judgements are intrinsic to *any* factual discourse, we are nevertheless able to infer from them, together with explanatory premisses, conclusions of a type which are *not* intrinsic to every factual discourse (those specified in (iii) and (iv)), we do have a transition here that goes against the grain of Hume's Law, however precisely that is supposed to be here interpreted or applied. On the other hand, if 'P is false' is value-neutral, then the inferences to 'P ought not be believed (CP)' and 'Don't believe (act upon) P (CP)' certainly seem inescapable.

2.   The suggestion that science itself presupposes, or embodies commitment to, certain values, such as objectivity, openness, integrity, honesty, veracity, consistency, coherence, comprehensibility, or explanatory power, should certainly be welcomed – suggesting, as it does, that the class of the 'value-neutral' is as empty as that of Austin's original 'constatives'.[32] But it does nothing either to rescue Hume's Law, or to deny the validity of inference-types (iii) and (iv), which turn on the special feature of the sciences of beliefs that commitment to truth and explanatory power entail the search for theories which will possess value-implications that cannot be regarded as conditions of, or as already implicit as anticipations in the organisation of, scientific-activity-in-general.

3.   It might be maintained that, although inference-type (iii) is valid,

(iv) is faulty, so that no commitment to any sort of action is entailed by the critical explanatory theory. But this is not so. For one can reason straight-away to action directed at removing the sources of false consciousness, providing of course one has good ground for supposing that it would do so, that no ill (or sufficiently overriding ill) effects would be forthcoming, and that there is no better course of action which would achieve the same end. Of course the inference scheme does not itself, conceived as a philo-sophical reconstruction, determine what such practical ('critical-revolutionary') action is; that is the task of substantive theory. Of course 'remove (annul, defuse, disconnect, dissolve, transform) sources of false consciousness' does not specify *what* the sources are, any more than 'lying is wrong' says which statements are lies.

Behind this objection, however, lie two considerations of some moment. First, the kind of theory underpinning (iv) may be different from that informing (iii). Diagnosis is not therapy. We may know that some-thing is causing a problem without knowing how to get rid of it or change it. Second, an explanatory critique of this type does not in general specify how we are to act after the source of mystification (false consciousness) is removed. It focuses on action which 'frees' us to act, by eliminating or disconnecting a source of mystification acting as an unwanted source of (co-)determination, replacing that source with another wanted (or perhaps just less unwanted) one, so achieving (absolute or relative) liber-ation from one stream of constraints or compulsions inherited from, as the causalities (and casualties) of the past. But it does not tell us what to do, if and when (and to the extent that) we are freed. Thus emancipated action may, and perhaps must, have a different logical form from emancipatory action.

The human sciences, then, must make judgements of truth and falsity, in virtue of their explanatory charter. And these, in the context of explan-atory theories, entail value-judgements of type (iii) and (iv). *Mutatis mutandis* similar considerations apply to judgements of rationality, consistency, coherence, and so on. Thus I.S.1 can be generalized in the cognitive direction represented in I.S.2 below, where C(P) stands for the contradictory character of some determinate set of beliefs.

$$\text{I.S.2} \quad T > P. \ T \exp C(P) \ \rightarrow \ -V(S \rightarrow C(P)) \ \rightarrow \ V\phi_{-s}$$

But the human sciences are of course not only concerned to explain what might be called 'cognitive ills'. Their manifest includes the explanation of the 'practical ills' of ill-health, misery, repression, and so on; and in between such ills and the cognitive ones, what might be called the communicative ills of deception (including self-deception), distortion, and so on.

This indicates two further lines of consideration. First I.S.1 can be straightforwardly generalized to deal with the explanation of such non-cognitive ills, with a corresponding deduction of value-judgements, as in I.S.3 below, where I-H stands for ill-health.

I.S.3   T exp I-H. $-V(I\text{-}H) \rightarrow -V(S \rightarrow I\text{-}H) \rightarrow V\phi_{-s}$

However, as will be immediately obvious, this deduction, despite its evident social and epistemic power, is now no longer from purely factual premisses, or from what is immediately or self-evidently constitutive of purely factual discourse. And so it cannot be used to achieve a formal refutation of Hume's Law. It is precisely on this rock that most previous attempts at its refutation, including Searle's notorious attempted derivation of an 'ought' from the rather tenuous institution of 'promising',[33] have broken. But further reflection shows another possibility here: namely that there are *non-cognitive* conditions, such as a degree of good health and the absence of marked asymmetries in political, economic and the other modalities of power, for discourse-in-general (including factual discourse) to be possible. If this is correct then a formal derivation of an 'ought' can proceed as in I.S.4 below:

I.S.4 $T > P$. $T \exp (I\text{-}H \rightarrow I(P)) \rightarrow -V(S \rightarrow I\text{-}H) \rightarrow V\phi_{-s}$

Is there a sense in which I.S.1 and I.S.2 are epistemically prior to their non-cognitive generalizations? Yes, in as much as empirically-controlled retroduction to explanatory structures always occurs in the context of, and typically (in science) assumes the form of, criticism of beliefs (consciousness): scientific, proto-scientific, lay and practical.

7 Depth Rationality

Level V: Depth-explanatory critical rationality

The most thoroughly explored applications of I.S.1 and I.S.2 involve the phenomena of psychological *rationalization* and *ideological mystification*. These phenomena are characterized by two distinctive features. First, a doubling of necessity between misrepresentation (P) and source (S); so that the, or some such, misrepresentation is not only causally necessitated by, but causally necessary for, the persistence or modulation, reproduction or limited (non-essential) transformation of its source. Secondly, an internal relationship between source (S) and object (O); so that the misrepresented object is either the same as, or at least causally dependent upon, the source of the misrepresentation.

Thus, in a simple depth-psychological model, an agent N may mis-describe her real (or the causally efficacious) reason, s, for some action, ψ, by p. If p is itself a contingently necessary releasing condition for ψ and s itself generates, in context, p then we have:

(5) $s \rightarrow p. \quad sp \rightarrow \psi.$

To explain this we now posit a structure S such that ψ is (perhaps con-tingently) necessary for its persistence or modulation, as in

(6) $S \rightarrow (s \rightarrow p. \quad sp \rightarrow \psi) \rightarrow S'.$

Given $s \neq p$ the deductions proceed as in I.S.1.

This paradigm may be easily extended to include 'outer' as well as 'inner' causes, including the self-mystification of forms of social life, or systems of social relations, in ideologies. Thus the contradictions which mystify Colletti[34] turn simply on the necessary co-existence in social reality of an object and a (categorially) false presentation of it, where it is the inner (or essential) structure of the object which generates the cate-gorially false presentation (or appearance).

Schema (7) is isomorphic with (5):

(7) $E \rightarrow A. \quad EA \rightarrow P;$

and (8) is isomorphic with (6):

(8) $R \rightarrow (E \rightarrow A. \quad EA \rightarrow P) \rightarrow R',$

where E = essence, A = appearance, P = practices, and R, R' = the modulated reproduction of the capitalist mode of production.

Are there any general conditions on the internal structure (E) of a self-reproducing system (T) which generates and contains within itself a func-tionally necessary misrepresentation (A) of itself? It seems plausible to suppose that E must possess at least sufficient internal differentiation to justify attributing to it a '*Spaltung*' or *split*; and that if T is to be capable of endogenous (essential) transformation, rather than merely modulated reproduction, the split must constitute, or be constituted by, *antagonistic* (opposed) *tendencies*. But apart from the Colletti-style contradiction built into the notion of the system's mis-representation of itself, it seems a priori unlikely that what the human sciences may empirically discover about the various structural sources of false consciousness will justify the application of a single, unified category of 'contradiction' to those structures. Instead one might conjecture a galaxy of concepts of contradiction, clustered around the core notion of the axiological indeterminacy generated by the logical archetype (together with the evaluative connotations this secretes). The specific concepts of contradiction would then achieve their individuation in the constraints they impose upon such indeterminacy and in their thematization of its form.

Perhaps the most famous depth-explanation, Marx's *Capital*, has the structure of a triple critique: of theories, of the practical consciousness such theories reflect or rationalize, and of the conditions explaining such consciousness. But in Marx, and the Marxist tradition generally, the criticized (discursive and practical) consciousness is regarded not just as false but as 'ideological' – where 'ideology' is counterposed to 'science'. In addition to the *critical* and *explanatory* conditions, one thus finds a further set of *categorial* conditions. Here beliefs are typically criticized for their *unscientificity* simpliciter, or for their inadequacy in sustaining the (irreducible) *specificity* of the subject-matter of their domains. Thus in reification, fetishism, hypostatization, voluntaristic conventionalism, organicism, and so on, social life is presented, in one way or another, in an asocial mode – a condition rooted, for Marx, in the alienation and atomization characteristic of capitalism as a specific form of class society. For example, on Marx's analysis, the wage-form collapses a power (labour-power) to its exercise (labour), the domain of the real to the actual, while the value-form fetishistically represents social relations in the guise of natural qualities. The critique of these gross categorial errors could be represented as:

I.S.9 $T > P. T \exp I(P). T \exp -S_c (P) \rightarrow -V(S \rightarrow -S_c. I(P))$
          $\rightarrow V\phi_{-s};$

and

I.S.10 $T > P. T \exp I(P). T \exp -S_o (P) \rightarrow -V(S \rightarrow -S_o. I(P))$
          $\rightarrow V\phi_{-s},$

where $-S_c$ and $-S_o$ stand for the unscientific and desocializing character of the forms in question.

What are we to make of Engels's celebrated rebuke to Lefargue: 'Marx rejected the "political, social and economic ideal" you attributed to him. A man of science has no ideals, he elaborates scientific results, and if he is also politically committed, he struggles for them to be put into practice. But if he has ideals, he cannot be a man of science, since he would then be biased from the start'?[35] While interests both predispose and motivate analyses (and their acceptance/rejection) in the human sciences, so that

Engels's scientistic repudiation of the V → F connection is disingenuous, it remains the case that no value-judgements other than those already bound up in the assessment of the cognitive power of Marx's theory are necessary for the derivation of a negative evaluation of the capitalist mode of production (CP) and a positive evaluation of action rationally oriented towards its transformation (CP) – so that the political commitment that Engels attributed to Marx as, so to speak, a contingent extra, can (on the assumption that Marx's depth-explanation is correct) be logically grounded in his scientific practice alone. Of course the theories now required to confirm, extend, develop or refute Marx's own analyses can only be consequent upon engagement in investigations of comparable scope and penetration.

Level VI: Depth rationality

Given that clear paradigms exist in the human sciences of I.S.1–4, most notably in the traditions inaugurated by Marx and Freud but also in some of the work of the theorists of the life-world of social interaction, is there a sense in which the *application* of these inference schemes, and hence of the type of explanatory critique they presuppose, is transcendentally necessary?

Now assume two interlocutors X and Y. Suppose X believes herself to possess a rational argumentative procedure R_A, a reasoned argument A_r and a conclusion Q; but that Y does not or cannot (perhaps 'in spite of herself') accept or act upon R_A, A_r or Q. (The reverse conditions may apply symmetrically to X, but we can ignore this complication here.) What is to be done when rational argument fails? Clearly there are three general kinds of possibility here:

(i)   Y continues to mistakenly believe (and act upon)−Q;

(ii) some non-discursive process (e.g. force, medication) induces in Y a belief in Q; or

(iii) X and Y jointly initiate an inquiry into the conditions blocking or compelling Y's beliefs.

Adoption of solution (i), the stoic acceptance of irrationality, error, and so on, is a counsel of despair. Moreover it cannot be generalized to the first-person case of·doubt (or more generally, choice) without vicious axiological regress. Solution (ii) can be ruled out on the grounds that drugs, for example, or force, can only simulate the acceptance of A_r or R_A. Further it is not emancipatory, in that it does not replace an unwanted with a wanted source of determination, but merely counteracts the effects of one unwanted source of determination with another. This has the corollary that inasmuch as the original source of determination is not defused, it may continue to exercise a latent power.

The alternative (iii) of a *depth-investigation* (D-I) is possible where reason fails but has not yet exhausted its resources; and it is practicable where Y's beliefs are generated or underpinned by unreflected (unacknowledged) processes, and Y seeks to understand, in order to undermine or abrogate, these processes. A depth-investigation may be defined generally as any co-operative inquiry, which includes the agent, into the structure of some presumed set of mechanisms, constituting for that agent an unwanted source of determination (which, whether cognitive or not, will always possess some cognitive manifestation), with a view to initiating, preserving or restoring that agent's ability to act and think rationally.

Four points must be immediately made about this definition. First, what is rational cannot be stipulated a priori, but must itself be discovered, in relation to antecedent notions of rationality (its nominal essences, so to speak), in the context of the explanatory critique such a depth-investigation presupposes. Secondly, although the concept of a depth-investigation has been introduced as an ideographic practically-oriented *application* of some or other determinate explanatory critique, the *theory* at the heart of the critique itself depends crucially for its own development and empirical confirmation on such investigations (whether on living or reconstructed, for instance, historical, materials). It follows from this that the links between theory and practice, and between pure and applied research, though not abrogating their distinctions, are bound to be tighter than in the natural sciences. Thirdly, corresponding to the different types of inference scheme outlined above, there will be different forms of depth-investigation. There must not, however, by hypostatized. For of course the explanation of cognitive ills will in general involve reference to practical and communicative ills, and vice versa. Finally the desire for emancipation which motivates the depth-investigation can neither be posited a priori (for although it is a necessary truth that people act on their wants, it is not a necessary truth that they act on their interests), nor predicted in historicist fashion on the basis of some particular theory of individual development or history. But as a socially-produced social object, the desire for emancipation will of course be a crucial topic for meta-investigations. And such investigations will need to be continually reflexively incorporated into the substantive theory of the practice from or for which emancipation is sought.

The structure of a simplified D-I may be elucidated as follows:

(1) Y is not capable of ϕ; scientific realism suggests there is a mechanism M preventing this.

(2) General theory T investigates the structure of blocking/compelling mechanisms, under the control of empirical data and researches.

(3) The application of T to Y depends upon the agent Y, as well as X. For it is Y's interpretations, actions and determinations that are at issue.

Subjectivity in the human sciences is not an obstacle; it is (an essential part of) the datum. But ontological authorship does not automatically carry over into epistemological authority. Now the Y-dependence of the D-I means that Y must have a motive or interest in disengaging M, or in a range of acts that M prevents. And that co-investigator X must not have an interest in the distortion of M-descriptions. Concretely, this raises the questions of the costs of emancipation for Y and of the conditions under which emancipation may be a second-best solution for Y; and for X it presupposes both the willingness to learn (in the general spirit of Marx's 'Third Thesis on Feuerbach')[36] and the continuing development of X's own self-understanding. At a deeper level, the success of the detailed investigation of the modus operandi of M in or for Y must depend upon an *internal differentiation* within the experience of Y, so that the empiricist/utilitarian notion of emancipation as a process of the alteration of the circumstances of atomistic individuals must be rejected. Moreover it should be reiterated that cognitive emancipation will in general depend upon non-cognitive (and extra-discursive) conditions; and that cognitive emancipation is necessary, but insufficient, for full emancipation (as shown by the example of the slave who knows very well she is a slave but still remains a slave, unfree).

In fact *dissonance*, not liberation, may be the immediate result of enlightenment. And such dissonance may lead either to 'revolutionary-critical' activity or to despair. Moreover constraints upon cognitive emancipation itself are imposed by the pre-formation of thought-contents (in psychoanalysis), the projects of others (in social phenomenology) and the non-discursive aspects of social reality (in historical materialism). Hence emancipation cannot be conceived either as an internal relationship within thought (the idealist error) or as an external relationship of 'educators', 'therapists' or 'intellectuals' to the 'educated', 'sick' or 'oppressed' (the empiricist error).

Now I want to propose that the possibility of a depth-investigation is a transcendental condition for any human science and hence (at a remove) for any science at all; and that in particular *to inquire into the nature of the real grounds for beliefs is the same thing as to inquire into the possibility of rationalization, self-deception, deception of others, counterfinality and systemic mystification*; and that to inquire into the conditions of possibility of these cognitive-communicative malaises immediately raises the question of the conditions of the possibility of practical ones – from ill-health to brutal oppression. The issue of the causes of belief and action, presupposing a distinction between *real* and *possible* (including assumed or fancied) *grounds*, can only be taken up by the depth human sciences. But a moment's reflection shows that this distinction, and hence the possibility of a depth-investigation at the psychoanalytical, phenomenological and historical levels, is a condition of every rational praxis or authentic act of self-understanding at all. It is necessitated by the existential intransitivity and enabled by the causal interdependency of the phenomena of sociality. Thus in the human sciences the problem of error (oppression, or whatever) must make way for the problem of the causes of this error (oppression, and so on), as part of the programme, paramorphic (but non-identical) to that of Kepler, Galileo and Newton, of the investigation of the underlying structures producing the manifest phenomena of social life.

The object of the depth-investigation is *emancipation*. Emancipation may be conceived either as the process of the changing of one mode of determination D_1 into another D_2, or as the act of switching from D_1 to D_2, both D_1 and D_2 perduring but D_1 in an inactivated condition. Now if the emancipation is to be *of* the human species, then the powers of the emancipated human being and community must already exist (although perhaps only as powers to acquire or develop powers) in an unactualized state. The key questions for substantive theory then become: what are the conditions for the actualization of the powers?: are they stimulating (cf. the socialist tradition) and/or releasing (cf. the anarchic/liberal traditions)?; do they lie in social organisation and/or individual initiatives etc?[37]

8 Conclusion

Can anything be said about the conditions of the possibility of emancipatory practices in general? I think that, for emancipation to be possible, four general types of condition must be satisfied.

First, *reasons must be causes*, or discourse is ontologically redundant (and scientifically inexplicable). But the potentially emancipatory discourse, given the TMSA and the general conception of an open world, can only co-determine action in an already pre-structured, practical and collective context.

Second, *values must be immanent* (as latent or partially manifested tendencies) in the practices in which we engage, or normative discourse is utopian or idle. I think that Marx, in conceiving socialism as anticipated in the revolutionary practice of the proletariat, grasped this. And it is on this feature that Habermas's deduction of speech-constitutive universals also turns.[38] But if there is a sense in which the ideal community, founded on principles of truth, freedom and justice, is already present as an anticipation in every speech inter-action, might one not be tempted to argue that equality, liberty and fraternity are present in every transaction or material exchange; or that respect and mutual recognition are contained in the most casual reciprocated glance?[39] It is an error to suppose that ethics must have a linguistic foundation; just as it is an error to suppose that it can be autonomous from science or history.

Third, critique must be *internal to* (and conditioned by) *its objects*; or it will lack both epistemic grounding and causal power. But it follows from this that it is part of the very process it describes, and so subject to the same possibilities, of unreflected determination and historical super-session, it situates. Hence continuing self-reflexive auto-critique is the *sine qua non* of any critical explanatory theory.

Finally, for emancipation to be possible *knowable emergent laws must operate*.[40] Such laws, which will of course be consistent with physical laws, will be set in the context of explanatory theories elucidating the structures of cognitive and non-cognitive oppression and the possibility of their transformation by women and men. Emancipation depends upon the untruth of reductionist materialism and spiritualistic idealism alike. On reductionism – if the physical process level is L_p, and the level at which emancipation is sought is L_e, then either L_p completely determines L_e and no qualitative change is possible; or qualitative change is possible, and the laws of L_p are violated. On idealism – either emancipation is entirely intrinsic to thought, in which case it is unconditioned and irrationality is inexplicable; or if it is conditioned, it cannot be intrinsic to thought. Emancipation depends upon explanation depends upon emergence. Given the phenomenon of emergence, an emancipatory politics or therapy depends upon a realist science. But, if and only if emergence is real, the development of both are up to *us*.

The possibility of emancipation is not of course the reason why an emergent powers theory, if it is, is true. It is rather that if human beings, and social forms in general, are emergent from but conditioned by nature, then there is at least the possibility that the human sciences, provided they 'do not anticipate the new world dogmatically, but rather seek to find the new world through criticism of the old',[41] could still be of some benefit to the greater majority of humankind.

Dialectics, Materialism and Theory of Knowledge

1 Dialectics

Dialectics is possibly the most contentious topic in Marxist thought, raising the two main issues on which Marxist philosophical discussion has turned, namely the nature of Marx's debt to Hegel and the sense in which Marxism is a science. The most common emphases of the concept in the Marxist tradition are as (a) a method, most usually scientific method, instancing *epistemological* dialectics; (b) a set of laws or principles, governing some sector or the whole of reality, *ontological* dialectics; and (c) the movement of history, *relational* dialectics. All three are to be found in Marx. But their paradigms are Marx's methodological comments in *Capital*, the philosophy of nature expounded by Engels in *Anti-Dühring*, and the 'out-Hegeling Hegelianism' of the early Lukács in *History and Class Consciousness* – texts which may be regarded as the founding documents of Marxist social science, dialectical materialism, and Western Marxism respectively.

There are two inflections of the dialectic in Hegel: (a) as a logical process; and (b) more narrowly, as the dynamo of this process.

(a) In Hegel the principle of idealism, the speculative understanding of reality as (absolute) spirit, unites two ancient strands of dialectic, the Eleatic idea of dialectic as *reason* and the Ionian idea of dialectic as *process*, in the notion of dialectic as a self-generating, self-differentiating and self-particularizing *process of reason*. The first idea begins with Zeno's paradoxes, moves through the differing Socratic, Platonic and Aristotelian dialectics, on via the practice of medieval disputation to Kantian critique. The second typically assumes a dual form: in an *ascending* dialectic, the existence of a higher reality (e.g. the Forms or God) is demonstrated; and in a *descending* dialectic, its manifestation in the phenomenal world is explained. Prototypes are the transcendent dialectic of matter of ancient scepticism and the immanent dialectic of divine self-realization of neo-Platonic and Christian eschatology from Plotinus and Eriugena onwards.

Combination of the ascending and descending phases results in a quasi-temporal pattern of original unity, loss or division and return or reunification; or a quasi-logical pattern of hypostasis and actualization. Combination of the Eleatic and Ionian strands results in the Hegelian Absolute – a logical process or *dialectic* which actualizes itself by alienating itself, and restores its self-unity by recognizing this alienation as nothing other than its own free expression or manifestation; and which is recapitulated and completed in the Hegelian System itself.

(b) The motor of this process is dialectic more narrowly conceived, which Hegel calls the 'grasping of opposites in their unity or of the positive in the negative'.[1] This is the method which enables the dialectical commentator to observe the process by which categories, notions or forms of consciousness arise out of each other to form ever more inclusive totalities, until the system of categories, notions or forms as a whole is completed. For Hegel truth is the whole and error lies in onesidedness, incompleteness and abstraction; it can be recognized by the contradictions it generates, and remedied through their incorporation in fuller, richer, more concrete conceptual forms. In the course of this process the famous principle of *sublation* is observed: as the dialectic unfolds no partial insight is ever lost. In fact the Hegelian dialectic progresses in two basic ways: by bringing out what is implicit, but not explicitly articulated, in some notion, or by repairing some want, lack or inadequacy in it. 'Dialectical', in contrast to 'reflective' (or analytical), thought grasps conceptual forms in their systematic interconnections, not just their determinate differences, and conceives each development as the product of a previous less developed phase, whose necessary truth or fulfilment it is; so that there is always a tension, latent irony or incipient surprise between any form and what it is in the process of becoming.

The most important phases in the development of Marx's thought on Hegelian dialectic are (i) the brilliant analysis of its 'mystified' logic in the *Critique of Hegel's Philosophy of the State*, resumed in the final manuscript of the *Economic and Philosophical Manuscripts*, where Hegel's idealist concept of labour moves centre-stage; (ii) in the immediately following works, *The Holy Family*, *The German Ideology*, and *The Poverty of Philosophy* the critique of Hegel is subsumed under a ferocious polemical assault on speculative philosophy as such; (iii) from the time of the *Grundrisse* on, a definite positive re-evaluation of Hegelian dialectic occurs. The extent of this re-evaluation remains a matter of lively controversy. Two things seem, however, beyond doubt: that Marx continued to be critical of the Hegelian dialectic as such and yet believed himself to be working with a dialectic related to the Hegelian one. Thus he says à propos of Dühring: 'He knows very well that my method of development is *not* Hegelian, since I am a materialist and Hegel is an idealist. Hegel's dialectics is the basic form of all dialectics, but only *after* it has been stripped of its mystified form, and it is precisely this which distinguishes my method'.[2] And in *Capital* he writes: 'The mystification which the dialectic suffers in Hegel's hands by no means prevents him from being the first to present its general forms of motion in a comprehensive manner. With him it is standing on its head. It must be inverted to discover the rational kernel within the mystical shell.'[3] These two metaphors – of the inversion and of the kernel – have been the subject of almost theological speculation. The kernel metaphor seems to indicate that Marx thought it possible to extract part of the Hegelian dialectic – against both (i) the Young Hegelian and Engelsian view that a complete extraction of the dialectical method from Hegel's system is possible and (ii) the view of positivistically-minded critics from Bernstein to Colletti that no extraction at all is possible, that the Hegelian dialectic is totally compromised by Hegel's idealism. Unfortunately Marx never realized his wish 'to make accessible to the ordinary human intelligence, in two or three printer's sheets, what is *rational* in the method which Hegel discovered and at the same time mystified'.[4]

Whatever Marx's debt to Hegel, there is a remarkable consistency in his criticisms of Hegel from 1843 to 1873. (a) Formally, there are three principal targets of attack – Hegel's inversions, his principle of identity and his logical mysticism. (b) Substantively, Marx focuses on Hegel's failure to sustain the autonomy of nature and the historicity of social forms.

(a)   (1) Hegel is guilty, according to Marx, of a three-fold inversion of subject and predicate. In each respect Marx describes Hegel's position as an inversion, and his own position as an inversion of Hegel's – the inversion of the inversion. Thus Marx counterposes to Hegel's absolute idealist ontology, speculative rationalist epistemology, and substantive idealist sociology, a conception of universals as properties of particular things, knowledge as irreducibly empirical, and civil society (later modes of production) as the foundation of the state. But it is unclear whether Marx is merely affirming the contrary of Hegel's position or rather transforming its problematic. In fact, he is usually doing the latter: his critique is aimed as much at Hegel's terms and relations as his 'inversions'. Marx conceives infinite mind as an illusory projection of (alienated) finite beings and nature as transcendentally real; and the Hegelian immanent spiritual teleology of infinite, petrified and finite mind is replaced by a methodological commitment to the empirically-controlled investigation of the causal relations within and between historically emergent, developing humanity and irreducibly real, but modifiable nature. Nor does Marx clearly differentiate the three inversions which are identified in Hegel. Their distinctiveness is however implied by Marx's second and third lines of criticism, pinpointing Hegel's reductions of being to knowing (the 'epistemic fallacy') and of science to philosophy (the 'speculative illusion').

(2) Marx's critique of Hegel's principle of identity (the identity of being and thought *in* thought) is duplex. In his *exoteric* critique, which follows the line of Feuerbach's transformative method, Marx shows how the empirical world appears as a *consequence* of Hegel's hypostatization of thought; but in his *esoteric* critique, Marx contends that the empirical world is really its secret *condition*. Thus Marx notes how Hegel presents his own activity, or the process of thinking generally, transformed into an independent subject (the Idea), as the demiurge of the experienced world. He then argues that the content of the speculative philosopher's thought actually consists in uncritically received empirical data, absorbed from the existing state of affairs, which is in this way reified and eternalized. Figure 1 illustrates the logic of Marx's objection.

Marx's analysis implies (i) that conservatism or apologetics is intrinsic to the Hegelian method, not as the left Hegelians supposed, a result of some personal weakness or compromise, and (ii) that Hegel's logical theory is inconsistent with his actual practice, in that his dialectical steps turn out to be motivated by non-dialectical, unreflected, more or less crudely empirical considerations.

(3) Marx's critique of Hegelian 'logical mysticism', and the parthenogenesis of concepts and ideological conjuring tricks it allows, turns on a critique of the notion of the autonomy or final self-sufficiency of philosophy (and ideas generally). But here again it is unclear whether Marx is advocating (i) a literal inversion: the absorption of philosophy (or its positivistic supersession) by science, as is suggested by the polemics of the *German Ideology* period; or rather (ii) a transformed practice of philosophy as heteronomous: as dependent upon science and other social practices but with relatively autonomous functions of its own, as is indicated by his (and Engels's) own practice.

Figure 1   Marx's Critique of Hegel's Principle of Identity

(b) Marx's critique of Hegel in the *Economic and Philosophical Manuscripts* locates two conceptual lacunae: (1) of the *objectivity* of nature and being generally, conceived as radically other to thought, or as independently real and neither causally dependent upon nor teleologically necessitated by any kind of mind; and (2) of the distinction between *objectification* and *alienation* – for in rationally transfiguring the present, historically determined, alienated forms of human objectification as the self-alienation of an absolute subject, Hegel conceptually pre-empts the possibility of a truly human, non-alienated mode of human objectification. More generally, in contrast to Hegel for whom 'the only labour . . . is *abstract mental labour*'[5] labour for Marx always (1) presupposes 'a material substratum . . . furnished without the help of man'[6] and (2) involves real transformation, entailing irredeemable loss and finitude and the possibility of genuine novelty and emergence. So any Marxian dialectic will be objectively conditioned, absolutely finitist and prospectively open (i.e. unfinished).

One possibility raised by Marx's critique of Hegel's philosophy of identity is that the dialectic in Marx (and Marxism) may not specify a *unitary* phenomenon, but a number of *different* figures and topics. Thus it may refer to patterns or processes in philosophy, science or the world; being, thought or their relation (ontological, epistemological and relational dialectics); nature or society, 'in' or 'out of' time (historical or structural dialectics); which are universal or particular, trans-historical or transient and so on. And within these categories further divisions may be significant. Thus any epistemic dialectic may be metaconceptual, methodological (critical or systematic), heuristic or substantive (descriptive or explanatory); a relational dialectic may be conceived primarily as an ontological process (as in Lukács) or as an epistemological critique (as in Marcuse). Such dialectical modes may be related by (a) a common ancestry and (b) their systematic connections within Marxism *without* being related by (c) their possession of a common essence, kernel or germ, still less (d) one that can be read back (unchanged) into Hegel. Marx may still have been positively indebted to Hegelian dialectic, even if in his work it is totally *transformed* (so that neither kernel nor inversion metaphor would apply) and/or *developed* in a variety of ways.

The most common positive theories of the Marxian dialectic are (i) as a conception of the world (as suggested by Engels, dialectical materialism, Mao Tse-tung); (ii) as a theory of reason (suggested by Della Volpe, Adorno); and (iii) as essentially depending upon the relations between them (or thought and being, subject and object, theory and practice, etc.) (suggested by Lukács, Marcuse). There is little doubt that in Marx's own self-understanding the primary emphasis of the concept is *epistemological*. Often Marx uses 'dialectical' as a synonym for 'scientific' method. In

Capital he quotes the St Petersburg reviewer's distinctively positivistic description of his method, commenting 'when the writer describes so aptly . . . the method I have actually used, what else is he describing but the dialectical method?'[7] However, it seems clear that Marx's method, though naturalistic and empirical is not positivist, but rather *realist*; and that his epistemological dialectics commits him to a *specific* ontological and a *conditional* relational dialectics as well. In a letter Marx observes that 'the secret of scientific dialectics' depends upon comprehending '*economic categories as the theoretical expression of historical relations of production, corresponding to a particular stage of development of material production*'.[8] Marx's dialectic is scientific because it explains the contradictions in thought and the crises of socio-economic life in terms of the particular contradictory essential relations which generate them (ontological dialectic). And Marx's dialectic is historical because it is both rooted in, and (conditionally) an agent of, the changes in the relations and circumstances it describes (relational dialectic).

Corresponding to Marx's distinction between his empirically-controlled mode of inquiry and his quasi-deductive method of exposition, we can distinguish his *critical* from his *systematic* dialectics. The former, which is also a practical intervention in history, takes the form of a triple *critique* – of economic doctrines, agents' conceptions, and the generative structures and essential relations which underlie them – and it incorporates a (historicized) Kantian moment (first stressed by Max Adler), in which the historical conditions of validity and practical adequacy of the various categories, theories and forms under attack are meticulously situated. Marx's critical dialectics may perhaps best be regarded as an empirically open-ended, materially conditioned and historically circumscribed, dialectical phenomenology.

Marx's systematic dialectics begins in *Capital* vol. I, ch. 1, with the dialectics of the commodity and culminates in *Theories of Surplus Value* with the critical history of political economy. Ultimately, for Marx, all the contradictions of capitalism derive from the structurally fundamental contradictions between the use-value and the value of the commodity, and between the concrete useful and abstract social aspects of the labour it embodies. These contradictions, together with the other structural and historical contradictions they ground (such as those between the forces and relations of production, the production and valorization process, wage-labour and capital, and so on) are (i) real inclusive oppositions, in that the terms or poles of the contradictions existentially presuppose each other and (ii) internally related to a mystifying form of appearance. Such *dialectical contradictions* violate neither the principle of non-contradiction – for they may be consistently described; nor the law of gravity, for the notion of a real inverted (mis-)representation of a real object, generated by the object concerned is readily accommodated with a non-empiricist, stratified ontology, such as that to which Marx is committed. Marx conceives these fundamental structural contradictions as themselves a historical legacy of the separation of the immediate producers from (i) the means and materials of production, (ii) each other, and hence (iii) the nexus of social relations within which their action on (and reaction to) nature takes place. It is undeniable that there is more than a trace here of a modified Schillerian schema of history as a dialectic of original undifferentiated unity, fragmentation, and restored but differentiated unity. Thus Marx says: 'It is not the *unity* of living and active humanity with the natural, inorganic conditions of their metabolic exchange with nature, and hence their appropriation of nature, which demands explanation, or is the result of a historical process, but rather their separation from these inorganic conditions of human existence and this active existence, a separation which is completely posited only in the relation of wage-labour and capital.'[9] He may have regarded this as empirically established. But in any event it would be unduly restrictive to proscribe such a conception from science: it may, for instance, function as a metaphysical heuristic, or as the hardcore of a developing research programme with empirical implications, without being directly testable itself.

It is not Marx's so called 'dialectical' definitions or derivations, but his dialectical *explanations*, in which opposing forces, tendencies or principles are explained in terms of a common causal condition of existence, and *critiques*, in which inadequate theories, phenomena and so on are explained in terms of their historical conditions, which are distinctive. Why does Marx's critique of political economy take the apparent form of an *Aufhebung* (sublation)? A new theory will always set out to save most of the phenomena successfully explained by the theories it is seeking to supersede. But in saving the phenomena theoretically Marx radically transforms their descriptions, and in locating the phenomena in a new critical-explanatory ambit, he contributes to the process of their practical transformation. Is Marx indebted, in his critical or systematic dialectics, to Hegel's conception of reality? The three keys to Hegel's ontology are (1) realized idealism, (2) spiritual monism and (3) immanent teleology. In opposition to (1), Marx rejects both the Hegelian absolute and the figure of constellational identity, conceiving matter and being as irreducible to (alienations of) spirit and thought; against (2), Althusser has correctly argued that differentiation and complexity are essential for Marx, and Della Volpe has rightly stressed that his totalities are subject to empirical, not speculative, confirmation; as for (3), Marx's emphasis is on causal, not conceptual, necessity – teleology is limited to human praxis and its appearance elsewhere 'rationally explained'.[10] Most important of all, for Marx initiating a *science of history*, ontological *stratification* and *becoming* are irreducible, whereas in Hegel, where they are treated in the logical spheres of Essence and Being, they are dissolved into actuality and infinity respectively (and thence into the self-explanatory realm of the Notion). In all philosophically significant respects, Marx's ontology is as much at variance with Hegel's as it is with that of the atomistic empiricism, which is the target of Engels's later philosophical works, and which Marx in his youthful critique had shown that Hegelian idealism tacitly presupposes.

The three most common positions on dialectics are that it is nonsense (argued by Bernstein); that it is universally applicable; and that it is applicable to the conceptual and/or social, but not the natural, domain (argued by Lukács). Engels stamped his immense authority on the second, universalist, position. According to him, dialectics is 'the science of the general laws of motion and development of nature, human society and thought';[11] laws which can be 'reduced in the main to three'.[12] These laws are: (1) the transformation of quantity into quality and vice-versa; (2) the interpenetration of opposites; and (3) the negation of the negation.

There are ambiguities in Engels's discussion: it is unclear whether the laws are supposed to be more or less a priori truths or super-empirical generalizations; or indispensable for scientific practice or merely convenient expository devices. Besides the notorious arbitrariness of Engels's examples, the relevance of his dialectics for Marxism, conceived as a putative social science, may be questioned, especially as Engels is opposed to any reductive materialism. While the evidence indicates that Marx agreed with the general thrust of Engels's intervention, his own critique of political economy neither presupposes nor entails any dialectics of nature, and his critique of apriorism implies the a posteriori and subject-specific character of claims about the existence of dialectical or other types of processes in reality. The relations between the Marxian, Engelsian and Hegelian positions can be represented as in Figure 2.

The very supposition of a dialectics of nature has appeared to many critics, from Lukács to Sartre, as categorically mistaken, in as much as it involves anthropomorphically (and hence idealistically) retrojecting onto nature categories, such as contradiction and negation, which only make sense in the human realm. These critics do not deny that natural science, as part of the socio-historical world, may be dialectical; what is at issue is whether there can be a dialectics of *nature* per se. Patently there are differences between the natural and social spheres. But are their specific differences more or less important than their generic similarities? In effect the problem of the dialectics of nature reduces to a variant of the general problem of naturalism, with the way it is resolved depending upon whether dialectics is conceived sufficiently broadly and society sufficiently naturalistically to make its extension to nature plausible. Even then one

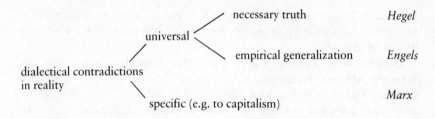

Figure 2

should not expect a unitary answer – there may be dialectical polarities and inclusive oppositions in nature, but not dialectical intelligibility or reason. Some apologists for Engels (for instance P. Ruben) have argued that (1) the epistemic interrogation of nature by man and (2) man's historical emergence from nature, presuppose Schellingian 'points of indifference' (or dialectical identity) to sustain the intelligibility of the 'transcategorial' links. Yet both epistemic homogeneization or equating (in measurement or experiment) and historical emergence (in evolution) presuppose the praxis-independence of the relevant natural poles. Any dialectical relation between humanity and nature takes the un-Hegelian aspect of an *asymmetrically* internal relation (social forms presuppose natural forms, but not the reverse); so that any epistemological or onto-logical identity occurs only within an overreaching materialist *non-identity*.

In the short run the paradoxical outcome of Engels's intervention was a tendency, in the evolutionist Marxism of the Second International, to a hypernaturalism and monism in many respects comparable to the posi-tivism advanced by Haeckel or Dühring, for instance, and which Engels had been consciously opposing. But in the longer run certain formal consequences of Engels's appropriation of the Hegelian dialectic (in which reflectionism acted as an epistemic surrogate for the principle of identity, and a processual world-view underpinned a homology of form) asserted themselves: the absolutization or dogmatic closure of Marxist knowledge, the dissolution of science into philosophy, even the transfiguration of the status quo (in the reconciling *Ansicht* of Soviet Marxism).

If Engels had unwittingly established the naturalized *process* of history as a 'new absolute', Lukács attempted to show that the *goal* of history was the true realization of that very absolute which Hegel had vainly sought in contemplative philosophy, but which Marx had finally found in political economy: in his discovery of the destiny and role of the proletariat as the identical subject–object of history. In both Engels and Lukács 'history' was effectively emptied of substance – in Engels, by being 'objecti-vistically' interpreted in terms of the categories of a universal process; in

Lukács, by being 'subjectivistically' conceived as so many mediations or moments of a finalizing unconditioned act of self-realization, which was its logical ground.

Despite these original flaws, both the dialectical materialist and Western Marxist traditions have produced some notable dialectical figures. Within Western Marxism, besides Lukács's own dialectic of historical self-consciousness or subject–object dialectics, there are Gramsci's theory/practice, Marcuse's essence/existence and Colletti's appearance/reality contradictions, all of more or less directly Hegelian provenance. In Benjamin dialectic represents the discontinuous and catastrophic aspect of history; in Bloch it is conceived as objective fantasy; in Sartre it is rooted in the intelligibility of the individual's own totalizing activity; in Lefebvre it signifies the goal of de-alienated humanity. Among the more anti-Hegelian Western Marxists (including Colletti), the Della Volpean dialectic consists essentially in non-rigid, non-hypostatized thinking, while the Althusserian dialectic stands for the complexity, preformation and overdetermination of wholes. Poised between the two camps, Adorno emphasizes, on the one hand, the immanence of all criticism and, on the other, non-identity thinking.

Meanwhile, within the dialectical materialist tradition, Engels's third law was unceremoniously dropped by Stalin and the first law relegated by Mao Tse-tung to a special case of the second, which from Lenin onwards increasingly discharged most of the burden of the dialectic. Certainly there were good materialist credentials (as well as political motives) for these moves. The negation of the negation is the means whereby Hegel dissolves determinate being into infinity. On the other hand, as Godelier has pointed out, dialectical materialists have rarely appreciated the differences between the Marxian *unity* and the Hegelian *identity* of opposites. Within this tradition Mao is noteworthy for a potentially fruitful series of distinctions – between antagonistic and non-antagonistic contradictions, principal and secondary contradictions, the principal and secondary aspects of a contradiction and so on – and for stressing, like Lenin and Trotsky, the 'combined and uneven' nature of their development.

In its long and complex history five basic threads of meaning of dialectic, each of which is more or less transformed within Marxism, stand out. (1) From Heraclitus, *dialectical contradictions*, involving inclusive oppositions or conflicts of forces of non-independent origins, are identified by Marx as constitutive of capitalism and its mode of production. (2) From Socrates, the elenchus or *dialectical argument* is, on the one hand, transformed under the sign of the class struggle, but, on the other, continues to function in some Marxist thought as, under 'ideal conditions' (in Gramsci, a communist society; in Habermas, an 'unconstrained consensus'), a norm of truth. (3) From Plato, *dialectical reason* takes on a range of connotations from conceptual flexibility and novelty – of the sort which, subject to empirical, logical and contextual controls, plays a crucial role in scientific discovery and development – through enlightenment and demystification (Kantian critique) to the depth rationality of materially grounded and conditioned practices of collective self-emancipation. (4) From Plotinus to Schiller, *dialectical process* of original unity, historical diremption and differentiated unity, remains, on the one hand, as the counterfactual limits or poles implied by Marx's systematic dialectics of the commodity form, and acts, on the other, as a spur in the practical struggle for socialism. (5) From Hegel, *dialectical intelligibility* is transformed in Marx to include both the causally generated presentation of social objects and their explanatory critique – in terms of their conditions of being, both those which are historically specific and praxis-dependent and those which genuinely are not.

2 Materialism

In its broadest sense, materialism contends that whatever exists just is, or at least depends upon, matter. (In its more general form it claims that all reality is essentially material; in its more specific form, that human reality is.) In the Marxist tradition, materialism has normally been of the weaker, *non-reductive* kind, but the concept has been deployed in various ways. The following definitions attempt some terminological clarity at the outset. Philosophical materialism is distinguished, following Plekhanov, from historical materialism, and, following Lenin, from scientific materialism generally. *Philosophical materialism* comprises:

(1) *ontological materialism*, asserting the unilateral dependence of social upon biological (and more generally physical) being and the emergence of the former from the latter;

(2) *epistemological materialism*, asserting the independent existence and transfactual activity of at least some of the objects of scientific thought;

(3) *practical materialism*, asserting the constitutive role of human transformative agency in the reproduction and transformation of social forms.

Historical materialism asserts the causal primacy of men's and women's mode of production and reproduction of their natural (physical) being, or of the labour process more generally, in the development of human history.

Scientific materialism is defined by the (changing) content of scientific beliefs about reality (including social reality). The so called '*materialist world-outlook*' consists of a looser set of (historically changing) practical beliefs and attitudes, a *Weltanschauung* (which may include a pro-scientific stance, atheism, and so on). This section is mainly concerned with philosophical materialism, but its relation to historical materialism is briefly taken up.

The principal philosophically significant connotations of Marx's '*materialist* conception of history' are: (a) a denial of the autonomy, and then of the primacy, of ideas in social life; (b) a methodological commitment to concrete historiographical research, as opposed to abstract philosophical reflection; (c) a conception of the centrality of human praxis in the production and reproduction of social life and, flowing from this, (d) a stress on the significance of labour, as involving the transformation of nature and the mediation of social relations, in human history; (e) an emphasis on the significance of nature for man which changes from the expressivism of the early works (especially the *Economic and Philosophical Manuscripts*) where, espousing a naturalism understood as a species-humanism, Marx conceives man as essentially at one with nature, to the technological Prometheanism of his middle and later works where he conceives man as essentially opposed to and dominating nature; (f) a continuing commitment to simple everyday realism and a gradually developing commitment to scientific realism throughout which Marx views the man–nature relationship as asymmetrically internal – with man as essentially dependent on nature, but nature as essentially independent of man.

Only (c), Marx's new practical or transformative materialism, can be considered in any detail here. It depends upon the view that human is distinguished from merely animal being or activity by a double freedom: a freedom from instinctual determination and a freedom to produce in a planned, premeditated way. The general character of this conception is expressed most succinctly in the *Theses on Feuerbach* (8th thesis): 'All social life is essentially *practical*. All mysteries which lead theory to mysticism find their rational solution in human practice and in the comprehension of this practice.'[13] The twin themes of the *Theses* are the passive, ahistorical and individualist character of traditional, contemplative materialism, and the fundamental role of transformative activity or practice in social life, which classical German idealism had glimpsed, only to represent in an idealized and alienated form. It was Lukács who first pointed out, in *The Young Hegel*, that the nub of Marx's critique of Hegel's *Phenomenology of Mind* was that Hegel had identified, and so confused, objectification and alienation; by conceiving the present, historically specific, alienated forms of objectification as moments of the self-alienation of an Absolute Subject, he at once rationally transfigured them and foreclosed the possibility of a fully human, non-alienated, mode of human objectification. But once this distinction has been made a three-fold ambiguity in Marx's own use of 'objectivity' and its cognates remains; and its clarification becomes essential for Marx's materialism from at least the time of the *Theses on Feuerbach* on. Thus the 1st Thesis implies, but does not clearly articulate, a distinction between (α) *objectivity* or externality as such and (β) objectification as the *production* of a subject; and the 6th Thesis entails a distinction between (β) and (γ) objectification as the *process* of the reproduction or transformation of social forms.

The 1st Thesis commits Marx to sustaining both the materialist insight of the independence of things from thought and the idealist insight of thought as an activity and hence to a distinction between (α) and (β), or in the terminology of the *Grundrisse* Introduction between real and thought objects, or in the terminology of modern scientific realism between the intransitive objects of knowledge and the transitive process or activity of knowledge-production. This distinction allows us to clarify the sense in which for Marx social practice is a *condition*, but not the *object*, of natural science; whereas it is *ontologically*, as well as *epistemologically* constitutive in the social sphere. Seen in this light, Marx's complaint against idealism is that it illicitly abstracts from the intransitive dimension, the idea of an independent reality; while traditional materialism abstracts from the transitive dimension, the role of human activity in the production of knowledge.

The 6th Thesis proclaims a critique of all individualist and essentialist social theory, focused upon Feuerbach's humanism, and isolates man's historically developing sociality as the true key to the ills Feuerbach anthropologically explained. And it entails the distinction between (β) and (γ), intentional human activity and the reproduction or transformation of the antecedently existing, historically social forms, given as the conditions and media of that activity, but reproduced or transformed only in it.

Failure to distinguish adequately (α) and (β), as two aspects of the unity of known objects, has led to tendencies to both epistemological idealism (reduction of (α) to (β) from Lukács and Gramsci to Kolakowski and Schmidt) and traditional materialism (reduction of (β) to (α) from Engels and Lenin to Della Volpe and the contemporary exponents of 'reflection theory'). And failure to distinguish adequately (β) and (γ), as two aspects of the unity of transformative activity (or as the duality of praxis and structure), has resulted in both sociological individualism, voluntarism, and spontaneism (reduction of (γ) to (β) as in Sartre for example) and determinism, reification, and hypostatization (reduction of (β) to (γ) as in Althusser for example). The 9th and 10th Theses expressly articulate Marx's conception of the differences between his new and the old materialism: 'The highest point reached by that materialism which does not comprehend sensuousness as practical activity, is the contemplation of single individuals and of civil society.' 'The standpoint of the old materialism is civil society; the standpoint of the new is human society, or social humanity.' The problem-field of traditional materialism is based on an abstract ahistorical individualism and universality: isolated Crusoes, externally and eternally related to one another and to their common naturalized fate. For Marx, this conception underlies the traditional problems of epistemology, and indeed of philosophy generally. For the contemplative consciousness, disengaged from material practice, its relation to its body, other minds, external objects, and even its own past states, becomes problematic. But neither these philosophical problems nor the practices from which they arise can be remedied by a purely theoretical therapy. In opposition to the Young Hegelian Stirner who believes 'one has only to get a few ideas out of one's head to abolish the conditions which have given rise to those ideas',[14] Marx argues that 'the resolution of *theoretical* oppositions is possible only in a *practical* way, and hence is by no means a task of knowledge but a task of *actual* life; which philosophy could not resolve because it grasped the task *only* as a theoretical one'.[15] Hence 'the philosophers have only *interpreted* the world in various ways; the point is to *change* it' (11th Thesis).

It would be difficult to exaggerate the importance of Engels's more cosmological cast of materialism, elaborated in his later philosophical writings, especially *Anti-Dühring, Ludwig Feuerbach*, and *Dialectics of Nature*. It was not only the decisive moment in the formation of the leading theorists of the Second International (Bernstein, Kautsky, Plekhanov) but, as the doctrinal core of what subsequently became known as dialectical materialism, it provided the axis around which most subsequent debates have revolved. Writing in a context imbued with positivist and evolutionist (especially social Darwinist) themes, Engels argued: (a) against mechanical or 'metaphysical' materialism, that the world was a complex of processes, not fixed and static things; and (b) against reductive materialism, that mental and social forms were irreducible to, but emergent from, matter (as indeed its highest product). The immediate target of Lenin's later influential *Materialism and Empirio-Criticism* was the spread of Mach's positivist conceptions among his Bolshevik comrades such as Bogdanov.

Both Engels and Lenin utilize a number of different notions of materialism and idealism, which are treated as mutually exclusive and completely exhaustive categories, and generally speak of ontological and epistemological definitions of materialism as though they were immediately equivalent. But the mere independence of matter from human thought does not entail its causal primacy in being; it is consistent with the objective idealisms of Plato, Aquinas and Hegel. Certainly it is possible to argue that (1) and (2) above are intrinsically connected – in that if mind emerged from matter then a Darwinian explanation of the possibility of knowledge is feasible and, conversely, that a full and consistent realism entails a conception of man as a natural causal agent nested within an overreaching nature. But neither Engels nor Lenin specified the links satisfactorily. Engels's main emphasis is undoubtedly ontological and Lenin's epistemological; and may be represented thus:

the natural world is prior to and causally independent of any form of mind or consciousness, but not the reverse (Engels);

the knowable world exists independently of any (finite or infinite) mind, but not the reverse (Lenin).

A noteworthy feature of Engels's materialism is his stress on the practical refutation of scepticism. Pursuing a line of thought favoured by among others Dr Johnson, Hume and Hegel, Engels argued that scepticism – in the sense of suspension of commitment to some idea of an independent reality, known under some description or other – is not a tenable or serious position. Although theoretically impregnable, it was continually belied or contradicted by practice (including, he could have added, as Gramsci was later to intimate in his notion of theoretically implicit consciousness, the sceptic's own speech practice), particularly 'experiment and industry'. 'If we are able to prove the correctness of our conceptions of a natural process by making it ourselves . . . then there is an end to the Kantian ungraspable "thing-in-itself"'.[16] Whereas in Engels there is a pervasive tension between a positivistic concept of philosophy and a metaphysics of science, in Lenin there is clear recognition of a relatively autonomous Lockean or underlabourer role for philosophy in relation to historical materialism and the sciences generally. This is accompanied by (i) a clear distinction between matter as a *philosophical category* and as a *scientific concept*; (ii) emphasis on the practical and interested character of philosophical interventions, in his doctrine of *partinost* (partisanship); (iii) the attempt to reconcile scientific change with the idea of progress (and, normatively, to counter dogmatism and scepticism respectively) in a distinction between 'relative' and 'absolute' truth.

The hallmark of the dialectical materialist tradition was the combination of a dialectics of nature and a reflectionist theory of knowledge. Both were rejected by Lukács in the seminal text of Western Marxism, *History and Class Consciousness*, which also argued that they were mutually inconsistent. Gramsci, redefining objectivity as such in terms of a universal inter-subjectivity, asymptotically approached in history but only finally realized under communism, went even further, claiming: 'It has been forgotten that in the case of [historical materialism] one should put the accent on the first term – "historical" – and not on the second – which is of metaphysical origin. The philosophy of praxis is absolute "historicism", the absolute secularization and earthliness of thought, an absolute humanism of history'.[17] In general, where Western Marxism has been sympathetic to dialectical motifs it has been hostile to materialism. For Sartre, for instance, 'no materialism of any kind can ever explain [freedom]'[18] which is precisely what is distinctive of the human-historical situation. On the other hand, where Western Marxism has advertised its materialism, this has usually been of an exclusively epistemological kind, as in Althusser, Della Volpe and Colletti; and, where ontological topics have been broached, as in Timpanaro's important reemphasis on the role of nature,[19] and of the biological 'substructure' in particular, in social life, their discussion has often been vitiated by an unreflected empirical realism in ontology.[20]

In any discussion of materialism there lurks the problem of the definition of matter. For Marx's practical materialism, which is restricted to the social sphere (including of course natural science) and where 'matter' is to be understood in the sense of 'social practice', no particular difficulty arises. But from Engels on, Marxist materialism has more global pretensions, and the difficulty now appears that if a material thing is regarded as a perduring occupant of space capable of being perceptually identified and reidentified, then many objects of scientific knowledge, although dependent for their *identification* upon material things, are patently immaterial. Clearly if one distinguishes scientific and philosophical ontologies, such considerations need not, as Lenin recognized, refute philosophical materialism. But what then is its content? Some materialists have subscribed to the idea of the exhaustive knowability of the world by science. But what grounds could there be for this? Such cognitive triumphalism seems an anthropocentric, and hence idealist, conceit. On the other hand, the weaker supposition that whatever is knowable must be knowable by science, if not tautologous, merely displaces the truth of materialism onto the feasibility of naturalism in particular domains.

For such reasons one might be tempted to treat materialism more as a *prise de position*, a practical orientation, than as a set of quasi-descriptive theses, and more specifically as: (a) a series of denials, largely of claims of traditional philosophy – for instance concerning the existence of God, souls, forms, ideals, duties, the absolute and so on, or the impossibility (or inferior status) of science or earthly happiness; and (b) as an indispensable ground for such denials, a commitment to their scientific explanation as modes of false or inadequate consciousness or ideology. However, such an orientation both presupposes some *positive* account of science (ideology, and so on) and is in principle vulnerable to a request for normative grounding itself, so that a pragmatist reconstruction of materialism is hardly an advance on a descriptivist one. In both cases the problem of justification remains. In fact it may be easier to justify materialism as an account of science and scientificity than it is to justify materialism per se; and perhaps only such a *specific* explication and defence of materialism is consistent with Marx's critique of hypostatized and abstract thought (in, for instance, the 2nd Thesis on Feuerbach).

Post-Lukácsian Marxism has typically counterposed Marx's premises to Engels's conclusions. But on contemporary realist reconstructions of science there is no inconsistency between refined forms of them. Thus a conception of science as the practical investigation of nature entails a *non-anthropocentric ontology* of independently existing and transfactually efficacious real structures, mechanisms, processes, relations and fields.[21] Moreover such a *transcendental realism* even partially vindicates the spirit, if not the letter, of Engels's 'Two Great Camps Thesis'. For (a) it stands opposed to the *empirical realism* of subjective idealism and the *conceptual realism* of objective idealism alike, (b) pinpointing their common error in the reduction of being to a human attribute – experience or reason – in two variants of the 'epistemic fallacy' and (c) revealing their systematic interdependence – in that epistemologically, objective idealism presupposes the reified facts of subjective idealism and ontologically, subjective idealism presupposes the hypostatized ideas of objective idealism; so that upon inspection of their respective fine structures they may be seen to bear the same Janus-faced legend: empirical certainty/conceptual truth. Historical investigation also gives some grounds for Engels's view that materialism and idealism are related as dialectical antagonists in the context of struggles around changes in scientific knowledge and, more generally, social life. Finally it should be mentioned that a transcendental realist explication of materialism is congruent with an emergent powers naturalist orientation.[22]

The importance of this last consideration is that, since Marx and Engels, Marxism has conducted a double polemic: against idealism and against vulgar, reductionist or 'undialectical' materialism, for example contemplative (Marx) or mechanical (Engels) materialism. And the project of elaborating a satisfactory 'materialist' account or critique of some subject matter, characteristically celebrated by idealism, has often amounted in practice to the endeavour to avoid *reductionism* (for instance of philosophy to science, society or mind to nature, universals to particulars, theory to experience, human agency or consciousness to social structure) – the characteristic 'materialist' response – without reverting to a *dualism*, as would more than satisfy idealism. This in turn has usually necessitated a war of position on two fronts – against various types of '*objectivism*', including metaphysics, scientism, dogmatism, determinism, reification, and against various formally counterposed, but actually complementary, types of '*subjectivism*', including positivism, agnosticism, scepticism, individualism, voluntarism. It would be misleading to think of Marxist materialism as seeking a via media or simple Hegelian synthesis of these historical duals – it is rather that, in transforming their common problematic, both the errors and the partial insights of the old antagonistic symbiotes are thrown, from the new vantage point, into critical relief.

As defined at the outset, none of (1)–(3) entails historical materialism, which is what one would expect of the relations between a philosophical position and an empirical science. On the other hand, historical materialism is rooted in ontological materialism (1), presupposes a scientific realist ontology and epistemology (2), and consists in a substantive elaboration of practical materialism (3). Only the first proposition can be further commented upon here. Both Marx and Engels were wont to defend historical materialism by invoking quasi-biological considerations. In *The German Ideology* they state: 'The first premiss of all human history is, of course, the existence of living human individuals. Thus the first fact to be established is the physical organisation of these individuals and their consequent relation to the rest of nature. . . . [Men] begin to distinguish themselves from animals as soon as they begin to *produce* their means of subsistence, a step which is conditioned by their physical organisation'.[23] Marxists have, however, for the most part considered only one side of the natural–social relation, that is, technology, describing the way in which human beings appropriate nature, effectively ignoring the ways (putatively studied in ecology, social biology, and so on) in which, so to speak, nature reappropriates human beings.

3 Theory of Knowledge

It is a truism that the tensions in Marxist thought between positivism and Hegelianism, social science and philosophy of history, scientific and critical (or humanist or historicist) Marxism, materialism and the dialectic, and so on, are rooted in the ambivalences and contradictory tendencies of Marx's own writings. Despite this, it is possible to reconstruct from his work perspectives (a) *in* and (b) *on* the theory of knowledge which transcend and partially explain the dichotomies within Marxism.

(a) Two epistemological themes predominate in Marx: (α) an emphasis on *objectivity*, the independent reality of natural, and the relatively independent reality of social, forms with respect to their cognition (which is realism, in the ontological or 'intransitive' dimension); (β) an emphasis on the role of work or *labour* in the cognitive process, and hence on the social, irreducibly historical character of its product, knowledge (which is 'practicism', in the narrowly epistemological or 'transitive' dimension). (α) is consistent with the practical modification of nature and constitution of social life; and Marx understands (β) as dependent on the mediation of intentional human agency or praxis. Objectification in the senses of the *production* of a subject and of the *reproduction* or transformation of a social process must be distinguished both from objectivity qua externality, as in (α), and from the historically specific, or alienated, forms of labour in particular societies – so 'objective' and its cognates have a four-fold meaning in Marx. These two inter-related themes – objectivity and labour – entail the epistemological supersession of empiricism and idealism, scepticism and dogmatism, hyper-naturalism and anti-naturalism alike.

In his early writings Marx essayed a forceful and sporadically brilliant critique of idealism, which was the medium of his biographical *Ausgang* from philosophy into substantive socio-historical science, and provides the key to the subject matter of his new science. But he never engaged a comparable critique of empiricism. His anti-empiricism is available only in the practical, untheorized state of the methodological commitment to scientific realism implicit in *Capital*, together with a few scattered philosophical *aperçus*. One consequence of this critical imbalance has been the relative intellectual underdevelopment of the realist in comparison with the practicist pole within Marxist epistemology, and a tendency for it to fluctuate between a sophisticated idealism (roughly (β) without (α)) and a crude materialism (roughly (α) without (β)).

Marx's critique of idealism, which incorporates a vigorous critique of apriorism, consists in a double movement: in the first, *Feuerbachian* moment, ideas are treated as the products of finite embodied minds, and in the second, distinctively *Marxian* moment, such embodied minds are in turn conceived as the products of historically developing ensembles of social relations. The first moment includes critiques of Hegel's subject–predicate inversions, the reduction of being to knowing (the 'epistemic fallacy') and the separation of philosophy from social life (the 'speculative illusion'). In the second anti-individualist moment, the Feuerbachian humanist or essentialist problematic of a fixed human nature is replaced by a problematic of a historically developing sociality and/or of a human nature expressed only in it. 'The human essence is no abstraction inherent in each single individual. In its reality it is the ensemble of social relations'.[24] 'The sum of the forces of production, capital and forms of social intercourse, which each individual confronts as something given, is the real foundation of . . . the "essence of man"'.[25] At the same time Marx wished to insist that 'history is *nothing* but the activity of men in

pursuit of their ends'.[26] Thus Marx works his way towards a conception
of the reproduction and transformation of the social process in and
through human praxis; and of praxis as in turn conditioned and made
possible by that process: 'Men make their own history but they do not
make it just as they please; they do not make it under circumstances
chosen by themselves, but under circumstances directly encountered,
given and transmitted by the past'.[27] Did Marx suppose that under
communism men and women would make history as they pleased, that
process would be dissolved into praxis? The evidence is ambiguous. In any
event, the subject matter of *Capital* is not human praxis, but the structures, relations, contradictions and tendencies of the capitalist mode of
production: 'individuals are dealt with here only in so far as they are the
personifications of economic categories, the bearers (*Träger*) of particular
class relations and interests'.[28]

Marx is never seriously disposed to doubt (1) simple *material object
realism*, the idea that material objects exist independently of their cognition; but his commitment to (2) *scientific realism*, the idea that the
objects of scientific thought are real structures, mechanisms or relations
ontologically irreducible to, normally out of phase with and perhaps in
opposition to the phenomenal forms, appearances or events they generate,
is arrived at only gradually, unevenly and relatively late. However, by the
mid-1860s scientific realist motifs provide a constant refrain: 'all science
would be superfluous if the outward appearances and essences of things
directly coincided'.[29] 'Scientific truth is always paradox, if judged by
everyday experience, which catches only the delusive appearance of
things'.[30] In opposition to vulgar economy Marx claims to give a scientific, and in opposition to classical political economy a categorically adequate (non-fetishized, historicized), account of the real underlying
relations, causal structures and generative mechanisms of capitalist economic life. Marx's method in fact incorporates three aspects: (a) a *generic
scientific realism*; (b) *a domain-specific qualified (or critical) naturalism*;
and (c) *a subject-particular dialectical materialism*. At (a) Marx's
concern is, like that of any scientist, with a consistent, coherent, plausible
and empirically-grounded explanation of his phenomena. At (b), his
naturalism is qualified by a series of differentiae of social, as distinct
from natural, scientific inquiry – the most important of which are
the praxis-, concept- and space-time-dependence of social forms, the
historical reflexivity necessitated by the consideration that the critique
of political economy is part of the process it describes and the fact
that neither experimentally established nor naturally occurring closed
systems are available for the empirical control of theory (entailing reliance
on explanatory, non-predictive criteria of confirmation and falsification).
(In this respect the 'power of abstraction' which Marx invokes in

Capital[31] neither provides a surrogate for 'microscopes' and 'chemical reagents' nor does justice to Marx's actual empirical practice.) At (c), the particular character of Marx's explanations is such that they take the form of an *explanatory critique* of an object of inquiry which is revealed, on those explanations, to be *dialectically contradictory*. Marx's scientific critique is both of (i) conceptual and conceptualized entities (economic theories and categories; phenomenal forms) and of (ii) the objects (systems of structured relations) which necessitate or otherwise explain them. At the first level, the entities are shown to be false *simpliciter* (for instance the wage form), fetishized (for instance the value form) or otherwise defective; at the second level, Marx's explanations logically entail *ceteris paribus* a negative evaluation of the objects generating such entities and a commitment to their practical transformation. The particular systemic dialectical contradictions, such as between use-value and value, which Marx identifies as structurally constitutive of capitalism and its mystified forms of appearance give rise, on Marx's theory, to various historical contradictions which, on that theory, both tendentially subvert its principle of organization and provide the means and motive for its supersession by a society in which 'socialized mankind, the associated producers, regulate their interchange with nature rationally [bringing] it under their conscious control, instead of being ruled by it as by some blind power'.[32]

If for Marx idealism is the typical fault of philosophy, empiricism is the endemic failing of *common-sense*. Marx sets himself against both the idealist ontology of forms, ideas or notions with its conceptual (or religious) totalities and the empiricist ontology of given atomistic facts and their constant conjunctions, in favour of the real world, conceived as structured, differentiated and developing and, given that we exist, a possible object of knowledge for us. Thus the essence of Marx's critique, in the *Theses on Feuerbach*, of the old 'contemplative materialism' is that it desocializes science and destratifies reality; so that, at best, it can merely prompt, but not sustain '*scientificity*'. And the essence of Marx's critique, in the final manuscript of the *Economic and Philosophical Manuscripts* and elsewhere, of the culmination of classical German idealism in the philosophy of Hegel is that it destratifies science and then dehistoricizes reality; so that it prompts, but cannot sustain '*historicity*'. So we arrive at the twin epistemic motifs of Marx's new science of history: materialism signifying its generic form (as a science), dialectic its particular content (as a science of history). But it is an index of the epistemological lag of philosophical Marxism behind Marx that, whether fused in dialectical materialism or separated in Western Marxism, its dialectic has remained cast in an essentially idealist mould and its materialism expressed in a fundamentally empiricist form.

Marx (and Engels) usually associate dogmatism with idealism and rationalism, and scepticism with empiricism; and in the *German Ideology* they firmly reject both. Their premises, they announce, are not 'arbitrary dogmas' but can be verified 'in a purely empirical way'.[33] At the same time, they lampoon the kind of 'new revolutionary philosopher' who has 'the idea that men were drowned in water only because they were possessed with the *idea* of gravity'.[34] Thus, on the one hand (in the transitive dimension), they initiate the idea of Marxism as an empirically open-ended research programme; and, on the other (in the intransitive dimension), they register their commitment to an objective ontology of transfactually active structures.

(b) Marx's position *on* epistemology also revolves around two interrelated themes: an emphasis (α) on the *scientificity* and (β) on the *historicity* of the cognitive process (the themes, of course, of the new science of history brought to bear on the theory of knowledge). On the one hand Marx represents himself as engaged in the construction of a science, so that he is seemingly committed to certain epistemological propositions (such as criteria demarcating science from ideology or art); and, on the other, he conceives all sciences, including his own, as the product of (and a potential causal agent in) historical circumstances, and must therefore be committed to the possibility of historically explaining them. (α) and (β) constitute two aspects (the 'intrinsic' and 'extrinsic' aspects) of the cognitive process: (α) without (β) leads to *scientism*, the dislocation of science from the socio-historical realm and a consequent lack of historical reflexivity; (β) without (α) results in *historicism*, the reduction of science to an expression of the historical process and a consequent judgemental relativism. These two aspects are united in the project of an explanatory critique of historically specific epistemologies.

However, the peculiar character of Marx's route from philosophy into science was such that, as in the case of his scientific realism, the nature of his commitment to the intrinsic aspect remained untheorized. Indeed, following an early phase in which Marx visualizes the realization of philosophy in and through the proletariat, his expressly articulated views abruptly halt at a second positivistic phase in which philosophy seems to be more or less completely superseded by science: 'When reality is depicted, philosophy as an *independent* [emphasis added] branch of knowledge loses its medium of existence. At the best, its place can only be taken by the summing up of the most general results, abstractions which arise from the observation of the historical development of men'.[35] This abstract-summative conception of philosophy was given the imprimatur of the later Engels and became the orthodoxy of the Second International. However there is a patent contradiction between Engels's theory and practice: his practice is that of an engaged underlabourer for historical materialism – a Lockean function which Marx clearly approved. More-over it is difficult to see how Marxism can dispense with epistemological interventions, and hence positions, so long as social conditions give rise not just to the (philosophical) 'problem of knowledge', but to knowledge as a (practical, historical) problem. In any event, if there is a third position implicit in Marx's practice, it is one in which philosophy (and a fortiori epistemology) is conceived as dependent upon science and other social practices – heteronomously, as a moment of a practical–cognitive ensemble. As such it would have nothing in common with either the old Hegelian 'German professorial concept-linking · method' or the Lukácsian-Gramscian view of Marxism as a philosophy, rather than a (naturalistic) science, characterized by a totalizing vantage point of its own.

The main characteristics of the later Engels's immensely influential philosophical intervention were: (1) a conjunction of a positivistic con-ception of philosophy and a pre-critical metaphysics of the sciences; (2) an uneasy synthesis of a non-reductionist (emergentist) cosmology and a monistic (processual) dialectics of being; (3) espousal of such a universal dialectical ontology in harness with a reflectionist epistemology, in which thought is conceived as mirroring or copying reality; (4) a vigorous critique of subjectivism and an emphasis on natural necessity combined with a stress on the practical refutation of scepticism. *Anti-Dühring* was the decisive influence in the Marxism of the Second International, while the combination of a dialectics of nature and reflection theory became the hallmark of orthodox philosophical Marxism – styled 'dialectical materialism' by Plekhanov (following Dietzgen). Unfortunately Engels's critique of the contingency of the causal connection was not comple-mented by a critique of its actuality (a notion shared by Hume with Hegel) or with co-equal attention to the mediation of natural necessities in social life by human praxes. Moreover despite his great insight into particular episodes in the history of science – for instance his remarkable (post-Kuhnian!) Preface to *Capital* II – the effect of his reflectionism was the truncation of the transitive dimension and a regression to contemplative materialism. Thus the mainstream of the Second International, at its best in the works of Kautsky, Mehring, Plekhanov and Labriola, came to embrace a positivistic and rather deterministic evolutionism (in Kautsky's case, arguably more Darwinian than Marxian); and concerned itself for the most part with systematizing, rather than developing or extending, Marx's work. Paradoxically – because if the main theme of Engels's inter-vention was materialism, its express intention had been to register and defend the specific autonomy of Marxism as a science – its outcome was a *Weltanschauung* not so very different from the hypernaturalist monisms – the 'mechanical' and 'reductive' materialisms – of Haeckel, Dühring and others, which Engels had set out to attack.

Lenin's distinctive contributions were his insistence on the practical and interested character of philosophical interventions, and a clearer conception of the relative autonomy of such interventions from day-to-day science, both of which partially ameliorated the objectivist and positivist cast of Engels's thought. Lenin's philosophical thought moved through two phases: *Materialism and Empirio-Criticism* was a reflectionist polemic designed to counter the spread of Machian ideas in Bolshevik circles (e.g. by Bogdanov); while in the *Philosophical Notebooks* Engels's polar contrast between materialism and idealism gradually took second place to that between dialectical and non-dialectical thinking. There was a robust, if short-lived, debate in the Soviet Union in the 1920s between those who, like Deborin, emphasized the dialectical side and those who, like Bukharin, emphasized the materialist components of dialectical materialism. Thus of the two terms of Engels's epistemological legacy – 'dialectics' and 'materialism' – both were rejected by Bernstein, they were accentuated at different times by Lenin, then externalized as an internal opposition within Soviet philosophy between Deborin and the mechanists before its codification under Stalin as '*Diamat*'; henceforth they were to be represented by antithetical currents within Western Marxism.

In the thought of Adler and the Austro-Marxists, Marxist epistemology became self-consciously critical, in Kantian terms, in two senses: analogously, in that Marx, like Newton, had enabled the formulation of a Kantian question, 'how is socialization possible?'; and directly, in that sociality was a condition of the possibility of experience in exactly the way that space, time and the categories are in Kant. For Adler, Marx's theory is to be understood as an empirically controlled critique, whose object – socialized humanity – is subject to quasi-natural laws, which depend for their operation upon intentional and value-oriented human activity.

None of the thinkers considered so far doubted that Marxism was primarily a science (cf. e.g. Bukharin's *Historical Materialism*). At the same time there was little, if any, emphasis on the authentically dialectical or Hegelian elements within Marx; for which, no doubt, the difficulties of Marx's exposition of the theory of value in *Capital* and the late publication of key early works were largely responsible. This situation now changed. Indeed, in the Hegelian Marxism expounded by Lukács[36] which stimulated the work of the Frankfurt School and the genetic structuralism of Goldmann and provided an interpretative canon for Marx almost as influential as that of Engels, in Korsch[37] and in Gramsci[38] the main emphases of the Engelsian tradition are dramatically reversed.

The chief generic features of their theory of knowledge are (1) historicism, the identification of Marxism as the theoretical expression of the working class, and of natural science as a bourgeois ideology, entailing the collapse of the intrinsic aspect of the cognitive labour process together with a rejection of Marxism as a social science in favour of Marxism as a self-sufficient or autonomous philosophy or social theory, with a comprehensive totalizing standpoint of its own; (2) anti-objectivism and anti-reflectionism, based on the idea of the practical constitution of the world, leading to the collapse or effective neutralization of the intransitive dimension of science and a corresponding epistemological idealism and judgemental relativism; (3) recovery of the subjective and critical aspects of Marxism (including in Lukács case, the rediscovery of an essential ingredient of Marx's theory: the doctrine of fetishism), submerged in the positivistic scientism of the Second International.

Marxism is now fundamentally the expression of a subject, rather than the knowledge of an object; it is 'the theoretical expression of the revolutionary movement of the proletariat'.[39] Moreover it is not just self-sufficient – containing as Gramsci puts it, 'all the fundamental elements needed to constitute a total and integral conception of the world'[40] – but distinguished precisely and only by this self-sufficiency. Thus for Lukács 'it is not the primacy of economic motives that constitutes the decisive difference between Marxism and bourgeois thought, but the point of view of the totality [a position reiterated in his later *Ontology of Social Being*] . . . the all-pervasive supremacy of the whole over its parts is the essence of the method which Marx took over from Hegel'.[41] From this standpoint natural science itself expresses the fragmentary, reified vision of the bourgeoisie, creating a world of pure facts, segregated into various partial spheres and unrelated to any meaningful totality. Thus Lukács inaugurates a long tradition within Marxism which confounds science with its positivistic misrepresentation and starkly counterposes dialectical to analytical thought.

For Lukács the proletariat is the identical subject–object of history, and history (in the Lukácsian circle) is its realization of this fact. Historical materialism is nothing other than the self-knowledge of capitalist society, or (on the circle) the ascribed consciousness of the proletariat which, in becoming self-consciously aware of its situation as the commodity on which capitalist society depends, already begins to transform it. *Capital* I, ch. 1, sect. 4, on commodity fetishism 'contains within itself the whole of historical materialism, and the whole self-knowledge of the proletariat, seen as the knowledge of capitalist society'.[43] Lukács's epistemology is rationalist and his ontology idealist. More particularly, his totality is (as Althusser has pointed out) 'expressive', in that each moment or part implicitly contains the whole; and teleological, in that the present is only intelligible in relation to the future – of achieved identity – it anticipates. What Marx's ontology has, and both the Engelsian ontology (highlighting process) and the Lukácsian ontology (highlighting totality) lack, is structure.

For Gramsci the very idea of a reality-in-itself is a religious residue, and the objectivity of things is redefined in terms of a universal inter-subjectivity of persons; i.e. as a cognitive consensus, asymptotically approached in history but only finally realized under communism, after a practical one has been achieved. Gramsci remarks that 'according to the theory of praxis it is clear that human history is not explained by the atomistic theory, but that the reverse is the case: the atomistic theory, like all other scientific hypotheses and opinions, is part of the super-structure'.[43] This encapsulates a double collapse: of the intransitive to the transitive dimensions, and the intrinsic to the extrinsic aspects, of science. In the first respect Gramsci's remark reminds one of Marx's jibe against Proudhon that like 'the true idealist' he is, he no doubt believes that 'the circulation of the blood must be a consequence of Harvey's theory'.[44] The historicity of our knowledge (as well as the distinct historicity of its objects) on which Gramsci quite properly wishes to insist does not refute, but actually depends upon, the idea of the otherness of its objects (and their historicity).

Lukács, Gramsci and Korsch all reject any dialectics of nature of an Engelsian type, but whereas Lukács does so in favour of a dualistic, romantic anti-naturalism, Gramsci and Korsch ·do so in favour of a historicized anthropomorphic monism. Whereas Lukács argues that the dialectic, conceived as the process of the reunification of original subject and estranged object, only applies to the social world, Gramsci and Korsch maintain that nature, as we know it, is part of human history and therefore dialectical. While in Gramsci's achieved (being-knowing) iden-tity theory, intransitivity is altogether lost, on Lukács's theory, on which identity is the still-to-be-achieved outcome of history, intransitivity remains in two guises: (i) as an epistemically inert nature, not conceived in any integral relation to the dialectic of human emancipation; (ii) as the realm of alienation in human history, prior to the achievement of pro-letarian self-consciousness.

The principal epistemological themes of the 'critical theory' of Horkheimer, Adorno, Marcuse and (in a second generation) Habermas and their associates are (1) a modification of the absolute historicism of Lukácsian Marxism and a renewed emphasis on the relative autonomy of theory; (2) a critique of the concept of labour in Marx and Marxism; and (3) an accentuation of the critique of objectivism and scientism.

(1) is accompanied by a gradual decentering of the role of the pro-letariat and eventually results in the loss of any historically grounded agency of emancipation, so that – in a manner reminiscent of the Young Hegelians – revolutionary theory is seen as an attribute of individuals (rather than as the expression of a class) and displaced onto the normative plane as a Fichtean 'Sollen' or 'ought'. The consequent split between

theory and practice, poignantly expressed by Marcuse – 'the critical theory of society possesses no concepts which could bridge the gap between present and future, holding no promise and showing no success, it remains negative'[45] – underscored a pessimism and judgementalism which, together with its totally negative – romantic and undialectical – conceptions of capitalism, science, technology and analytical thought, place its social theory – conceived (as in historicist Marxism) as the true repository of epistemology – at some remove from Marx's. By the same token, this allowed it to illuminate problems which Marx's own optimistic rationalism and Prometheanism had obscured.

(2) The pivotal contrast of critical theory between an emancipatory and a purely technical or instrumental reason came increasingly, from Horkheimer's 'Traditional and Critical Theory'[46] to Habermas's *Knowledge and Human Interests*,[47] to be turned against Marx himself, in virtue of his emphasis on labour and his concept of nature purely as an object of human exploitation. Thus Marcuse[48] conceives an emancipated society as one characterized neither by the rational regulation of necessary labour nor by creative work but rather by the sublimation of work itself in sensuous libidinous play. According to Habermas, Marx recognizes a distinction between labour and interaction in his distinction between the forces and relations of production but misinterprets his own practice in a positivistic way, thereby reducing the self-formation of the human species to work. However, it may be argued that Marx understands labour not just as technical action, but as always occurring within and through a historically specific society and that it is Habermas, not Marx, who mistakenly and uncritically adopts a positivistic account both of labour, defining it as technical action, and of natural science, which he sees as adequately represented by the deductive–nomological model.

(3) Habermas's attempt to combine a conception of the human species as a result of a purely natural process with a conception of reality, including nature, as constituted in and by human activity illustrates the antinomy of any transcendental pragmatism. For it leads to the dilemma that if nature has the transcendental status of a constituted objectivity it cannot be the historical ground of the constituting subject; and, conversely, if nature is the historical ground of subjectivity then it cannot simply be a constituted objectivity[49] – it must be *in-itself* (and, contingently, a possible object for us). This is a point which Adorno, in his insistence on the irreducibility of objectivity to subjectivity, seems to have appreciated well. Indeed Adorno[50] isolates the endemic failing of First Philosophy, including Marxian epistemology, as the constant tendency to reduce one of a pair of mutually irreducible opposites to the other (for instance in Engelsian Marxism consciousness to being, in Lukácsian Marxism being to consciousness) and argues against any attempt to base thought on a

non-presuppositionless foundation and for the immanence of all critique.

It will be convenient to treat together the work of (i) humanist Marxists, such as E. Fromm, H. Lefebvre, R. Garaudy, A. Heller and E.P. Thompson; (ii) existentialist Marxists, such as Sartre and Merleau-Ponty; (iii) East European revisionists, such as L. Kolakowski, A. Schaff and K. Kosik; and (iv) the Yugoslav *Praxis* group of G. Petrović, M. Marković, S. Stojanović and their colleagues. Despite their diverse formations and preoccupations, all share a renewed emphasis on man and human praxis as 'the centre of authentic Marxist thought',[51] an emphasis lost in the Stalinist era, whose recovery evidently owed much to the *Economic and Philosophical Manuscripts* (and, to a lesser extent, the new humanistic readings of Hegel's *Phenomenology* proposed by for example A. Kojève and J. Hyppolite). Two points are worth stressing: first, it is assumed that human nature and needs, although historically mediated, are not infinitely malleable; second, the focus is on human beings not just as empirically given but as a normative ideal – as de-alienated, totalizing, self-developing, freely creative and harmoniously engaged. The first signals an undoubted partial return from Marx to Feuerbach. Among these writers, Sartre's *oeuvre* is the most far-reaching and sustained attempt to ground the intelligibility of history in that of individual human praxes. But, as has been noted before, Sartre's starting point logically precludes his goal: if real transformation is to be possible then a particular context, some specific ensemble of social relations, must be built into the structure of the individual's situation from the beginning – otherwise one has: inexplicable uniqueness, a circular dialectic and the abstract a-historical generality of conditions (from 'scarcity' to the 'practico-inert').

By and large anti-naturalist Western Marxism from Lukács to Sartre has shown little concern with either ontological structure or empirical confirmation. These biases are separately corrected in the scientific rationalism of Althusser and other structuralist Marxists (such as Godelier) and the scientific empiricism and neo-Kantianism of Della Volpe and Colletti. In Althusser one finds, most sharply formulated in *For Marx* and (with E. Balibar) *Reading Capital*: (1) a novel anti-empiricist and anti-historicist conception of the social totality; (2) rudiments of a critique of epistemology coupled with a collapse of the extrinsic aspect ('theoreticism'); and (3) a form of scientific rationalism influenced by the philosopher of science G. Bachelard and the meta-psychologist J. Lacan, in which the intransitive dimension is effectively neutralized, resulting in a latent idealism.

(1) Althusser reasserts the ideas of structure and complexity, on the one hand, and of irreducible sociality, on the other, in his view of the social totality as an overdetermined, decentred complex, pre-given whole, structured in dominance. Against empiricism, it is a whole and structured, and

its form of causality is not Newtonian (mechanistic); against historicism and holism it is complex and overdetermined, not an 'expressive totality', susceptible to an 'essential section' or characterized by a homogeneous temporality, and its form of causality is not Leibnizian (expressive). Against idealism, the social totality is pre-given; and against humanism, its elements are structures and relations, not individuals, who are merely their bearers or occupants. However, while Althusser wishes to insist against sociological eclecticism that the totality is structured in dominance, his own positive concept of structural causality is never clearly articulated.

(2) Although opposed to any reduction of philosophy to science or vice-versa, in maintaining that criteria of scientificity are completely intrinsic to the science in question, Althusser leaves philosophy (including his own) without any clear role; in particular, the possibilities of any demarcation criterion between science and ideology, or critique of the practice of an alleged science, seem ruled out. Epistemological autonomy for the sciences is accompanied by and underpins their historical autonomy, and the dislocation of science from the historical process presupposes and implies the inevitability of ideology (conceived as mystification or false consciousness) within it – a view at variance with Marx's.

(3) Although Althusser insists upon a distinction between the real and thought, the former functions merely as a quasi-Kantian limiting concept within his system, so that it easily degenerates into an idealism, shedding the intransitive dimension completely, as e.g. in 'discourse theory'. It is significant that just as Althusser sees Spinoza, not Hegel, as the true precursor of Marx, his paradigm of science is mathematics, an apparently a priori discipline, where the distinction between the sense and reference of concepts, and the theory-dependence and theory-determination of data, can be obscured. In short Althusser tends to buy theory at the expense of experience, as he buys structure at the price of praxis and the possibility of human emancipation.

If Lukács expresses the Hegelian current within Marxism in its purest form, Della Volpe draws out the positivist themes most exactly. The aim of his important work, *Logic as a Positive Science*, is the recovery of historical materialism as a tool of concrete empirically oriented research and the revindication of Marxism as a materialist sociology or a 'moral Galileanism'. Della Volpe situates Marx's critique of Hegel as the historical climax of a line of materialist critiques of a priori reason extending from Plato's critique of Parmenides to Kant's critique of Leibniz. In it, Marx replaces the Abstract-Concrete-Abstract (A-C-A) Circle of the Hegelian dialectic with its 'indeterminate abstractions' by the Concrete-Abstract-Concrete (C-A-C or better C-A-C') Circle of materialist epistemology with its 'determinate rational abstractions', thus effecting a transition from 'hypostasis to hypothesis, from a priori assertions to experimental forecasts'.[52] Any knowledge worthy of the name is science',[53] and science always conforms to this schema, which Marx is said to have elaborated in the Introduction to the *Grundrisse*, and which, as Della Volpe interprets it, boils down to the familiar hypothetico-deductive method of Mill, Jevons and Popper.

Only four kinds of problems with the Della Volpean reconstruction can be indicated here. (1) It is supposed to apply indifferently to social science and philosophy as well as natural science. The upshot is a hypernaturalist account of social science and a positivist-proleptic conception of philosophy shackled on to a view of science which is monistic and continuist within and across disciplines and buttressing a conception of Marx's own development as linear and continuous. (2) C-A-C is a purely formal procedure which works equally well for many theoretical ideologies. (3) Della Volpe never clearly differentiates theoretical precedents from historical causes: a latent historicism underpins the overt positivism of his work. (4) Most importantly, there are crucial ambiguities in the definition of the C-A-C′ model. Does 'C' refer to a conceptualized problem or a concrete object, i.e. does the circle describe a passage from ignorance or from being to knowledge? If it is designed to do both, then the consequent empirical realism, in tying together transitive and intransitive dimensions, destratifies reality and dehistoricizes knowledge. Does 'A' refer to something real, as in transcendental realism and Marx, or merely ideal, as in transcendental idealism and pragmatism? Finally, does 'C′' refer to (i) presentation, (ii) test or (iii) application? The distinction between (i) and (ii) is that between Marx's order of presentation and inquiry; (ii) and (iii) that between the logics of theoretical and applied activity; (i) and (iii) that between the hierarchy of presuppositions of capitalist production elaborated in *Capital* and the kind of analysis of determinate historical conjunctures (the 'synthesis of many determinations' of the *Grundrisse* Introduction) which Marx essayed in the *18th Brumaire* or *The Civil War in France*.

The best known member of the Della Volpean school, Colletti, rejected even Della Volpe's restricted, purely epistemological, dialectics, contending that any dialectic excluded materialism, and criticized Della Volpe's hypernaturalist reconstruction of Marx for omitting the critical themes of reification and alienation. Colletti has, however, had great difficulty in reconciling these themes with his own unstratified empirical realist ontology and neo-Kantian conception of thought as other than being; and seems eventually to have settled on a split between the positive and critical dimensions of Marxism, thereby abandoning the notion of a scientific critique, prior to an eventual vehement renunciation of Marxism itself. There is in the work of Colletti, as in that of Habermas and Althusser (probably the three most influential recent writers on Marxist epistemology), a pervasive dualism: between thought as truth and as situated, objectivity as something in itself and as the objectification of a subject, man as a natural being and as the genus of all genera (the point at which the universe comes to consciousness of itself). While Colletti's work has been criticized in Italy (for instance by Timpanaro) for neglecting the ontological aspects of materialism, both the Althusserian and Della Volpean tendencies in general seem vulnerable to scientific realist reconstructions of knowledge and Marxism. Between the theory of knowledge and Marxism, there will always, however, remain a certain tension. For, on the one hand, there are sciences other than Marxism, so that any adequate epistemology will extend far beyond Marxism in its *intrinsic* bounds; but, on the other, science is by no means the only kind of social practice, so that Marxism has greater *extensive* scope. There will thus always be a tendency for one or the other to be subsumed – as, within the concept of Marxist epistemology, epistemology becomes critically engaged and Marxism submits itself to a reason it displaces.

Rorty, Realism and the Idea of Freedom

A liberal society is one which has no ideal except freedom (CC p. 13)*

Richard Rorty has given us an eloquent critique of the epistemological problematic, from which contemporary philosophy is gradually emerging. But I want to suggest that he has provided us with only a partial critique of a problem-field, to which he remains in crucial respects captive. These passing notes are not of course innocent. They are written from a particular perspective, that of a Lockean underlabouring interest in human sciences which partly do and partly do not (yet) exist – which are in the process of struggling to come into being. Such sciences would provide that sort of consiousness of our natural and social past and present as to allow us to change both ourselves and the conditions under which we live (cf. *PMN* p. 359) in such a way that 'the distinction between the reformer and the (violent) revolutionary is no longer necessary' (*CC* p. 13). More specifically, I want to claim that we shall only be able 'to see how things in the broadest possible sense of the term, hang together, in the broadest possible sense of the term' (*CP* p. xiv) from this perspective if we are committed to:

(i) an *ontologically* oriented philosophically realist account of science, on which the world is explicitly construed, contrary to Humean ontology, as structured, differentiated and changing; and

---

*The following abbreviations will be used in this chapter. Works by Richard Rorty: *CC* – 'The Contingency of Community', *London Review of Books*, 24 July 1986. *CL* – 'The Contingency of Language', *London Review of Books*, 17 April 1986. *CP* – *The Consequences of Pragmatism*, Harvester Press, Brighton 1982. *CS* – 'The Contingency of Self', *London Review of Books*, 8 May 1986. *PMN* – *Philosophy and the Mirror of Nature*, Basil Blackwell, Oxford 1980.

Works by Roy Bhaskar: *PON* – *The Possibility of Naturalism*. Pagination refers to 2nd ed. Harvester Press, Hemel Hempstead 1989. *RTS* – *A Realist Theory of Science*, 1st ed. Leeds 1975, 2nd ed. Harvester Press, Brighton 1978. *SR* – *Scientific Realism and Human Emancipation*, Verso, London 1986.

(ii) a *critical* naturalist account of the human sciences, which will sustain the idea of an explanatory critique of specific structural sources of determination and their emancipatory transformation.

Rorty remains, I am going to contend, a prisoner of the implicit ontology of the problematic he describes. My aim is to carry the dialectic of 'de-divinisation' (*CC* p. 10) a stage or two further by conceiving reality, being, the world (precisely as it is known to us in science) as only *contingently* related to human being; and therefore as not *essentially* characterizable as either empirical or rational or in terms of any other human attribute. This is the mistake of what I call the 'epistemic fallacy': the definition of being in terms of knowledge (cf. *RTS* pp. 36ff.). A picture has indeed held philosophy captive.[1] It is the picture of ourselves or our insignia in any picture – the picture as invariably containing our mirror-image or mark. Philosophical post-narcissism (see *CS* p. 12) will be evinced in the exercise of our capacity to draw non-anthropomorphic pictures of being. This is my main post-Rortian point. But I shall also be pursuing one or two subsidiary theses. I shall argue that Rorty's remarks on science reveal an unacceptable positivist–instrumentalist and Humean–Hempelian bias, and that his account of science is based on a half-truth. Further I shall contend that *Philosophy and the Mirror of Nature* is characterized by a central tension – roughly that of Kant's '"existentialist" distinction between people as empirical selves and as moral agents' (*PMN*, p. 382), a fault-line parallel to that of the Kantian resolution of the Third Antinomy, on which *PMN* is 'stuck fast'. Moreover, as in Kant's case, it is Rorty's ontology which is responsible for his failure to sustain an adequate account of agency and a fortiori of freedom as involving inter alia emancipation from real and scientifically knowable specific constraints rather than merely the poetic redescription of an already-determined world.

1 Rorty's Account of Science

'Kuhn himself . . . occasionally makes too large concessions to the tradition, particularly when he suggests that there is a serious and unresolved problem about why the scientific enterprise has been doing so nicely lately' (*PMN* p. 339). Rorty goes on to interpret the unease felt by Kuhn at the absence of a solution to the problem of induction as merely the expression of 'a certain inarticulate dissatisfaction' (*PMN* p. 341). Still this does raise the question of the characterization of science. In particular in what has science been so successful lately? – Rorty supposes that it has succeeded in 'the prediction and control of nature' (*PMN* pp. 341, 356).

He assumes that the aim of science is prediction and control – Comtean *'savoir pour prévoir, prévoir pour pouvoir'*; and that explanation is deductive–subsumptive and symmetrical with prediction, that is, Hempelian in form (*PMN* pp. 347, 356) – a bias he shares with Habermas.[2] Such explanations of course presuppose Humean causal laws. The truth of physicalism and regularity (Humean) determinism (*PMN* pp. 28n., 205, 354, 387) is rendered consistent with the truth of non-physicalistic statements by reference to Davidsonian theory, on which singular causal claims or heteronomic (non-strictly Humean) generalizations entail that a homonomic, strictly Humean description exists.[3] Thus Rorty is committed to a basically positivist account of the logical form of sentences in science, and of the structure of scientific theories. This in turn presupposes that the world is at least fundamentally (though not necessarily exclusively) Humean–Laplacean in form, that is, that it is constituted by atomistic events or states of affairs or molecular state descriptions and their *constant conjunctions*.

That Rorty can presuppose as much has to be explained by a critical lacuna in his dialectical reconstruction of the recent history of analytical philosophy of science. Roughly speaking, there have been two main axes of criticism of the standard positivist view of science of the sort against which Popperians, Wittgensteinians and Kuhnians reacted. There has been criticism of its *monistic* theory of scientific development, turning on the social, historical and/or discontinuous character of scientific knowledge – of the kind advanced by Sellars, Feyerabend and Kuhn. But there has also been criticism, from Scriven on, of the *deductivist* theory of scientific structure, turning especially on the stratification of scientific knowledge. Although Rorty is aware of this line of criticism (see *PMN* p. 168), it plays no role in his narrative.[4] It is a line which is especially salient for debates about the *Geisteswissenschaften*, where explanations conforming to the deductive–nomological model are completely unavailable[5] and where any generalizations have to be formulated 'normically' as allowing for exceptions.[6]

There are two main moments in the anti-deductivist critique of Humean and Hempelian theory. The first, whose prototype was provided by Kant's critique of Hume, which was later repeated and refined by Campbell's critique of Duhem, and then by Hesse and Harré's critique of Hempel, involves the denial that constant conjunctions are *sufficient* for causal laws, explanations, or scientific theories. But it is the second on which I wish to focus here. This involves the denial that constant conjunctions are even *necessary*. This 'transcendental realist' position may be motivated by reflection on the nature of experimental and applied scientific activity (see *RTS* chs. 1 and 2). Analysis of experimental activity shows that the regularities necessary for the empirical identification of laws hold only under special and in general artificially produced closed conditions; but, for at least a large class of fundamental laws,[7] analysis of applied activity shows that these laws are presumed to prevail in open systems, outside the conditions which permit their empirical identi- fication, where no constant conjunctions obtain. Such laws have to be analysed *transfactually* as tendencies. These tendencies are of novel kinds of thing. They are the relatively enduring generative mechanisms and structures of nature, initially hypothesized in the scientific imagination but sometimes subsequently found to be real, which produce the flux of events. There are no known laws in physics that conform to the Humean form. Generalizations can be empirical, or more broadly actual, or uni- versal, but not both – a consequence that Cartwright captures in the title of her book, *How the Laws of Physics Lie.*[8] Transcendental realism makes possible a reformulation of the Greek action/contemplation contrast (see *PMN* p. 11). There is 'a difference that makes a difference' between (a) 'it works because it's true' and (b) 'it's true because it works' (*CP* p. xxix). (a) gives the gist of applied explanations in open systems, (b) of theoretical corroborations in closed systems. Rorty notes that Newtonian mechanics was doubly paradigmatic for the founders of modern philosophy – as 'a method for finding truth' and as 'a model for the mechanics of inner space' (*PMN* p. 328n). But he remains under the spell of a third effect of the celestial closure achieved by Newtonian mechanics; namely its form- ing a model of phenomena as well as science, an ontological paradigm of an empirical actualist and regularity determinist cast. Galileo and Newton were misinterpreted by the Enlightenment. It is important to appreciate that in the battle between the gods and the giants (*CP* p. xv), the friends of the Earth no less than the friends of the Forms have been wrong about science.

Reflection on experimental and applied scientific activity reveals that science is committed to a non-anthropocentric and specifically non- Humean ontology – of structures and generative mechanisms irreducible to and often out of phase with the (normally artificially contrived) patterns of events which comprise their empirical grounds. In particular the laws of nature, as they are currently known to us, entail the (contingently counter- factual) possibility of a non-human world; that is to say, that they would operate even if they were unknown, just as they continue to operate (transfactually) outside the closed conditions which permit their empirical identification in science. It follows from this that statements about being cannot be reduced to or analysed in terms of statements about knowledge, so that what I have referred to as 'the epistemic fallacy' *is* a fallacy (*SR* p. 47). Accordingly we need two dimensions in which to talk about science: an ontological or 'intransitive' dimension and an epistemological or historical sociological or 'transitive' dimension (see *RTS* Ch. 1). The laws of nature, unlike their normally experimentally produced grounds, are not empirical, but real (tendencies). That the reality known to us in science is only contingently related to our experience of it, its knowledge, and more generally human being, is the only position consistent with a 'scientific realist' (*PMN* p. 381) world-view or congruent with Sellars's dictum which Rorty quotes approvingly that 'science is the measure of all things, of what is that it is, and of what is not that it is not'.[9]

One consequence of the argument which establishes the transfactual and non-empirical nature of laws is that a philosophical as distinct from a scientific ontology is *irreducible* in the philosophy of science. A philosophical ontology will consist of some general account of the nature of the world, to the effect that it is structured and differentiated, whereas a scientific ontology will specify the structures which, according to the science of the day, it contains and the particular ways in which they are differentiated (see *RTS* p. 29).[10] But a moment's reflection shows that a philosophical ontology is *inevitable* too. For one cannot talk about science – for instance about the logical form of causal laws – without implicitly presupposing something about the world known by science – about, that is to say, its ontological form, say to the effect that it is constituted by events which are constantly conjoined in space and over time. Commitment to empirical realism and in particular to the Humean theory of causal laws (empirical invariances as necessary or necessary and sufficient for laws) carries with it commitment to a (false) general account of the world.

A very damaging feature of empirical realism is the systematic tendency to conflate knowledge and being, as in the notion of the 'empirical world', or epistemological with ontological concepts and issues. Thus the transfactuality of laws is just one aspect of the existential intransitivity of objects – the condition that in general things exist (and act) independently of their descriptions (which is consistent with causal interdependency in the processes of the production of things and their descriptions, namely, in the social domain) (see *PON* p. 47). The idea of the existential intransitivity of objects (as a proposition in the intransitive dimension of the philosophy of science) is compatible with the idea of the social production of knowledge (as a proposition in the transitive dimension of the philosophy of science). Paradigmatically, we make facts and, in experimental activity, closed systems; but we find out about (discover and identify) things, structures and causal laws (cf. *CL* p. 3, *CP* p. xxxix, *PMN* p. 344). We could stipulate these as 'necessary truths'. But it is probably better to recognise that there is an inherent ambiguity or bipolarity in our use of terms like 'causes', 'laws', 'facts' and so on, and to be prepared, whenever necessary, to disambiguate them, distinguishing a transitive (social or making) from the intransitive (ontological or finding) employment of these terms.

Kuhn provides a famous case of transitive–intransitive (epistemological–ontological) ambiguity when he notoriously says, in a passage discussed by Rorty (*PMN* pp. 344–5), that we must learn to make sense of sentences like this: 'though the world does not change with a change of paradigm, the scientist afterward works in a different world'.[11] Once we disambiguate 'the world' into 'social, historical, transitive' and 'natural, (relatively) unchanging, intransitive' we can rewrite the sentence, without paradox, as follows: 'though the (natural) world does not change with a change of paradigm, the scientist afterward works in a different (social (or cognitive)) world'. I shall suggest in a moment that Rorty's argument trades in places on a similar paradox and ambiguity.

A consequence of the non-anthropocentric ontology to which science, but not Rorty, is committed is that it is not optional, but mandatory that we tell causal stories which make the laws of physics prior to and longer than the truths of biology and both of these the backdrop for human history. It is not just 'hard', but inconsistent with both the practical presuppositions and the substantive content of the sciences 'to tell a story of changing physical universes against the background of an unchanging Moral Law or poetic canon' (*PMN* pp. 344–5).

In any event, 'physics gives us a good background against which to tell our stories of historical change' (*PMN* p. 345) is ambiguous in the way of Kuhn's 'world'. If physics means 'the physical world' as described by [the science of] physics (hereafter physics$_{id}$ – or the physical world), then it is true and unparadoxical. If, however, physics means 'the set of descriptions' of the physical world in the science of physics (hereafter physics$_{td}$ – or the science of physics), then as a rapidly changing social product it is part of the process of historical change and so cannot form a background to it. Two other instances of this ambiguity may be cited. At *PMN* p. 342, Rorty claims that the reduction of the cognitive (fact, theory) to the non-cognitive (value, practice) would seem to ' "spiritualise" nature by making it like history or literature, something which men have *made* rather than *found*', whereas it would merely spiritualize (natural) science which has indeed been made rather than found. (The identity of nature and science only holds if one commits the epistemic fallacy or subscribes to the subject–object identity theory with which the fallacy is implicated – in which indeed it is founded.) Discussing the Nietzschean view of self-knowledge as self-creation (*CS* p. 11), Rorty remarks that 'the only way to trace home the causes of one's being as one is would be to tell the story of one's causes in a new language'. He continues: 'This may sound paradoxical, because we think of causes being discovered rather than invented – but even in the natural sciences we occasionally get genuinely new causal stories, the sort of story produced by what Kuhn calls "revolutionary science"'. However what are told in revolutionary science are new – or revolutionary – stories$_{td}$ about the causes$_{id}$ of natural phenomena. Moreover in social life the principle of existential intransitivity holds just the same. Thus redescribing$_{td}$ the past in a revolutionary way can cause$_{id}$ radical new changes, including a new identity, self-definition or auto-biography: but it cannot retrospectively cause$_{id}$ old changes, alter the past (as distinct from its interpretation). It is not surprising that Rorty should slip from transitive to intransitive uses of terms like 'cause' – it is endemic to empirical realism, the epistemological definition of being in terms of (a particular empiricist concept of) experience.

One odd feature of Rorty's account of science may be briefly mentioned. He seems to think that it may be possible to have a plurality of comprehensive closed theories of strictly Humean form: 'There are *lots* of vocabularies in the language within which one might expect to get a comprehensive theory phrased in homonomic generalisations, and science, political theory, literary criticism and the rest will, God willing, continue to create more and more such vocabularies' (*PMN* p. 208). He seems here to be committed to a most implausible form of what might be called a 'multiple aspect theory'.

2 De-divinizing Ontology and the Inexorability of Realism

The principle of the existential intransitivity of objects, that things in general exist and act independently of their descriptions, must be complemented by the principle of the historical transitivity of knowledge, that we can only know them under particular descriptions (cf. *RTS* p. 250; *SR* p. 99). But it does not follow from the principle of the historical transitivity of knowledge that we cannot know that what is known (under particular descriptions) exists and acts independently of those descriptions. Rorty is correct that there is 'no inference from "one cannot give a theory-independent description of a thing" to "there are no theory-independent things"' (*PMN* p. 279). But equally there is no inference from 'there is no way to know a thing except under a particular description' to 'there is no way to know that that thing exists (and acts) independently of that particular description'. In fact one can know that scientifically significant reality existed and acted prior to and independently of that relative latecomer science as a truth in (a result of) sciences (of cosmology and geogony, biology and anthropology) and one can know that it exists and acts independently of science as a practical presupposition of the social activity of science (and a truth in philosophy). Of course what is known – in the discourse of philosophy – to exist and act independently of science will always be known in some more or less specific way – whether in the relatively neanderthal forms of Peircian 'secondness' (*PMN* p. 375) or Maine de Biran's 'intransigence'[12] or what Putnam has called '19th century . . . village atheism'[13] or in the form of a more fully elaborated ontology.

Such generic characterizations of the world can and do play a significant role in the practice of science; and some ontology, or general account of being, and hence some kind of realism, will in any event be implicitly presupposed, if it is not explicitly theorized, in a philosophical discourse on science. The crucial questions in philosophy are not whether to be a realist or an anti-realist, but *what sort* of realist to be (an empirical, conceptual, transcendental or whatever realist); whether one explicitly theorizes or merely implicitly secretes one's realism; and whether and how one decides, arrives at or absorbs one's realism. While arguing that we never encounter reality *except under a chosen description* (*CP* p. xxxix), Rorty unwittingly imbibes and inherits Hume's and Kant's chosen descriptions of the reality known by the sciences.

Ontology is irreducible partly because different (for instance cognitively-oriented) practices presuppose different and incompatible accounts of the world. It is not sufficient to '[explain] rationality and epistemic authority by reference to what society lets us say' (*PMN* p. 174) precisely because 'what society lets us say' can itself always be '[placed] in the logical space of reasons, of justifying [and, we must add, criticizing] and being able to justify [and criticize] what one says' (*PMN* p. 182). That is to say, what society or one's peers and contemporaries *ought* to let one say is always a legitimate question, especially in the case of *conflicts*, actual or potential, between different language-games, as is chronically the case in the contested and quandarous human sciences.

We can now also begin to appreciate why we need to sustain the concept of an ontological realm distinct from our current claims to knowledge of it. First, for the intelligibility of their establishment, involving, as they do, creative redescription of, and active intervention in, nature. Second, for the possibility of their criticism and rational change (see *RTS* p. 43). (I will deal with Rorty's claim that the transitions between normal discourses, paradigms or language-games, though caused, cannot be reasoned (*CC* pp. 10–11) below). Rorty's 'transcendentalia' (*PMN* pp. 310–11) now become, from this perspective, necessary features of the immanent practice of the sciences. And even his welcome warnings about the dangers of reifying or hypostatizing truth become misleading (and ecologically irresponsible) if they are taken to imply that there are no real world constraints on beliefs or to license a poetic or practical Prometheanism to the effect that there are 'no non-human forces to which human beings should be responsible' (*CC* p. 10).

I now want to isolate and comment on five pivotal presuppositions of Rorty's work. Rorty assumes that:

(1) Science can get by without philosophy, and in particular metaphysics and ontology;

(2) Any (philosophical) realism must be a truth-realism;

(3) The only kind of realism science needs is what Putnam calls an 'internal realism' (*PMN* pp. 298, 341) – which is required for purposes of Whiggish historiography;

(4) The Humean theory of causal laws (at least as modified by Davidson) and the deductive–nomological accounts of explanation and prediction (and a fortiori their symmetry) are in order and correct;

(5) Their truth is compatible with the possibility of the *Geisteswissenschaften* and in particular the *wirkungsgeschichtliches Bewusstsein* (*PMN* p. 359), central to the project of 'edification' and emancipatory social science alike.

None of these assumptions withstand critical scrutiny.

Rorty accepts Kant's conflation of the a priori and the subjective (criticized in *SR* pp. 11 ff.), (see *PMN* pp. 8–9, 258) and thus sees the only possible locus of necessity as 'within the mind' (*PMN* p. 189). He thus assumes that any transcendental philosophy is going to be primarily epistemological or epistemologically oriented (*PMN* p. 381). This prematurely forecloses the possibility of a philosophy of or for science which was no longer concerned to 'ground' knowledge or find certain foundations for it; but which was instead concerned to ask what the *world* must be like for certain characteristic (practical and discursive) social activities of science to be possible.[14] Such a philosophy would be a transcendental realism not idealism; ontologically, rather than epistemologically, geared; and unafraid of recognizing epistemically relativist implications – which are anyway quite consistent with judgementally rationalist results (*PON* pp. 57–8).

From such a philosophical perspective, reality can be unequivocally (and no longer anthropocentrically or epistemologically) accorded to things. It would be wrong to hold, for instance, to the slogan that 'to be is to be the value of a variable'.[15] For the way things are in the world takes no particular account of how human beings are, or how they choose to represent them. Moreover from such a perspective, (natural) necessity would, like reality, when appropriate, be unequivocally ascribed to the efficacy of causal laws and generative mechanisms and the existence of some properties of structures and things (*RTS* ch. 3.3 & 3.5). It would reflect a superstitious anthropomorphism to believe that 'necessity resides in the way we say things, and not in the things we talk about'.[16] Also from such a perspective, there would remain no temptation to identify or treat as synonyms the 'ontological' and the 'empirical' (see *PMN* p. 188). For such a philosophy would have a use for the category of the 'real but non-empirical', for example in designating the transfactual operation of causal laws prior to, outside and independently of human experience.

Finally such a transcendental philosophy would unashamedly acknowledge as a corollary of its realism, the historicity, relativity and essential transformability of all our knowledge. Putnam's disastrous 'meta-induction'[17] loses its force if one no longer conflates ontological realism and epistemological absolutism and thinks of absolutism and irrationalism as the only alternatives. Indeed from this standpoint it should even be welcomed – as underlining the historicity and potential transformability of all our cognitive achievements. Rorty evades the 'relativist predicament' (*CC* p. 11) by the twin expedients of deploying an epistemic absolutism for normal science and an epistemic irrationalism for abnormal science, or more generally discourse. In the former case he invokes Davidson's arguments against alternative conceptual schemes and assumes that within a language-game or discourse 'everybody agrees on how to evaluate everything everybody else says' (*PMN* p. 320). In the later case he stipulates that what is believed or said, though, like Davidsonian metaphors (*CS* p. 14), caused, cannot be reasoned, so that 'the most human beings can do is to manipulate the tensions within their own epoch in order to produce the beginnings of the next epoch' (*CC* p. 11). This is a counsel of despair. It stems partly from the over-normalization of normal discourse, ignoring its holes, silences and incommensurabilities – and also its ambiguities and ambivalences, its open texture and rich potentialities for development. Partly too from the failure to allow anything like immanent critique (including the possibility of meta-critique (*SR* pp. 25–6)) as a process of rational disputation and change in the synchronic and diachronic space or overlap between language-games, where all the interesting (and truly dialectical) arguments take place and develop, and without which there would be nothing very much, if at all, to say (see *PON* p. 148).[18]

To sum up on point (1) above, then, we can reaffirm with Rorty that there is no Archimedean point outside human history and no 'third thing' called correspondence standing between the world and language. But that doesn't mean that we do not need a philosophical de-divinized ontology, in which to think (i) the contingency of our origins, of human experience and human reason (and hence the possibility of an unexperienced or an a-rational(-ized) world); (ii) the finitude of human being (including the uncompleted or unfinished character of human lives); and (iii) the historicity of human knowledge (within what I have called the transitive dimension of the philosophy of science).

Contrary to (2) above, I suggest that what is required to underlabour for science is not an epistemologically-slanted truth realism of the sort that the pre–1976 Putnam and the tradition have sought to provide, but an ontologically-primed causal powers and tendencies of things realism of the sort I sketched in *A Realist Theory of Science* and Harré and Madden elaborated in *Causal Powers*.[19]

As regards (3), there are places (for instance at *PMN* pp. 282, 341) where the sort of internal realist historiography which Rorty reckons a sufficient realism might appear to differ little from the account a transcendental realist might provide. But there are differences in metaphysics, ideological intent and rhetorical style. Transcendental realists are unblushingly falliblist and historicist about science. They feel no need to be uncritical and 'complimentary' about everything that passes for knowledge or is done in science's name (cf. *PMN* p. 298); no reason to 'buy in' to shoddy science (see *RTS* p. 188); no compunction about admitting to occasional intra-scientific perplexity or 'stuckness'. Nor do they feel under any imperative to write the story of science Whiggishly as one long continuous success story – without blemishes or periods of stasis and even regression. For they never forget that science is something that human beings have made, in causal interaction with the things they have found, in nature.

As for (4), we have already seen that Humean and Hempelian theory are inconsistent with the practical activity and substantive content of science. (5) will be considered in sections 4–6 below.

It is true that nature has no preferred way of being represented; that nature speaks being', like the Heideggerian 'language speaks man' (*CC* p. 11), is only a metaphor. But the following should be borne in mind. Despite the indisputable formal underdetermination of theory by evidence at any moment of time in most scientific domains most of the time, there are only one or two plausible theories consistent with the data. Theories are islands in oceans of anomalies. Secondly, in what might be called the 'epistemic stance' to nature,[20] we do 'read' the world, as we read the time off a clock or sentences off a page *as if* it were constituted by facts or under the descriptions of a theory (see *SR* ch. 3.6). To say that theory conditions our beliefs in epistemically significant perception is not to say that theory determines them. Theory and nature may be co-determinants of beliefs in a notional parallelogram of forces (see *SR* pp. 189–91); and we may appeal to either (in propositionalized form) in a justificatory context. (In fact Rorty allows for the control of theory by observation in the guise of 'control by less controversial over more controversial beliefs' (*PMN* pp. 275–6n.) – but beliefs of the former kind may be less controversial precisely because they were formed in or as a result of (theoretically-informed) observation.) Finally we must never forget the immense effort that goes into that nitty-gritty practical laboratory activity which Bacon called 'twisting the lion's tail'[21] designed precisely to create or induce the conditions under which grounds for a theoretical judgement will become available. Such practical activity, comprising social trans-actions between human beings and their material transactions with nature, constitutes the woof and warp of getting into 'the logical space of reasons, of justifying and being able to justify what one says' (*PMN* p. 182), the staple diet of normal science.

3 Epistemology and Anti-epistemology

The highest point reached by contemplative materialsm, that is, materialism which does not comprehend sensuousness as practical activity, is the contemplation of single individuals and of civil society.

The standpoint of the old materialism is civil society; the standpoint of the new is human society, or social humanity.[22]

What is the epistemological problematic, which Rorty identifies and partially describes, but in which, in my view, he remains entrapped? For Rorty, it is a problem-field, which is also a project or quest and a theory or solution-set. The project is to identify certain foundations for knowledge, which philosophy purports to do on the basis of its special understanding of the nature of knowledge and of mind. The Cartesian–Lockean–Kantian tradition has conceived philosophy as foundational, knowledge as repre-sentational and the mental as privileged and even incorrigible. At the core of philosophy has been the quest for certainty, in response to the possi-bility of Cartesian (sceptical) doubt. This, in its dominant empiricist form it has found in the immediate deliverances of sense (rather than, or some-times as well as, in self-evident truths of reason – or their analytical proxy's, such as meanings).

Rorty's sustained polemic against foundationalism in *PMN* is accom-panied by a vigorous assault on its attendant ocular metaphors, mirror imagery and overseer conception of philosophy. Most of this I whole-heartedly endorse. In *PMN* he isolates one particular moment in the genesis of foundationalist epistemology of special importance. This is what I call the '*ontic fallacy*' (*SR* p. 23). It consists of the effective onto-logization or naturalization of knowledge, the reduction of knowledge to being or its determination by being, in what may best be regarded as a species of *compulsive belief-formation* (see *PMN* pp. 158, 374–7). (Thus Plato focused 'on the various parts of the soul and of the body being compelled in their respective ways by their respective objects' (*PMN* p. 158).) Rorty sees that this involves the dehumanization of discursive, justifying subjects, and the collapse, in the alleged moment of cognition,

of the *pour-soi* to the *en-soi*, of justification to para-mechanical explanation. ('It is the notion of having reality unveiled to us . . . with some
unimaginable sort of immediacy which would make discourse and
description superfluous' (*PMN* p. 375).[23]) But – and this is one sense in
which *PMN* is based on a half-truth – Rorty does not see that it is the
epistemic dual or counterpart of the ontic fallacy, namely the human-
ization of nature, in an anthropomorphic, epistemological definition of
being (in empiricism, in terms of the concept of experience) in the
epistemic fallacy, which prepares the way and paves the ground for the
ontologization (eternalization and divinization) of knowledge in a
subject–object identity or correspondence theory. Such a theory effectively
welds together the transitive or social–epistemic and intransitive or ontic
dimensions of science (see *SR* pp. 66, 253). On it knowledge is naturalized
and being epistemologized.

This problematic, which may be fairly called 'epistemological', has
ontological and sociological conditions and consequences. The drive to
certainty, powered by epistemology's sceptical foil, sets up a dialectic in
which correspondence must give way to, or be philosophically underpinned by, identity. Similarly, accuracy of representation must pass over
into immediacy of content. Then, in its dominant empiricist form, the
objects intuited in experience and their constant conjunctions come, in the
ideology of empirical realism, to define the world, stamp being in a
Humean mould. The sociological precondition of the atomistic and
uniform ontology of empirical realism is an individualism, comprised of
autonomized units, conjoined (if at all) by contract, passive recipients of a
given and self-evident world rather than active agents in a complex,
structured and changing one. For such isolated consciousnesses, disengaged from material practice, their relation to their bodies, other minds,
external objects and even their own past selves must become doubtful.
Philosophy's task – that of the traditional 'problems of philosophy' – now
becomes to reconstruct and indemnify our actual knowledge in a way
congruent with these conceptions of man and being.

What explains this problematic? There seems little doubt about the role
of the fundamentalist exercise. It is surely, as Rorty suggests, a misguided
attempt to eternalize the normal discourse of the day (*PMN* pp. 9–10,
333n.). Moreover it is philosophy's fundamentalist ambitions which justify
its ontology. This ontology, formulated in the antiquated vocabulary of
Newtonian and Humean mechanics is now seriously 'interfering with' (*CL*
p. 5) our efforts to investigate and change social being. What explains it?
Could it be anything other than the conception of man – of single individuals in civil society – at the heart of it? Perhaps the real meaning of
the epistemological project is not epistemological at all, but ontological: to
reconstitute the (known) world in the self-image of bourgeois man.

If this, or something like it, is part of the meaning of the episte-mological tradition which has come down to us from Descartes and Locke through Hume and Kant and their descendants, what should be said about the role of epistemology within the context of the transcendental realist philosophy of science I have been advocating here? We can approach the need for *some*, anti-traditional epistemology by reflecting on the irreducible normativity of social practice which Rorty notes (*PMN* p. 180n.). This begins to show us why we need something other than the historical sociology of knowledge in the transitive dimension of the philosophy of science. It shows us why, from the standpoint of what I have called the 'axiological imperative', namely the condition that we must act (and other than by scrutinizing the antecedents of what we will do) (*PON* p. 87), we need an intrinsic (intentional, justifying) as well as (and, when it is efficacious, within the context of) the extrinsic (historical, explaining) aspect of science (see *SR* pp. 16ff.).

I think, despite his polemics against epistemology (as normally under-stood[24]) *per se*, Rorty half-concedes this point when talking of the 'bi-focality' of science: 'From the point of view of the group in question these subjective conditions are a combination of commonsensical practical imperatives (e.g. tribal taboos, Mill's methods) with the standard current theory about the subject. From the point of view of the historian of ideas or the anthropologist they are the empirical facts about the beliefs, desires and practices of a certain group of human beings. These are incompatible points of view, in the sense that we cannot be at both viewpoints simul-taneously'. (*PMN* p. 385) An epistemology or criteriology for science is required just in so far as science is an irreducibly normative activity, oriented to specific aims (in theory, the structural explanation of manifest phenomena) and characterized by specific methods of its own (see *RTS* ch. 3).

Now if value judgements of one sort or another are irreducible in the sciences, does this mean that they neither require nor can receive grounds other than the agreement of one's peers (see *PMN* p. 176)? Certainly not. For, in the first place, a value judgement, including one of truth, typically incorporates a descriptive or evidential component alongside its prescrip-tive, imperatival or practical component (see *SR* p. 183). To ignore the former, the descriptive ('factual' or ontological) grounds in virtue of which some belief or action is commended and recommended, could be called the emotivist or more generally *anti-naturalistic fallacy* in axiology. But can such grounds be cashed in any way other than by reference to what some community or, at the limit, what an agent believes about the world? Most certainly.

Outside science, a belief or action may be justified (or criticized) by refer-ence to what the (relevant) scientific community believes. But generally *inside* (the relevant part of) science, we cannot justify, say, an explanatory claim in this way. This may be partly because what is at stake (what stands in need of justification or criticism) is precisely what the community believes. But it will also be partly because at some point the explanatory query *in* science will take the form, 'Why is the world this way?', whereas the explanatory query *about* science will take the form, 'Why does the community believe such-and-such?' The answer to the former question will not consist of intellectual-cultural history or the natural sociology of belief, but of a (scientifically-) ontologically grounded, or justified, scientific explanation. Intra-scientific justifications (in the intrinsic aspect of science) will appeal to formal proofs, plausible models, decisive experiments, reliable apparatus, newly discovered phenomena, consistency with established theory, and so forth. Together they will amount to a justification, couched in the terms of some substantive scientific ontology, of the explanation offered of the puzzling phenomenon, rather than a sociological explanation (in the extrinsic aspect of science) of that community's (or agent's) belief. To confound the two would be to commit all over again a transposed variant of the Lockean mistake of confusing justification and explanation, which Rorty mercilessly exposes in *PMN* ch. 3. Of course, justifications within science are a social matter – but they require and are given ontological grounds. In failing to recognize this, Rorty has furnished us with a post-epistemological theory of knowledge without justification which matches his account of science without being. The result is just the opposite of what he intended: the epistemologization of being and the incorrigibility (uncriticizability) of what passes for truth.

4 The Essential Tension of *Philosophy and the Mirror of Nature* – or, A Tale of Two Rortys

> *Reason would overstep all its limits if it took upon itself to* explain how *pure reason can be practical. This would be identical with the task of explaining* how freedom is possible.[25]

A pervasive tension runs through *PMN* between (α) a hard-boiled scientistic naturalism of a physicalistic determinist cast, prominent to the fore, and (β) an acceptance of the autonomy of the *Geisteswissenschaften* and espousal of hermeneutics, accentuated towards the aft. Indeed the book is a veritable tale of two Rortys – tough-minded Humean versus tender-minded existentialist. Rorty's subsequent trajectory has further tautened the tension – the actualism of *PMN* culminating in the apotheosis of contingency in the 1986 Northcliffe Lectures (henceforth *NL*) (published as *CL*, *CS* and *CC*). Rorty is aware of the tension in *PMN*. So it is good to have his views on the apparent (and, I shall argue, real) incompatibility set out in two series of pithy paragraphs (on pp. 354–5 and 387–9). For I want to claim that Rorty is unable to sustain either (i) an intelligible account of scientific activity (which involves, *inter alia*, causal intervention in nature to win 'epistemic access' to transfactually efficacious laws) or (ii) of the world known by science or (iii) an adequate idea of human freedom, or (iv) of the compatibility between (α) and (β).

'Physicalism is probably right in saying that we shall some day be able, "in principle", to predict every movement of a person's body (including those of his larynx and his writing hand) by reference to microstructures within his body' (*PMN* p. 34; see also pp. 28n., 204–5, 387).

Against this, I am going to argue that a person's neurophysiology, or more generally physical microstructure, cannot constitute a closed system. This can be seen most easily by considering social interaction of an every-day sort. Suppose A goes into a newsagent's and says to B '*The Guardian*, please' and B hands A a copy of it. On the physicalist thesis we must suppose that for any physical movement there is a set of antecedent physical (neurophysiological, or microstructural) states sufficient for it. Call B's action 'ϕ_B'. We must now suppose either (1) that ϕ_B is determined by some set of antecedent physical states $N_1 \ldots N_n$ such that ϕ_B would have been performed without A's speech action, ϕ_A: or (2) that A's speech action, ϕ_A, as understood by B, was causally efficacious in bringing about ϕ_B.

(1) involves the supposition that B would have performed the action of handing A a copy of *The Guardian*, ϕ_B, or the movements in which it physically consists, even if A had performed some quite different action such as asking for the *Independent* or a packet of chewing gum or B to marry him, or dancing a jig, and even if A had not been present at all. This is absurd. But (2) involves an action of A's, as understood by B, inter-vening in the allegedly closed circuit constituted by B's neurophysiology (or microstructure). That is to say, it involves A's speech act as part of a causal sequence between some prior set of neurophysiological states of B and ϕ_B – just as ϕ_B intervenes between A's contemporaneous physical states and his subsequent action, ψ_A, of giving B 30p. (We cannot suppose that A's movement would have occurred if B had said 'Sorry, sold out' or passed him a copy of *The Sun* or slapped his face or ignored him.) So B's (and A's) neurophysiology (or microstructure) cannot constitute a closed system. Thus in the context of social interaction a person's body cannot form a closed system (see *PON* pp. 104–6).

This argument may be extended to cover the broader cases of open systemic behaviour generally, animal behaviour[26] and emergent natural powers. Here I consider only the first. Suppose C takes a stroll. It starts to rain. So she opens her umbrella. We must now suppose either (1') that C would have done so even if it had remained fine or (2') that the allegedly deterministic chain of neurophysiological (or microstructural) states is broken – in this case, by the weather.

There is a line of last resort that the reductionist might employ at (2), (2'), namely to deny that a single person's microstructure comprises a closed system. But now physicalism loses its distinctiveness as a philosophical thesis applicable to *individual human beings* (see *PMN* p. 387) and reduces merely to a barren form of Laplacean determinism, against which I have argued enough elsewhere (see *RTS* especially ch. 2). What of (1) and (1')? It might be urged here that as a matter of fact ϕ_B and only ϕ_B will occur in response, as it appears, to ϕ_A; that given the state of B's microstructure nothing else could have occurred. What we are left with now is a bizarre variety of Leibnizian pre-established harmony of monads, in which each person's microstructure is so synchronised with every other's that it appears *just as if* they were talking and dancing, batting and bowling, laughing and crying; and so synchronised with the microstructure of every other object in the universe that it appears *just as if* they were eating and drinking, building and digging, weaving and welding.

Only an emergent powers materialism, I want to claim, can sustain the phenomenon of agency (see *PON* 3.4–5; *RTS* 2.5; *SR* 2.1) and this entails the breakdown of the thesis of regularity determinism at the physical level. But we have already seen that the laws of nature, and the principles posited in scientific theories, cannot be construed as constant conjunctions. They do not have a closed systemic, regularity deterministic form. Rather they must be taken transfactually, as real tendencies operating on and whatever (when their antecedent – stimulus and releasing – conditions are satisfied) the flux of events. Events, for their part, whether the fall of an autumn leaf, the collapse of a bridge, the purchase of a newspaper, the composition of a poem or the decline of a civilization are not determined before they are caused (see *RTS* p. 107).

Rorty's next paragraph begins: 'The dangers to human freedom of such success is minimal, since the "in principle" clause allows for the probability that the determination of the initial conditions (the antecedent states of microstructures) will be too difficult to carry out except as an occasional pedagogical exercise' (*PMN* p. 354). This is disastrous. Freedom cannot be grounded in ignorance. Or else we would have to reckon a falling man free in virtue of his ignorance of gravity or the law of fall. And most free would be the least *pour-soi* (*PMN* p. 352), the furthest from 'the logical space of reasons, of justifying and being able to justify what one says' (*PMN* p. 389).

Rorty continues: 'The torturers and the brainwashers are, in any case, already in as good a position to interfere with human freedom as they would wish; further scientific progress cannot improve their position'. Two brief comments. First, torturers and brainwashers achieve their results by intervening in causal series, bringing about various physical effects, ultimately sounds, inscriptions and so on – which, but for their machinations, would not *ceteris paribus* (unless those effects were over-determined) have been forthcoming. Second, the idea that technical progress couldn't improve their position seems to me like wishful thinking. It would be rash to assume that subliminal advertising or market research were wasted. The more the manipulators know about the immediate determinants of human action (*CP*), the more successful, or so it would seem, they are likely to be.

Rorty's next paragraph may be broken down into:

(I) 'The intuition behind the traditional distinction between nature and spirit, and behind romanticism, is that we can predict what noises will come from someone's mouth without knowing what they mean'.

(II) 'Thus even if we could predict the sounds made by the community of scientific inquirers of the year 4000, we should not yet be in a position to join in their conversation.'

(III) 'This intuition is quite correct' (*PMN* p. 355).

Proposition (II) is quite correct. If we *were* able to predict verbal behaviour, we still might not be able to know what the agents *meant*. Thus, as Winch has pointed out, we might be able to compute the statistical probability for the occurrence of certain sounds, say, words in Chinese, without being able to understand what was being said[27] – and the converse is also the case (see *PON*, p. 137). But Rorty's intuition is faulty. For the reason why we cannot in general predict the sounds or inscriptions that people make unless we know what they mean to say is because it is the latter which determines the former. It is the state of the conversation, not physiology, which will explain the sounds and marks of the community of scientific inquirers for the year 4000, though these sounds and marks must be consistent with their physiology. Equally, it is the state of the economy that determines the use of machines and thus selects the initial and boundary conditions under which certain mechanical principles apply. In human agency, the agent puts matter in motion, setting the conditions for the operation of various neurophysiological and physical laws, the outcome of which is not pre-determined before it has actually been caused – by the agent in the context of her bio-psycho-social life. If the concept of human agency – as manifest in such phenomena as catching buses or writing poems – as distinct from mere bodily movement – as manifest in such phenomena as catching colds and digesting cakes – is to be sustained, it must be the case that the agent is causally responsible for some but not other of her bodily movements (see *PON* p. 92).

I now have enough material to attempt a diagnosis of Rorty's reconciliation of the pervasive tension of *PMN*. It is a variant of Kant's resolution of the Third Antinomy. Now this does not work for Kant, and it does not work for Rorty. The problem for Kant is how we can be held responsible for the things we do, involving as they do bodily movements (including those of our larynxes and our writing hands), if all our physical movements are fully determined by antecedent phenomenal causes. It is a problem for Rorty too. Kant has no answer to it – if we discount the idea of an original choice outside time (presumably an expedient not open to the naturalist Rorty). And whether we discount it or not, in either case, our ordinary system of causal imputation in the human world, and, with it our moral accountancy, collapses.

What prevents an adequate resolution of the antinomy for Kant is his empirical realism, his thoroughgoing actualism and determinism, as detailed in the Analogies, to which he is wedded in his account of the phenomenal realm. For it is this which necessitates placing 'free man' in a realm, albeit one said to be possibly real (as distinct from merely apparent), outside and beyond the purchase of science. It is the ontology implicit in Kant's account of science, as manifest in his comprehensive actualism, that prevents him sustaining an adequate account of human causal agency, and *a fortiori* of freedom as a possible property or power of embodied agents in space and time.

Rorty comes to replicate the problematic of the Kantian solution. The basic distinction he invokes is that of Kant's ' "existentialist" distinction between people as empirical selves and as moral agents' (*PMN* p. 382). We are determined as material bodies, *qua* empirical selves, but free as writing and speaking (or discursive) subjects, *qua* moral agents. Actually this is not quite as he puts it, but I will justify the interpretation and elaboration in a moment. The point for Rorty is not an ontological, so much as a linguistic one. Whereas Kant gives us at an least two worlds model, Rorty gives us an at least two languages model. The autonomy of the social and other less physicalistic sciences is rendered consistent with a comprehensive empirical actualism by allowing that physics (or the physical sciences) can describe every bit of the phenomenal world but that some bits of it, for instance the human, can also be truly redescribed in a non-physicalistic way (*PMN* pp. 28n., 205, 354, 387).

The problem for Rorty, as for Kant, is how if the lower-order level is completely determined, what is described in higher-order terms can have any effect on it. And of course the answer is that it cannot. If the intentional level, at which we cite reasons for actions and offer justifications and criticisms of beliefs is merely a redescription of movements which are already sufficiently determined by antecedent physicalistic causes, then the *causal irrelevance of reasons* for the states of the phenomenal world of bodily movements and physical happenings (including the production of sounds and marks) immediately follows. Given this, both the particular reasons adduced in explanations, and the status of reason explanations in general, appear as arbitrary and the practices (from the *wirkungsge-schichtliches Bewusstsein* of edification (*PMN* p. 359) to the creative redescriptions of strong poets (*CS* pp. 11ff.)) upon which they are based appear as illusory (See *PON* pp. 88–9).

Here again, as in Kant, it is Rorty's thoroughgoing actualism, determinism and deductivism which prevent an adequate account of human agency, and a fortiori responsibility and freedom. There is a further difference here in that the relation between reality and appearance is inverted. In Kant the phenomenal world is merely apparent, but the noumenal world is real, which is what makes freedom possible. In Rorty, on the other hand, the phenomenal actualistically described world must be taken as real, with freedom dependent on our ignorance of (or decision to hold in abeyance) those deterministic descriptions of it. But the structure of the problem-field is the same. In both cases, reason explanations become arbitrary, and the only way to change the material world is by operating on sub-social (physical) causes. Science becomes unintelligible, social science impossible and freedom cognitively unattainable.

5   Further Considerations on the Autonomy of the *Geisteswissenschaften* and Rorty's Idea of Freedom

Man is always free to choose new descriptions (for, among other things, himself)
(*PMN* p. 362n.)

The pivotal opposition between a phenomenal or empirical realm subject to strictly deterministic laws known to science and an intelligible realm of human being (or intentionalistic redescription) where agents are free is a familiar one. The Manichean world of late-nineteenth-century German culture fused this broadly Kantian cleavage with Hegelian dichotomies to found distinctions between *Erklären* (causal explanation) and *Verstehen* (interpretive understanding), the nomothetic and the ideographic, the repeatable and the unique, the domains of nature and of history. Since then, the pivotal contrast has usually been accompanied by the claim that, in the case of the intelligible order and its denizens, science must at least be complemented (the neo-Kantian position) and at the most be replaced (the dualist anti-naturalist position) by another practice, method or approach – namely 'hermeneutics'. The ground for hermeneutics lies in the uniquely meaningful, linguistic or conceptual character of its subject matter – in virtue of which it is precisely intelligible. So it is with Rorty too. But before we can see this, there is some unravelling to do.

The underlying distinction for Rorty is, as we have seen,

(A) the Kantian so-called ' "existentialist" distinction between people as empirical selves and as moral agents' (*PMN* p. 382).

It is this, or something very like this, distinction which underpins his critique of epistemology as based on a confusion of 'explanation' and 'justification' (*PMN* chs. 3–4) and his praise for Sellars (see *PMN* p. 180n.) for insisting on the irreducibility of norms, values and practices to facts and descriptions. (This is compatible with his critique of value-free discourse (*PMN* p. 364). For Rorty wants to stress the irreducible normativity of the social and defactualize the social so achieved. (Hence there are no objective (factual) constraints in social reality.)) It is grounded, or so I shall argue, in the consideration that it is discourse which is distinctive of human beings: 'people *discourse* whereas things do not' (*PMN* p. 347). Without discourse no statement (or description) could be true or false. Also without discourse, there would be no abnormal discourse, hence no hermeneutics and no edification; no choice and therefore no *pour-soi*. It is in this sense, I have suggested, that we could sum up his reconciliation of the poles constituting the pervasive tension of *PMN* by saying that we are determined as material bodies but free as speaking and writing (discursive) subjects. In ch. 8 of *PMN* (A) explicitly comes to the fore as the irreducibility of the *pour-soi* to the *en-soi*.

But before we get to ch. 8, Kant's 'existentialist' distinction (which structures *PMN* as a whole), has already become displaced or transposed in ch. 7 onto

(B) the 'linguistified'[28] and Kuhnian distinction between normal and abnormal discourse.

Later, by the time of *NL*, this distinction has made way for, or passed over into:

(C) the romantic distinction between what might be called 'alter-determination' and self-creation (*CS* p. 12).

But there are already clear premonitions of this in *PMN*, for instance in the attempt to distance the romantic notion of man as self-creative from

Cartesian dualism and Kantian constitution (*PMN* pp. 346, 358). Alter-determination consists of being made rather than making oneself, and leads to stasis or replication; whereas self-creation consists in self-transformation or self-overcoming. So (C) leads readily to:

(D) the Nietzschean distinction between the will to truth and the will to self-overcoming (*CL* p. 5; *CS* p. 12).

(C) is also the distinction between romanticism and moralism (*CC* p. 14) and (D) that between philosophy and poetry.

By now the whole ontological backcloth has shifted. The comprehensive actualism of the naturalistic Rorty has given way to a celebration of contingency. (This is really only the other side of the Humean coin – they are linked in symbiotic interdependency.) Already prefigured in ch. 8 (*PMN* p. 381n.), this familiar existentialist motif is elaborated into an ontology of the particular, idiosyncratic, accidental and unique. Thus the individuation of human beings – ideographic particulars – is to be achieved by capturing their uniqueness in a unique, and so novel way. Only in this way can we avoid the fate of being a product of some pre-existing set of programmes or formulae, and so a copy, replica or instance of a type (or universal) rather than an *individual*. (It might be argued that the concept of contingency only makes sense in relation to that of necessity, which is officially (for Quinean reasons) disallowed. But Rorty can say that his use of it is a deliberate polemical reactive one, designed to make an (anti-) philosophical point.)

(B), (C) and (D) constitute the linguistic, romantic and Nietzschean displacements of Rorty's original (in *PMN*) Kantian problematic. I am going to claim that discourse is the central unifying category in Rorty's later thought; and that it determines the progression from (A) through to (D).

In so far as it is discourse that is distinctive of human beings, we have the possibility of creating new languages (vocabularies, descriptions and so on), of unfamiliar uses of existing noises and marks (metaphors) (*CL* p. 6), of abnormal and incommensurable, including reactive and potentially edifying (including non-constructive) discourses – and hence of *hermeneutics*. Hermeneutics is the generic term for the activity of rendering intelligible what is at present unintelligible (*PMN* p. 321). It is the attempt to normalize discourse, which is paradigmatically discourse (from within some normal discourse) about abnormal rather than normal discourse (*PMN*, p. 346). Hermeneutics is a kind of meta-discourse; but one which is only needed in the case of some incommensurable, and therefore (from the viewpoint of the hermeneutical enquirer) abnormal, discourse. It is the attempt to establish a 'common context of utterance' or 'mutual horizon' (*PON* pp. 154ff.). Note that 'there is no requirement that people should be more difficult to understand than things: it is merely that hermeneutics is only needed in the case of incommensurable discourses, and that people discourse whereas things do not. What makes the difference is not discourse versus silence but incommensurable versus commensurable discourses' (*PMN* p. 347).

In Part 3 of *PMN* hermeneutics is somewhat oddly counterposed to epistemology, and the latter is thereby severed from its specific connections to science, scepticism, the theory of knowledge and philosophy. What they share in common is that they are both meta-discourses, discourses not about the world, but about our knowledge (epistemology) or discourse (hermeneutics) about the world. What differentiates them is that epistemology presupposes universal commensuration, underpinned by the figure of what I have called the 'ontic fallacy' (see p. 157 above); whereas hermeneutics does not, and in fact is necessary just when this assumption breaks down – when we must 'savour' or 'bandy about', in order to literalize or normalize, a new or different (alien) way of speaking (see *CL* p. 6). A directly connected peculiarity is Rorty's restriction of hermeneutics to discourse about abnormal (or incommensurable normal) rather than normal discourse. This is explained by Rorty's 'overnormalisation' of normal discourse (noted on p. 155 above). By contrast, I would argue that hermeneutics, or the interpretive understanding of meaningful objects, is *always* necessary in social life – and *within* it, as well as about it. (Thus there is hermeneutics in normal physics or chemistry.)

On the interpretation of Rorty I am developing, the fundamental feature of human beings, their discursivity, gives us their ontological duality: as both 'generators of new descriptions' and 'beings one hopes to be able to describe accurately', 'as both *pour-soi* and *en-soi*, as both described object and describing subject' (*PMN* p. 378). As describing subjects, human beings can redescribe every object, including themselves, in new, including potentially abnormal (and hence incommensurable normal) ways – which is to say that because human beings are describing subjects, new, and potentially incommensurable, descriptions can become true of *any* object.

But Rorty does not clearly or explicitly distinguish the case (a) where any object (including human beings) may *change*, and so require a new, potentially incommensurable, description from the case (b) where any object (including human beings) may, though *unchanged*, be redescribed in a new, potentially incommensurable, way. To make this distinction explicitly requires disambiguating intransitive from transitive change. Thus it is characteristic of Rorty that, having allowed that 'for all we know, it may be that human creativity has dried up, and that in the future it will be the *non*human which squirms out of our conceptual net' (*PMN*

p. 351), he goes on to add that in such a case 'it is natural to start talking about an unknown language – to imagine, for example, the migrating butterflies having a language in which they describe features of the world for which Newtonian mechanics has no name' (*PMN* p. 352).

For Rorty then:

(i) all things may be redescribed, even if they do not change, possibly in terms of an incommensurable vocabulary;

(ii) all things may exhibit novelty, and so require a new, potentially incommensurable, discourse;

(iii) only human beings can discourse (normally or abnormally, literally or metaphorically); and

(iv) only human beings can overcome themselves, their past and their fellow human beings. They do so in and by (creating a new) discourse in terms of a new incommensurable vocabulary.

It should be stressed that for Rorty everything is susceptible to a new, possibly incommensurable, description. He says that: 'It would have been fortunate if Sartre had followed up his remark that man is the being whose essence is to have no essence by saying that this went for all other beings also' (*PMN* pp. 361–2 n. 7). And he adds that the point is 'that man is always free to choose new descriptions (for, among other things, himself)'. But of course the addendum is not true of beings other than man. Snakes and stones, migrating butterflies and runner beans are not free to choose new descriptions. Of course some kinds of things (carbon atoms, dogs) but not others (tables, chairs) have essences (*RTS* p. 210). But can Rorty be interpreted as meaning anything other than (a) that discourse is the essence of man[29] and/or (b) that in so far as man has no specific essence (no 'species being') he is the being whose essence, qua describing and redescribing subject, is to be the essence or measure of all beings, qua describable and redescribable objects.[30] Discourse, then, is the essence of man; and, through man, of being. This, if the interpretation is correct, is the residue of Rorty's 'linguistic turn'. It chimes in well with Gadamer's dictum that 'being is manifest in language', which itself reflects Heidegger's proposition that 'language is the house of being'.[31]

What is the connection between (A) and (B)? There is a contingent overlap between them in the sense that the science–nonscience distinction gives way to the normal–abnormal discourse distinction and, as it so happens, the redescribable world of human beings (culture) is caught less well than the redescribable world of nature by the normal (scientific) discourse of the day (for any or all of reasons (i) – (iv)). Thus there is no historiographically relevant demarcation criterion, 'no deeper difference than that between what happens in "normal" and in "abnormal" discourse' – a 'distinction which cuts across [and effectively replaces] the distinction between science and nonscience' (*PMN* p. 333). And 'that portion of the field of inquiry where we feel rather uncertain that we have the right vocabulary at hand and that portion where we feel rather certain that we do . . . does, at the moment, roughly coincide with the distinction between the fields of the *Geistes-* and the *Naturwissenschaften* (*PMN* p. 352).

What then becomes of freedom? It ceases to be understood merely negatively, as grounded in our ignorance of physically determining laws, and becomes, through our capacity to *redescribe* that world (or relevant bits of it), something which is both positive and humanistically more recognisable – namely the capacity to create, and choose between, different vocabularies – that is, to speak or write *abnormally*. (Thus: 'Sartre tells us we are not going to have . . . a way of seeing freedom as nature (or, less cryptically, a way of seeing our creation of, and choice between vocabularies in the same "normal" way as we see ourselves *within* one of those vocabularies)' (*PMN* p. 380).) Freedom then is shown in the exercise of our capacity for abnormal discourse – for instance in fantasy and metaphor. Such discourse is of course always parasitic on the weighty existence of normal, literal, public, 'stodgy' discourse (*CC* p. 14). Moreover it presupposes a degree of leisure and the absence of debilitating toil or pain (*CS* p. 14).

Freedom as the capacity to engage in abnormal discourse is closely linked to 'freedom as the recognition of contingency' (*CS* p. 11). Recognition here consists of the use or appropriation of particular contingencies for symbolic purposes – 'which amounts to redescribing them' (*CS* p. 14). However it appears to be only the human world, where things are meaningful in character, which can be reappropriated in this way. This is particularly clear in the case of our dealings with fellow human beings. 'In coping with other persons . . . we can overcome contingency and pain . . . by appropriating and transforming their language'. But in relation to the 'non-human, the non-linguistic, we no longer have the ability to overcome contingency and pain, but only the ability to recognise [it]' (*CS* p. 14). This is, as it were, a Davidsonian variant of the Vichian *facimus*. We can know the social world not so much in so far as we have made it, but in so far as we have re-made or reappropriated it by redescribing it in our own terms. 'The final victory of poetry in its ancient quarrel with philosophy – the final victory of metaphors of self-creation over metaphors of discovery – would consist in our becoming reconciled to the thought that this is the only sort of power over the world which we can hope to have. For that would be the final abjuration of the notion that truth, and not just power and pain, is to be found "out there"' (*CS* p. 14).

We have got slightly ahead of ourselves. So let us retrace our steps. Though determined as material bodies (which includes the movements of our larynxes and writing hands), we are free as writing and speaking (discursive) subjects – a freedom shown most signally in the exercise of our capacity for abnormal discourse. A criterion of political value flows directly from this:

(B'): 'It is central to the idea of a liberal society that, in respect of words as opposed to deeds, persuasion as opposed to force, anything goes' (*CC* p. 11).

What is Rorty's highest value, his *summum bonum*? It is (C) romantic self-creation, which becomes, by the time of *NL*, (D) Nietzschean self-overcoming. Man is the describing, redescribing being. Among the entities man can redescribe in a new, and abnormal, way, is himself. By making a new, incommensurable description of herself 'stick', she makes it true; and thus 'gives birth to' (to use Harold Bloom's term) or 'creates' herself – which is to say 'overcomes' her previous or past self. Moreover, only by describing herself in a totally novel way can she capture or express her idiosyncrasy, uniqueness – or rather achieve it, achieve her individuation – for anything else would reduce her to a (more or less complex set of) formula(e), a token of a type (or set of types). Such radical self-redescription (which could be nicknamed 'me-' or 'we-' description) is the highest form of description. For not only does the redescription redescribe the redescriber; but in the process of redescription – of winning it, of making it stick, of achieving recognition for it – it makes the (re)description true; so achieving the identity of subject and object, by *creating* it. This, *if* it were possible, would be the historic goal of philosophy achieved in a romantic or Nietzschean mode.[32]

Man, then, by redescribing himself, a redescribing subject, in a totally new way and winning acceptance for it, creates a new identity or subjectivity for herself – and thus (potentially) for every other object in the universe too, which can be redescribed in accordance with the new image, in her own way. (For she is the genus of all genera, the *anima mundi* through which language speaks.) Self-creation by self-overcoming is the reconciliation of man as empirical self and as moral agent, as described object and describing subject; the realization of the reconciliation between nature and spirit which Kant vainly tried to achieve in *The Critique of Judgement* by recourse to a divinizing as-if, now achieved in the process of discursive self-formation. Freed from the shackles of nature by her poetic power or discursive agency, by creating new descriptions of herself or tradition which stick, or 'take' in the community (perhaps after her death), and so become true; she overcomes, or remakes, herself, or her tradition.

Such overcoming redescriptions are redescriptions of redescriptions of a
(fully determined) physical world; and there is no criterion for their truth
other than their acceptance. 'The Nietzschean substitution of self-creation
for discovery substitutes a picture of the hungry generations treading each
other down for a picture of humanity approaching closer and closer to the
light' (*CL* p. 6). On this moving staircase of history stories replace stories,
and there is nothing more to this process other than the prosaic quasi-
Darwinian fact that some stories which are told stick around for a while
(are re-told), while most do not.

Is the romantic/Nietzschean ideal – of total self-creation, full self-
overcoming – possible? Clearly not. Nor does Rorty think it attainable.
On the contrary, the new way of speaking can only be (a) marginal or
partial and (b) recognised *post festum* and retrospectively justified; and it
is (c) conditional on future acceptance or usage. (a) A total transformation
would leave the discursive agent and her community without the linguistic resources to recognize or refer to her achievement; nor could it be
literalized in the community unless there was some continuity or com-
munality in usage. 'Overcoming' is always piecemeal and partial – transformation, not replacement; and it respects the existential intransitivity of
the self or past to be overcome. (b) Clearly the self-overcoming discourse
must be abnormal. But if it is abnormal, how can it come to be understood, or normalized? Rorty's answer is that 'If it is savoured rather than
spat out, the sentence may be repeated, caught up, bandied about. Then it
will gradually require a habitual use, a familiar place in the language
game' (*CL* p. 6). I would prefer to consider the way in which something
akin to a logic of analogy, metaphor and new meaning or use is implicit in
for instance our scientific, literary, artistic, political judgements and practices. This would also be a logic of determinate negation and immanent
critique. (c) Because the self-overcoming process must be public[33] (for
Hegelian as well as Wittgensteinian reasons) 'there can be no fully
Nietzschean lives . . . no lives that are not largely parasitical upon an un-
redescribed past and dependent on the charity of an as yet unborn generation' (*CS* p. 15).

Despite the way Rorty refuses to find an identical subject–object here,
and so distances himself from the romantic and Nietzschean ideals, his
account of the social world is one in which the romantic and Nietzschean
processes are the vital ones, with the paradigmatic human being being the
strong poet (or utopian revolutionary) who manages to impose her
vision, even if only marginally, retrospectively and conditionally, upon a
tradition or a community. (In the former case she becomes a member
of a discontinuous series, whose fate is to be continually reappropriated in
a Whiggishly continuous narrative. In the latter case she becomes a
self whose self-description 'counts' and is acknowledged in the stories

which are told and repeated.) In any event Rorty has already subscribed to one identical subject–object – that implicit in the Humean–Kantian story of the world known by (at least natural) science,[34] which remains empirical, actual and contingent – rather than real, transfactually efficacious and characterized by natural necessity (cf. *RTS* ch. 3.3–3.6). And it is that world which, I argued in section 4, makes discursive, as well as any other socialized, open-systemic form of human agency, impossible. For such agency depends upon the agent 'making a difference' to the course of the material world.

(A)–(D) between them lets us score four progressively rich degrees of freedom in Rorty.

Freedom$_0$ – as susceptibility to new descriptions, discourses. This is freedom as caprice. It depends upon the sense in which, through man, discourse speaks being – the sense in which man is '*anima mundi*'.

Freedom$_1$ – as the capacity to give new descriptions, generate new discourses. This is the sense in which freedom is connected with being a moral agent, *pour-soi* and capable of justification and radical choice.

Freedom$_2$ – as the capacity to engage in metaphor, fantasy and abnormal discourse (revolutionary practice?). This is freedom as abnormal discourse – in which it is said, for instance, that the dangers to 'abnormal discourse do not come from science or naturalistic philosophy. They come from the scarcity of food and the secret police' (*PMN* p. 389). This is linked to freedom as the recognition of contingency, the contingencies which we seize on and appropriate in poetry and fantasy. Politically it licenses the slogan that 'in words, as opposed to deeds . . . anything goes' (*CC* p. 11). Its text is Mill's *On Liberty*.

Freedom$_3$ – as the capacity to generate radically new self-descriptions, and to break free from or overcome the past. This is the highest degree of freedom. It remains an individual project. Freudian or Nietzschean moral philosophy cannot be used to define social goals; nor is there any bridge between a private ethic of self-becoming and a public ethic of mutual accommodation (*CS* p. 12).

Freedom, then, as caprice, discourse, capricious discourse and creative discourse.

6 How is Freedom Possible?

What sort of freedom is at issue here? Freedom, for example, 'from the scarcity of food and the secret police' (*PMN* p. 389). Or from being so 'racked by pain' or 'immersed in toil' (*CS* p. 14) as to be unable to engage in abnormal discourse; or from being too uneducated to be capable of edification (*PMN* pp. 365–6); or from being too unleisured – to lack the time or the equipment – to create metaphors (*CS* p. 14), fantasies or poetry or generate a new description of oneself, one's culture or one's past. This kind of freedom – freedom$_1$ – freedom$_3$ – depends, I am going to argue, upon the explanatory-emancipatory critical human sciences. Such sciences do not yet exist – but they are struggling to burst into being. We stand to them today in the same kind of position as Descartes and Hobbes stood to the infant giant of mechanics (*PMN* p. 131). And the present book seeks to 'underlabour' for these new sciences in the way, a little later, Locke sought to underlabour for mechanics (see *CC* p. 11).

How then is such freedom possible? Very briefly and schematically:

(1) The *sui generis* reality and causal efficacy of social forms, on a strictly physical criterion, in terms of their making a difference to the state of the material world which would otherwise have occurred (from soil erosion and acid rain through to the production of some rather than other noises and marks), has to be recognised (see *PON* p. 39).

(2) The existence of objective social structures (from languages to family or kinship systems to economic or state forms), dependent on the reproductive and transformative agency of human beings, must be granted. Such structures are not created by human beings – for, they pre-exist us and their existence is a necessary condition for any intentional act. But they exist and persist only in virtue of our activity, which reproduces or transforms them. In our everyday practices of substantive *poiesis* or making, which consist in or involve the transformation, in various media, of what is to hand – (paper, a musical score, raw meat, steel) – we reproduce or transform the social world itself. In general, changes in social structures will reflect or be reflected in changes in the transformative agency which would otherwise reproduce them.

These social structures are concept-dependent, but not merely conceptual. Thus a person could not be said to be 'unemployed' or 'out of work' unless she and the other relevant agents possessed some (not necessarily correct or fully adequate) concept of that condition and were able to give some sort of account of it, namely, to describe (or redescribe) it. But it *also* involves, for instance, her being physically excluded from certain sites, definite locations in space and time. That is to say, social life always has a material dimension (and leaves some physical trace) (see *PON* p. 136).

(3) It follows from this that Rorty's distinction between 'coping with other persons' and 'coping with the non-human, the non-linguistic', namely by redescription and recognition respectively, (noted on p. 170 above) needs to be reworked – on several counts. First, there is more to coping with social reality than coping with other people. There is coping with a whole host of social entities, including institutions, traditions, networks of relations and the like – which are irreducible to people.[35] In particular, it would be a mistake to think that we had overcome a social structure, like the economy, state or family, if we were successful in imposing our description of it on the community. This holds in the case of people (including ourselves) too – we need to explain and sometimes change them (ourselves) as well as to (re-)describe them adequately (productively, fruitfully and so on). Think once more of the Rortian ideal – the strong poet (or utopian revolutionary) who can redescribe the already-determined world in accordance with their vision – who can, retrospectively, by making their descriptions of themselves or their society true (by winning acceptance for them), (re-)make themselves or their society. If there are objective social and psychic (as well as natural) structures – structures which need to be tackled before or so that we can become free (even in order to do poetry) – such a victory may prove a Pyrrhic one.

This point may also be put by saying that there is more to normative social science than creative redescription. Rorty says: 'To see a common social practice as cruel and unjust . . . is a matter of redescription rather than discovery. It is a matter of changing vocabularies rather than of stripping away the veil of appearances from an objective reality, of experimentation with new ways of speaking rather than of overcoming "false consciousness"' (CC p. 14). But the identification of the *source* of an experienced injustice in social reality, necessary for changing or remedying it, involves much more than redescription, even if it depends on that too centrally. It is a matter of finding and disentangling webs of relations in social life, and engaging explanatory critiques of the practices which sustain them. This may indeed often involve the detection of various types of false and otherwise unhappy consciousness (and more generally being). And this may in turn lead on to *critiques* of the vocabularies and conceptual systems in which they are expressed, and the additional social practices with which they are implicated. Moreover such explanatory critiques will lead, *ceteris paribus*, to action rationally directed to transforming, dissolving or disconnecting the structures and relations which explain the experience of injustice and the other ills theoretically-informed practice has diagnosed. Poets, like philosophers, need to think of explaining to change, rather than just reinterpreting or redescribing to edify, the world.

On the other hand, there is more to coping with nature than mere recognition – or that plus redescription. For a start, as I have already suggested, we need hermeneutics in everyday natural science and not just to render intelligible abnormal theoretical redescriptions of nature. Secondly, it should be stressed that just as our conscious interventions in nature, for instance in natural science and technology, are symbolically mediated; so we intervene in nature in all our causal interactions with the world, including our dialogues with the fellow members of our kind. The social world is not a cut-off redescription of nature. Rather it is both inscribed within and in continuous dynamic causal interaction with (the rest of) nature. To fail to see this, and in particular that there are physical (natural) constraints on human social life – namely 'non-human forces to which we must be responsible' (CC p. 10) and responsive – is a charter for ecological disaster, if not indeed (species) suicide.

The social and the socially conditioned or affected parts of the natural world are potentially transformable by human beings. But there may be some absolutes (universals, constants) of significance for human beings – which they just have to accept or 'recognize'. For example, fundamental laws of nature, the scarcity of some natural resources, upper limits to ecologically sustainable economic growth, aspects of human nature, the fact of the finitude (if not the precise duration) of human existence. The existence of *absolute* must not be confused with the existence of *objective* structures. Social structures may be just as objective, and transfactually efficacious within their geo-historical domain, as natural laws. Moreover both alike typically impose limits and constraints upon the kinds of action (including speech action) possible to human beings, without (normally) rigidly determining what we do within those limits or constraints (see RTS ch. 2.5).

The other side of the supposition that our movements are determined is the notion that our talk, discourse, is free. What does it mean, in this context, to hold that 'man is always free to choose new descriptions (for, among other things, himself)' (PMN p. 362n.)? I have argued in section 3 against Rorty that we are not *compelled* or determined in our beliefs or descriptions (any more than we are in most of our other states or actions – all of which depend on or manifest themselves in or through the movements of our bodies). But it does not follow from this that nature or society does not impose *constraints* on our rationally justifiable talk. Suppose this doctrine is coupled with the collapse of the intransitive dimension, in which current theory takes the place of the ontological realm (a realm which, I have argued (on p. 153 above), we need, philosophically, precisely to think the objective existence and efficacy of structures independently of our current theory of them). It is now easy to see how the notion that 'man is always free to choose new descriptions' can encourage the voluntaristic position that man is always free to choose *any* description – at any rate, any description that society, in the form of his peers (in the transitive dimension), will let him get away with – which is more or less the Rortian doctrine here (see *PMN* pp. 176 ff.).[36]

Such voluntarism may not do much damage in the normal discourse of the natural sciences, but in the abnormal discourses of the social sciences and the other humanities which are already in crisis and do appeal not just to irrelevant but to absurd and patently inapplicable philosophies (like positivism (see *PON* ch. 2; *SR* ch. 3.7)), it may encourage a superficial theoretical Maoism which masks or screens the absence of real intellectual progress (or social change – where it may be a case of '*plus ça change, plus c'est la même chose*'). The successful poet's life may now become an incessant succession of fleeting paradigm shifts in which even aesthetic enhancement begins to pale.

Of course these (intransitive) objective structures at work in nature and society, whether transhistorical or not, must always be described in a (transitive) more or less historically transient language, i.e. in terms of potentially transformable descriptions.[37] (But there will be objective constraints on rational linguistic change too – constraints other than those imposed by sheer poetic power, although the latter will, in context, be among them.)

(4) In virtue of the fact that efficacious reasons are causes of intentional behaviour, not just redescriptions of them, the agent's account of her reasons has a special authority, which a neo-Kantian dualism cannot ground (see *PON* ch. 3.2; *SR* ch. 2.6) – but this authority is not absolute. Rather it is subject to negotiation, as we come to understand better, both in general and in the individual case, 'how we work' (contra *PMN* p. 258), that is, what makes us do the apparently irrational or otherwise explanatorily interesting things which we do. (One consequence of this is that language can change us, as in 'the talking cure' but also when inspired by poetry (contra *PMN* p. 185).) Unconscious motivation and tacit skills are only two of the sources of opacity in social life; others are unacknowledged conditions and unintended consequences (*SR* ch. 2.2). So although society is a skilled accomplishment of agents, it does not follow from this that theoretical social science (informed by participants' understanding) is redundant. The task of the theoretical social sciences will be to establish the structural conditions, consequences and contours of the phenomenologically experienced world. In some, perhaps many, cases the critical redescription and structural explanation of that experience, and the accounts given in or based on it, will be necessary.

(5) Insofar as an agent is interested in preserving or extending or deepening or gaining some freedom, this will always involve trying to understand, in the sense of explaining, the character of some social or socially

conditioned or affectable entity, structure or thing – in order to maintain (reproduce) or change (transform) or otherwise dissolve or defuse, or to stimulate or release it. To become or remain 'free', in the simple sense of being 'unconstrained', always *potentially* involves both a theory of those constraints and, insofar as the freedom is feasible, a practice of liberation or liberty preservation. One may be free or desire freedom, in this sense, from any kind of thing.

On the other hand, emancipation, and more especially self-emancipation, involves

(1) a stronger sense of being 'free', namely as knowing, possessing the power and the disposition to act in or towards one's real interests (cf. *SR* p. 170); and

(2) a stronger sense of 'liberation', namely as consisting in the transformation of unneeded, unwanted and oppressive to needed, wanted and empowering *sources* of determination.

Emancipation, that is to say, depends upon the transformation of structures rather than just the amelioration of states of affairs. And it will, at least in the case of self-emancipation, depend in particular upon a conscious transformation in the transformative activity or praxis of the social agents concerned. As such, emancipation is *necessarily* informed by explanatory social theory.

The emancipatory social sciences may, for their part, take as their starting point some human need or aspiration (say for poetry) and inquire into the natural and social conditions (if any) of its non-fulfilment. Or they may begin with an immanent critique of prevailing social theories or ideologies, which may move on to the explanatory critique of falsity-generating (see *PMN* p. 282) or other malevolent (ill-producing) social structures (see *SR* chs. 2.5–2.7). In either case, the social sciences will be participants in a theory–practice dialectic or spiral with the emancipatory practices concerned. In this process, the kind of creative radical self or society redescriptions, to which Rorty calls our attention, may play a vital role in individuation or identity (including group and kind (or species) identity) formation. And this activity of *seeing themselves under a new description which they have helped to create*, will generally figure crucially in the *transformed transformative praxis* of the self-emancipating agents.

There is no need to deny either social scientific knowledge or a meta-theory of it to make the world safe for poets. For a society (or person) that has no use for poetry will *need* it more than most; and for that it will require that kind of knowledge of its situation which only the emergent human sciences can aspire to provide. Such sciences will always depend on poets; just as poets to be free, among other things to write or speak their lines, may, in the contemporary world, have to have recourse to the explanatory sciences as well as to their redescriptive powers. As for philosophers, if they follow the sounder part of Rorty's advice and give up the search for permanent neutral a-historical compulsive foundations of knowledge (which I have called the 'ontic fallacy'), they may find that by focusing on the historical arts and sciences and the other social practices, as they are, have come down to us and may yet develop, there is more than a little critical underlabouring (including further de-divinizing) to do . . .

What is Critical Realism?

1 The Emergence of Transcendental Realism

In this chapter I want to readdress the question of the exact form of the realism required (a) to combat both empiricism, as it is manifest in the ideology of the so-called 'new realism', and idealism, of the kinds at work in the temples of post-structuralism; and (b) more generally, to aid and empower the sciences, and especially the human sciences, in so far as these illuminate and inform projects of human self-emancipation. In particular I want to clarify the interrelationships between transcendental realism, scientific realism and critical realism – terms which I have variously employed to describe my philosophical position. It may help if I approach these issues in a quasi-biographical way.

The problem-field in the early–mid 1970s in the philosophy of science was characterized by two main lines of criticism of the recently hegemonic positivist account of science. There was an anti-monistic strand, typified by the work of writers such as Popper, Lakatos, Feyerabend, Sellars and Kuhn, which focused on the social character of science and highlighted the phenomena of scientific change and development. This strand I wove into my account of the 'transitive' or epistemological dimension in the philosophy of science. Then there was an anti-deductivist strand, represented by philosophers like Scriven, Hesse and Harré, which paid attention to the role of models and analogies in science and sustained some notion of the stratification of scientific knowledge. This feature of the second strand formed the base-line for my account of the 'intransitive' or ontological dimension in the philosophy of science.

As I developed the anti-deductivist moment in *A Realist Theory of Science* (henceforth RTS),[1] it became clear that it had two principal aspects:

(1) the critique of the lack of *sufficiency* of Humean criteria for laws, Hempelian criteria for explanation (Nagelian criteria for reduction and so on), turning on the failure of the positivistic account to sustain the *necessity* of nomological or law-like knowledge;

(2) the critique of the lack of *necessity* of Humean criteria for laws, Hempelian criteria for explanation (Nagelian criteria for reduction and so on), turning on the failure of the positivistic account to sustain the *universality* – or, as I also put it, the *transfactuality* – of nomological or law-like knowledge.

(1) was manifest in notorious problems such as that of induction (see RTS chapter 3.5–3.6), (2) in that of the applicability of our knowledge in open systems (see RTS chapter 2.4) or in what I subsequently called the problem of 'transduction'.[2] The decisive step here was (2). For it marked the difference between explicit rejection and tacit acceptance of the empiricist ontology of empirical realism in the critique of empiricism: the difference between transcendental realism and transcendental idealism of the sort represented by Rom Harré's *The Principles of Scientific Thinking.*[3] By developing the line of critique in (2) it became possible to isolate the crucial realm of the non-actual (and hence non-empirical) real (see RTS p. 56) and to identify the three-phase schema of scientific development, on which a science passes iteratively through empiricist, Kantian and (transcendental) realist stages (see RTS p. 145). It was this which was to constitute the meta-epistemological break in contemporary philosophy of science.

Rom Harré had talked of a 'Copernican revolution' in the philosophy of science[4] to refer to his inversion of the standard relationship between deductive skeleton and animating model. I took over the rhetoric of Copernicanism. But for me Harré's declension of it was ultimately vulnerable to empiricist counter-attack (see RTS chapter 3.2). I used it rather to connote two other ideas – one exoteric, the other esoteric. The exoteric meaning signalled the switch *within ontology* from events, states of affairs and the like to the structures and mechanisms which generated them. But the esoteric meaning signalled the switch *within philosophy* from epistemology to ontology, or from implicit to explicit ontology – predicated on the irreducibility of ontology and the isolation of the fundamental category mistake of the 'epistemological tradition'. This mistake is the *epistemic fallacy*, the definition of being in terms of knowledge (see RTS pp. 36ff) – or, in a displacement of this, in terms of language or discourse, the *linguistic fallacy*[5] – fallacies rendered plausible by the actualist account of laws exoteric Copernicanism had broken from. It was a small step from here to unearth the meaning of the epistemic fallacy in the *ontic fallacy* (SR pp. 23, 66 and chapter 3) – the ontologization and hence naturalization (and thence eternalization) of knowledge, and so its compulsive determination by being. It is this fallacy which Rorty notices in *Philosophy and the Mirror of Nature.*[6] But Rorty, remaining wedded to the epistemic fallacy – inasmuch as he stays committed to the Humean–Hempelian view of science which presupposes it – draws irrationalist-conventionalist conclusions from it.[7] On the Copernican view then, we move, like Copernicus but unlike Kant, to a conception of reality, including knowable reality, as only contingently, partially and locally humanized. To reclaim reality is (in the first instance) to de-anthropomorphize it: to let it be (non-coterminous with us).

2 Transcendental Realism, Science and Scientific Realism

Elsewhere I have sketched what I take to be an appropriate meta-philosophy for an adequate account of science.[8] On it, philosophy will incorporate Kantian, Hegelian, Marxian and Baconian-Bachelardian components and play two essential roles – namely as a Lockean under-labourer and occasional midwife, and as a Leibnizian conceptual analyst and potential critic. Now at first glance the discursive strategy I employed to establish transcendental realism in SR chapter 1 (and also chapter 2 above) appears different from that which I initially employed in RTS[9] – in that whereas in the latter case I seem to be deploying transcendental arguments positively, in the former I seem engaged in an immanent critique of current philosophies of science, deriving transcendental realism by, so to speak, a negative route. But on reflection these two apparently opposed procedures must amount to fundamentally the same thing. For the positive premises of interesting transcendental arguments will consist in descriptions of just those features of scientific practice which (currently dominant) philosophies of science (or philosophies in so far as they are oriented to or discourse about science – what I will call science-oriented philosophies) give prominence to; so that transcendental arguments of a novel or innovative sort will be in effect transcendental refutations of pre-existing accounts of science (see SR p. 14). In both cases one is engaged in a process of *determinate negation*. This may be schematized as follows:

(1) Take a science-oriented philosophy, which focuses on some more or less inadequately analysed activity, for example experiment, scientific education or training, conceptual change or development.

(2) Bring out the ontological, sociological and other presuppositions of the science-oriented philosophy, and hence set it in the form of a science-oriented realism, sociology and so on.

(3) Show how properly analysed the activity presupposes transcendental realism, or at any rate some position consistent with it and incompatible with that of the science-oriented philosophy thus critiqued.

One may differentiate a philosophy *of* science or a science-oriented philosophy from a philosophy *for* science or a scientific realism. Of course most philosophies of science are not scientific realisms. For to be a scientific realism a philosophy must be broadly consistent with the substantive contents of the sciences and oriented to the flourishing rather than the mere existence of science. Now transcendental realism, although the form in which scientific realism is I think best developed, is not of course the only scientific realism. For there are scientific realisms – say those of Smart or Sellars – with a fundamentally different analysis of science. And there are scientific realisms which attribute overwhelming evaluative and/or historical explanatory importance to science; or which scientistically identify the domain of truth with what can be known in science, or even reductively with some particular science, such as physics. For transcendental realism, science is not, contra Sellars 'the measure of all things, of what is that it is; and of what is not that it is not'.[10] Moreover transcendental realism can sustain a critical orientation, on a number of grounds, to the existing practice of a science. In particular, rejecting nominalism about science (as about any other scientifically significant object), it can criticize the practice of a science for a lack of scienticity (see SR p. 102).

The programme of transcendental realism, as it has developed in the last decade and a half, is to give an adequate account of science – more properly, the sciences, in all their differences and specificities as well as their unity – in three main dimensions: the intransitive or ontological dimension; the transitive or epistemological dimension; and the meta-critical dimension or the domain of critical theory (see SR p. 25). The last must be extended to include (a) the substantive as well as the philosophical and sociological presuppositions and commitments; and (b) of the historical practices of the sciences as well as their philosophical reconstructions or deconstructions. There is no need to rehearse the main themes of the transcendental realist account of science here. It is however worth stressing, in view of Ted Benton's and Alan Chalmers's critiques of my reappraisal in PON of the problem of naturalism in relation to a model of science drawn from transcendental reflection on experimental and fundamental or explanatory physics and chemistry,[11] that the account developed in RTS is not supposed to be an exhaustive account of physics and chemistry, let alone of all the sciences:[12] it is the hard core of a philosophical research programme – no more, no less. Its premises or data are historical practices and, as such, both the practices, and the knowledge (including the philosophical knowledge) they legitimate, are potentially – and essentially – corrigible. Its status is merely that of the best account currently available – in so far as it is at present uniquely consistent with the historical emergence, practical presuppositions and substantive contents of the sciences and reflexively self-consistent in that it can situate its own emergence (see SR pp. 302–3), fallibility and transformability (cf. PON pp. 170–1).

3 Transcendental Realism and Critical Naturalism: Limits on Naturalism and the Idea of an Explanatory Critique

Transposed to the context of the human sciences, transcendental realism appears immediately liberating. Orthodox accounts of science are based squarely on the dogmas of empirical-invariance and instance-confirmation (or -falsification): namely that laws are or depend upon empirical regularities and that they are confirmed (or falsified) by their instances (see RTS pp. 126–42). So these orthodox accounts are at once ontologically far too restrictive and (at least for entrenched theories) epistemologically far too permissive (see SR pp. 290–1 and PON chapter 4.2). If, on the other hand, laws are no longer constant conjunctions of punctiform events, but transfactual tendencies of relatively enduring structures, and if the deductive–nomological model is not only inapplicable but false and if the aim of science is not prediction and control but explanation and enlightenment, then, as I have expressed it elsewhere, there is at least a chance 'that the human sciences might be or become sciences in the same sense, though not of course in the same ways . . . as the experimental sciences of nature' ('Postscript to the 2nd Edition', PON, p. 167). It was this chance that I set out to explore in PON through transcendental deductions of the properties that societies and people must possess if they are to be (or demarcate the sites of) possible objects of knowledge. It is on the development of what I characterized as a *critical naturalist* position in the social, as distinct from the psychological, sciences that I wish to focus here. In PON chapter 2 I arrived at this via a transcendental argument from intentional agency as dependent on social material causes which the agent has not created, if he or she is to realize (or even formulate) his or her intention. But I could have approached this same (or an essentially similar) position through an immanent reconciliation of the antinomies of social theory – as Anthony Giddens did.[13]

The central line of my argument consisted in the elaboration of what I called the '*transformational* model of social activity'. Opposed to reification and voluntarism alike, the model allows us to sustain the conjoint dualities of structure and praxis – a conception of social structure existing only in virtue of the human praxis for which it is the indispensable condition and which that praxis (for the most part, unintentionally) reproduces or transforms (see PON chapter 2.2–2.4). Closely affiliated to this was an argument for the *relational* character of the subject-matter of sociology. Opposed to the dominant individualist or collectivist conceptions informing most social theory, this conceived that subject-matter as constituted through the position–practice system which individuals must enter to act and in so entering reproduce or transform, relationally defining (or redefining) the mediating or dual points connecting social structure and human agency – points such as positions in the family or the relations of production or the polity – (see PON chapter 2.1 and 2.4). From the transformational model of social activity I derived a series of limits on naturalism, or epistemogenically significant respects in which social objects are different (or emergent) from purely natural (paradigmatically physical) ones. These may be conveniently divided into ontological, epistemological, relational and critical differences – though the most salient other differences may also be deduced a priori from the ontological limits directly stemming from the transformational conception of social activity (see PON p. 53).

The chief *ontological* differences, other than the social-relation-dependence of social structures, are their praxis- and concept-dependence and their relatively greater material space–time specificity or substantial geo-historicity. Of course it is the case, as several critics have noticed, that a structure, say of power, may be reproduced without being exercised – but only in virtue of the human practices which sustain that structure in being. The conceptuality or concept-dependence of social life must be recognized without falling into that conceptual absolutization or reductionism (that concepts are not only necessary for, but exhaustive of, social life) which has so often characterized exclusively hermeneutical, linguistified, communication-oriented or discourse-theoretic approaches to social reality, in which the existence of extra-linguistic (although corrigibly conceptualized) aspects to and dimensions of social life is attenuated, at the limit, to zero (see PON chapter 4.3–4.5).[14] The faster dynamics (and, within a unified chronology, differential temporalities) and the associated spatial features of social life impart to it a more geo-historically specific character than the arcs of biological, geological and cosmological being within which it is successively inscribed. Social theory is also history and geography. Finally, recognition of the social-relation-dependence of all social structures should forewarn us against the hypostatization of the subject-matter of some specific social science – such as economics or linguistics or the sociology of scientific knowledge – as independent of the social totality.

The most significant *epistemological* feature of the social sciences is that social phenomena only ever occur in open systems, whereas in the natural sphere it is sometimes possible to contrive, or observe phenomena in, locally closed (in physics and chemistry) or quasi-closed (in biology)[15] systems. It follows from this that decisive test situations are in principle impossible;[16] so that criteria for theory-choice and theory-development must be exclusively explanatory and non-predictive. There are two extreme responses to the intrinsic openness of social systems. The first is to deny the possibility of *any* a posteriori controls on a theory independent of its practical applications.[17] This overlooks the possibility of non-predictive empirical test. The second is to regard the use of a battery of statistical techniques as a more or less fully adequate surrogate for experimental closure.[18] This neglects the qualitative limits on measurement and the use of statistical methods in the human sciences, as well as the probability that the social world is stochastically open.[19]

Of course this does not rule out conditional predictions in social science. Moreover a powerful explanatory theory will be capable of situating possibilities long before they are manifested; so that theory retains a prognostic function in the social domain. William Outhwaite has nicely caught the spirit of my position here, albeit in a slightly different context, when he characterises it as 'ontologically bold but epistemologically cautious.'[20] We can be sure that society exists and confident that it has certain general features (such as emergence, praxis-dependence, conceptuality, structural plurality, nomic transfactuality, spatio-temporality, totality). Its existence (and some of these features, such as stability of word meaning across uses, combined with the possibility of simile and metaphor) is a necessary condition for any knowledge, including knowledge in the natural sciences or everyday life. But we must exercise some circumspection in our cognitive claims about specific structures and mechanisms in social science, partly because of the absence of decisive test situations, and partly because of what Outhwaite calls, in a phrase redolent of the scientific research process, 'their general messiness and fluidity'.[21] However, critical naturalism does at least situate the possibility of adjudicating – in terms of their comparative explanatory power – between research programmes and between rival theories within them.[22]

The chief *relational* difference is that the objects of social scientific knowledge, although existentially intransitive (or independently real), are causally interdependent with the knowledge of which they are the objects (see PON p. 47). This leads on immediately to the principal *critical* difference, which turns on the breakdown, through the development of the concept of an *explanatory critique*, of the standard fact/value and theory/practice distinctions in a way which has merely weak and partial analogues in the natural sphere (see SR pp. 178, 189 n. 103). For if one can demonstrate the (contingently necessary) sufficiency of a structure (state of affairs or set of circumstances) for a false, inadequate or partial (one-sided) belief, then one can pass straight away *ceteris paribus* to a negative evaluation of that structure (or whatever) and *ceteris paribus* to a positive evaluation on action rationally directed at removing, transforming or dissolving it and thence *ceteris paribus* to such action (see PON chapter 2.6, SR chapter 2.5–7 and chapter 6 above). The point about this argument is not only that it formally refutes Hume's law,[23] nor that it *per se* delineates the structure of motivating argument for rational radical political commitment, but rather that it may be generalized from the critique of credibly false consciousness to take in the critique of all the other seemingly necessary ills (SR pp. 191–3) – amounting to the non-fulfilment of human needs, wants, potentialities, interests and aspirations – which together may constitute grounds for being say a socialist (that is committed to the deliberate transformation of society in a socialist direction).

Critical naturalism, as elaborated in PON and elsewhere, was an attempt to re-orient the human sciences away from the positivist and instrumentalist goals of prediction and control to the realist ones of depth explanation and human emancipation. The view of emancipation involved conceived it as, paradigmatically, a process of structural transformation – as a transformation *in* structures rather than a marginal adjustment of states of affairs and as a transformation *to* other (needed, wanted and empowering) structures rather than to a realm which magically escapes determination. Associated with this is a notion of freedom as consisting not merely in decreased restrictions, nor merely in these plus enhanced capacities under existing structures, but in emancipation from those unnecessary, undesired and oppressive (including exploitative) structures of power, domination and distorted need-recognition, opportunity and communication. To be free, on this view, is to know and to possess the power and disposition to act in or towards our real individual, social, species and natural interests. And for this the enlightenment which the depth human sciences may, but will not necessarily, bring is a necessary but insufficient condition.

It may be instructive if I conclude this section by looking briefly from a critical naturalist perspective at the two most influential Marxist philosophers since the mid sixties – Louis Althusser and Jürgen Habermas. It is well known that eminent philosophical personages – from Plato to Wittgenstein – always divide themselves into two (or, to the more discerning observer, three). I follow fashion in preferring the Althusser of *For Marx* and *Reading Capital* to that of the *Philosophy and the Spontaneous Philosophy of Scientists*[24] or *Reply to John Lewis*, let alone 'Marxism Today'.[25] Althusser's single most important achievement must surely lie in his attempt in his – inappropriately termed – concept of 'overdetermination' to capture:

(a) the multiple determination of events and phenomena generally in what are open systems; and

(b) the determination of these events and the mechanisms and structures that generate them in the 'structural unity' of the conjuncture (or convergence of mechanisms) in a nexus or of the structures in a (non-expressive, itself structured) totality (see SR p. 110, PON p. 170); and

(c) the hierarchical determination of these unities or totalities, in so far as differential causal force (and even unilateral structural determination) is consistent with the conjoint necessity and existential parity of their elements (cf. PON p. 43).

Unfortunately only a realist ontology and not a conventionalist epistemology can sustain what is valuable in these intuitions for the explanatory critical social sciences today.

Let us sharpen this by turning to Althusser's celebrated meta-epistemological distinction between the real object and the object of knowledge.[26] This does not correspond to the realist distinction between the intransitive and transitive objects of knowledge. For while, for the realist viewing knowledge in the transitive dimension as a process of production, the transitive object may be said to correspond to Althusser's Generalities I, the intransitive object of knowledge – what is known in and via this production process – is precisely the real object. It does not follow from the fact that we can only know in knowledge that we can only know knowledge! (or even knowledge of knowledge would be impossible). In the event, Althusser's failure to give any apodeictic status to the real object rendered it as theoretically dispensable as a Kantian thing-in-itself and helped to lay the ground for the worst idealist excesses of poststructuralism (see SR pp. 237–8 n. 9).[27]

To move across the Rhine, Habermas's early thesis of the interest–relativity of knowledge is quite consistent with the existential intransitivity of its objects. His failure to realize this – to break from the epistemic fallacy and to specifically thematize ontology – has a number of deleterious consequences for his work. Among these are the following:

(1) He remains ensnared in the antinomy of transcendental pragmatism – first formulated by McCarthy (see chapter 7, p. 141 above).[28]

(2) He tacitly inherits a positivist ontology as well as an instrumentalist–manipulative conception of the interest informing the natural, or later the empirical–analytical and purposive–rational, sciences and the sphere of labour as distinct from communicative interaction and from discourse (see SR pp. 230–1 n. 5). Explanation is not symmetrical with prediction in the natural sciences; nor is the latter tantamount to control.

(3) As Habermas's emancipatory interest is derivative from his communicative interest, his system readily takes on a dualistic anti-naturalist hue in which the extra-communicative or extra-discursive constraints on communicative interaction – identified with the exchange of speech acts – or (theoretical and practical) discourse – hermetically sealed off from action (such as experiment, class struggle) – are marginalized – only to reappear in his later *Theory of Communicative Action* in the guise of the colonization of the lifeworld by the reified systems of economy and polity coordinated by the media of money and power. This duality is that between externalist and internalist perspectives, the points of view of observer and participant – or, otherwise put, that between phenomenal system and noumenal lifeworld set at loggerheads with each other. Underpinning this magnificent, if Fichtean, construction is a *Sollen* or ought, an infinite striving already foreshadowed in his 1965 Frankfurt inaugural lecture: 'The human interest in autonomy and responsibility is not mere fancy, for it can be apprehended a priori. What raises us out of nature is the only thing whose nature we can know: language. Through its structure, autonomy and responsibility are posited for us. Our first sentence expresses unequivocally the intention of universal and unconstrained consensus'.[29] There is much that is valuable to be rescued from this, including a transcendental argument from language as a universal and necessary medium of discourse (rather than the coping-stone of the sciences and a fortiori of being) to a materialistically mediated conatus to consensus, if only it were set in a critical naturalist and transcendental realist perspective.

4 Critical Realism and its Implications

The upshot of the critical naturalist argument is an elucidation of how the ontological specificities of the subject-matter of social science permit a non-arbitrary procedure for arriving at (fallible and iteratively corrigible) real definitions of forms of social life, already identified and understood in a pre- or earlier-scientific way. Such definitions will be capable of generating explanatory hypotheses subject to non-predictive but empirical test. And such definitions and hypotheses will be embedded in research programmes (such as Marxism) yielding critiques of structures generating falsity and a range of other ills – from malnutrition and unemployment to famine and war (see PON pp. 49–53). Subject to qualification, both the models of theoretical and practical (or applied) explanations are operative in the social domain (see SR pp. 107–8, and chapter 6.2 above). Naturalism of a suitably qualified and critical type is vindicated; and the practice of social science as explanatory critique is embedded in the dialectic of the depth investigation (see SR chapter 2.7 and chapter 6.7 above), itself inscribed within the emancipatory spiral at work, if it is, in history.

I had called my general philosophy of science 'transcendental realism' and my special philosophy of the human sciences 'critical naturalism'. Gradually people started to elide the two and refer to the hybrid as 'critical realism'. It struck me that there were good reasons not to demur at the mongrel. For a start, Kant had styled his transcendental idealism the 'critical philosophy'. Transcendental realism had as much right to the title of critical realism. Moreover, on my definition of naturalism it amounted to realism, so to qualify it as critical realism made as much sense as to qualify it as critical naturalism. In either case, the hermeneutics involved in social science (and in the sociology and thence meta-critics of natural science) was a contingently critical one (see PON p. 138). Moreover the use of the adjective 'critical' rather than 'transcendental' brought out that the philosophy was critical in the strong sense – not just of other philosophies but potentially of scientitic practices, of common beliefs and of the praxis-dependent structures or circumstances that sustain them.

I now want to say something about the semantics of 'realism' and the use of critical realism as a critical tool at the political level. In philosophy 'realism' most usually connotes a position in:

(i) The theory of perception, where, opposed to (subjective) idealism, it stands for the idea that material objects exist independently of our perceiving them, and in the domain of the social sciences for the idea that the conceptual and the empirical do not jointly exhaust the real. Transcendental realism insists that the empirical is only a subset of the actual, which is itself a subset of the real (see RTS p. 56).

(ii) The theory of universals, where, opposed to nominalism, conceptualism and Wittgensteinian resemblance theory, it stands for the existence of universals independently (like Platonic realism) or as the properties of material things (like Aristotelian realism). Transcendental realism holds that some (typically scientifically significant) classes, or ways of classifying objects, constitute natural kinds, but most do not. Carbon and dogs possess real essences, defined respectively by their electronic structure and genetic code, but tables and chairs, chunks of graphite and puppies do not (see RTS pp. 209–13, 227).

(iii) The philosophy of science, where, opposed to the varieties of irrealism (SR p. 9), it asserts that the objects of scientific knowledge (such as causal laws) exist relatively or absolutely independently of their knowledge. Transcendental realism not only affirms this, but articulates the general character that the world must have (for instance it must be structured and differentiated, and characterized by emergence and change) if it is to be a possible object of knowledge for us.

Critical realism embraces a coherent account of the nature of nature, society, science, human agency and philosophy (including itself). Its intent is to underlabour for science, conceived as a necessary but insufficient agency of human emancipation. It is entirely natural, then, that it should be used as a critical tool in the diagnosis and criticism of the currently fashionable 'new realism' of the right wing of the labour movement in Britain today. But in transposing critical realism to an immediately political context there are a number of caveats that should be borne in mind.

'Realism' in International Relations Theory, and to some extent in political polemic generally, just means *realpolitik* or Machiavellianism. Again in Political Theory it sometimes means something akin to 'constitutionalism' or abiding by 'the rules of the game'.[30] Secondly, if the meta-thesis that makes the identification of the new realism as a realism, albeit of an impoverished and empirical realist sort, is that of the inexorability of some kind of ontology, and hence of some type or complex of types of realism, at any given level of discourse, then it is incumbent on the critic of the new realism to bring out the ontology of the 'fundamentalism' to which the 'revisionist' new realism opposes itself. This is by no means satisfactory. It combines aspects of an abstract conceptual realism with aspects of a romantic expressivist realism.[31] In contrast to the new revisionism and the old fundamentalism alike, a practically-oriented critical realist approach would seek to determine to what extent enduring underlying structures are being reproduced in novel forms and to what extent the structures themselves are being modified or even transformed. This is an open empirical question.

Thirdly the new realism – better empiricism – co-exists with a still dominant post-structuralism or 'new idealism' in the academy. Critical realists, myself included, have not so far engaged with this in the concreteness it merits. I plan to remedy this shortly.[32] In the meantime it must suffice to note that no writer has been as committed to an actualist ontology as Nietzsche, the direct or indirect (via Heidegger) provenance of most of the new idealism. A final caveat is necessary. In identifying particular philosophical positions – such as empirical realism – with political movements – such as the 'new realism' – and even more so with particular individuals, groups or episodes, there is a clear danger of essentialist theoretical reductionism. I avoided it in my analysis of positivism as an ideology generated by the dominant structures of normal science and bourgeois society in SR chapter 3 (see my insistence on a level (4) of analysis – of concrete historical particulars – not engaged in that text, at

SR pp. 234, 269 & passim). It is not clear that I altogether avoided it in chapter 1 above. That said, there is something about the market and what Marx called the value and wage forms which makes empirical realism the account of reality or ontology that is spontaneously generated therein. Within the capitalist mode of production critical realism is always going to seem a luxury its agents cannot afford. It is the argument of this book that it is a philosophy without which a socialist emancipation cannot be achieved.

Notes

Preface

1. J. Locke, *An Essay Concerning Human Understanding*, 'Epistle to the Reader'. ed. A.C. Fraser, New York 1959, Vol. I, p. 14.
2. K. Marx, *Concerning Feuerbach*, Thesis XI, *The Early Writings*, Harmondsworth 1975, p. 423.
3. Oxford 1980.
4. Oxford 1989.

Chapter 1

1. 'What is Enlightenment?' in *Kant on History*, ed. L.W. Beck, New York 1963, p. 3.
2. See my *Scientific Realism and Human Emancipation*, London 1986, p. 7.
3. K. Marx, *Capital* vol. III, London 1961, p. 798.
4. See my *Scientific Realism* p. 289.
5. Marx, *Capital* vol. I, p. 540.

Chapter 2

1. See for instance: G. Bachelard, *La Dialectique de la Durée*, London 1936, pp. 63–4; and T. Kuhn, *The Structure of Scientific Revolutions*, 2nd edition, Chicago 1970, p. 121.
2. See R. Harré, 'Surrogates for Necessity', *Mind* 1973, pp. 358–80.
3. See for instance C.G. Hempel, 'The Theoretician's Dilemma', in *Aspects of Scientific Explanation*, New York 1963.
4. Cf. H. Putnam, 'Realism and Reason', in *Meaning and the Moral Sciences*, London 1978, pp. 123–40.
5. L. Wittgenstein, *Tractatus Logico-Philosophicus*, London 1961, 6.35.
6. J.S. Mill, *A System of Logic*, London 1961, BK III, Ch. 3, Sect. 1.
7. G. Bachelard, *Le Matérialisme Rationnel*, Paris 1953, p. 411.
8. That is, in as much as the philosophy is to be at all *relevant* to the practice of science. As both Hume and Hegel realised, scepticism – in the sense of suspension of commitment to some idea of an independent reality – is not a tenable (or 'serious') position. Thus: 'whether your scepticism be as absolute and sincere as you pretend, we shall learn by and by, when the company breaks up; we shall then see whether you go out at the door or the window, and whether you doubt if your body has gravity or can be injured by its fall, according to popular opinion derived from our fallacious senses and more fallacious experience', Hume, *Dialogues Concerning National Religion*, New York 1948, p. 7. And: '[Scepticism] pronounces absolute disappearance and the pronouncement exists. . .; it

pronounces the nullity of seeing, hearing, etc., and it itself sees and hears, etc.; it pronounces the nullity of ethical realities, and acts according to them', Hegel, *The Phenomonology of Mind*, London 1949, p. 250. Cf. also Engels & Marx, *The German Ideology*, ed. C. Arthur, London 1970, p. 48.

9. G.W.F. Hegel, *The Phenomenology of Mind*, London 1949, pp. 154–5.

10. Cf. Hegel, ibid., pp. 131–45.

11. See R. Bhaskar, *A Realist Theory of Science*, 2nd edition, Hemel Hempstead 1978.

12. Ibid. ch. 2.

13. I. Kant, *Critique of Judgement*, New York 1972, pp. 249–58.

14. See for instance: R. Harré, *The Principles of Scientific Thinking*, London 1970, ch. 2; and M.B. Hesse, *The Structure of Scientific Inferences*, London 1974, chs 4 and 11.

15. See N.R. Hanson, *Patterns of Discovery*, Cambridge 1965, pp. 85ff.

16. It is important to note that science employs two criteria for the ascription of reality to a posited object: a perceptual criterion and a causal criterion. The causal one turns on the capacity of the entity to bring about changes in material things. Notice that a magnetic or gravitational field satisfies this criterion, but not a criterion of perceivability. On this criterion, to be is not to be perceived, but rather (in the last instance) just to be able to do.

17. See F. Dretske, *Seeing and Knowing*, London 1969, ch. 1.

18. See for instance T. Kuhn, 'Reflections on My Critics', in *Criticism and the Growth of Knowledge*, ed. I. Lakatos & A. Musgrave, Cambridge 1970, pp. 264–5.

19. See for instance K. Popper, *Objective Knowledge*, Oxford 1972, p. 308.

20. Cf. J. Locke, *Essay Concerning Human Understanding*, New York 1959, p. 14.

21. See R. Bhaskar, *The Possibility of Naturalism*, Hemel Hempstead 1979.

Chapter 3

1. G. Bachelard, *Le Nouvel Esprit Scientifique*, Paris 1934, translated as *The Philosophy of the New Scientific Mind*, New York 1968.

2. K.R. Popper, *Logik der Forschung*, Vienna 1934, translated as *The Logic of Scientific Discovery*, London 1959.

3. E. Meyerson, *La déduction relativiste*, Paris 1925.

4. See e.g. W. Heisenberg, *Physics and Philosophy*, London 1959.

5. D. Lecourt, *Marxism and Epistemology*, Verso 1975.

6. P. Feyerabend, *Against Method*, Verso 1975.

7. See my *Realist Theory of Science*, 1st ed. Leeds 1975, 2nd ed. Hassocks and New Jersey 1978 for a full development of the view presupposed here.

8. T.S. Kuhn, *The Structure of Scientific Revolutions*, 2nd ed. Chicago 1970, ch. II.

9. K.R. Popper, *Conjectures and Refutations*, London 1963, p. 34.

10. C.D. Broad, *The Philosophy of Francis Bacon*, Cambridge 1926.

11. Cf. K.R. Popper, *Objective Knowledge*, Oxford 1972, p. 81.

12. See especially *Criticism and The Growth of Knowledge*, ed. I. Lakatos & A. Musgrave, Cambridge 1970.

13. P.K. Feyerabend, 'Consolations for the Specialist', in Lakatos and Musgrave, *ibid*.

14. T.S. Kuhn, 'Reflections on my Critics', in Lakatos and Musgrave, *ibid*.

15. I. Lakatos, 'History of Science and its Rational Reconstructions', *Boston Studies in the Philosophy of Science Vol. VIII*, pp. 109–16.

16. Ibid., p. 110.

17. P. Duhem, *La Theorie Physique, Son Objet et Sa Structure*, Paris 1905 translated as *The Aim and Structure of Physical Theory*, Princeton 1954, part II, ch. IV.

18. I. Lakatos, 'Falsification and the Methodology of Scientific Research Programmes', in Lakatos and Musgrave, *The Growth of Knowledge*, p. 100–2.

19. Ibid., p. 100.

20. Ibid., p. 115.

21. M. Masterman, 'The Nature of a Paradigm', in Lakatos and Musgrave, *The Growth of Knowledge*, p. 71.

22. See M.B. Hesse, *Models and Analogies in Science*, London 1962.

23. G. Bachelard, *Le Rationalisme Appliqué*, Paris 1949.

24. 'Falsification', in Lakatos and Musgrave, *The Growth of Knowledge*, p. 133.

25. Ibid., p. 118 and 'History' *Boston Studies*, p. 100.

26. 'Falsification', in Lakatos and Musgrave, *The Growth of Knowledge*, pp. 177–8.

27. *Against Method*, p. 185.

28. P.K. Feyerabend, 'Against Science', *Radical Philosophy*, 11, p. 8.

29. Cf. 'History', *Boston Studies*, pp. 92 and 104.

30. P.K. Feyerabend, 'Problems of Empiricism', *Beyond the Edge of Certainty*, ed. R.G. Colodny, New Jersey 1965, esp. pp. 168–72 and 179–81; and T.S. Kuhn, *The Structure of Scientific Revolutions*, esp. ch. IX and X.

31. The idea of incommensurability may be illustrated by Gestalt phenomena in psychology, the absence of synonyms in natural languages and paradigm cases of scientific revolutions in which key concepts are involved. Thus imagine a stone falling to the ground. Do you conceive the earth, like Aristotle and Tycho Brahe, as fixed or, like Copernicus and Galileo, as moving? Try as you may, you cannot do both at once: the alternatives are exclusive. Or consider the phenomenon of wages. Do you conceive wages as payment for labour or as the means for the reproduction of the commodity labour power? *Against Method* contains a fascinating discussion of the 'incommensurability' of the archaic and non-archaic forms of life, as manifested in science, poetry and art.

32. This is the most plausible interpretation of Feyerabend's diagram in *Against Method*, p. 178.

33. In such a situation the appropriate direction of scientific advance will be determined by the significance of the facts in the domains over which the theories do not clash.

34. One aspect of incomplete overlap is 'Kuhn-loss': new theories often say nothing at all about, i.e. forget (repress), often indefinitely, not just contradict or redescribe, some known phenomena.

35. *Against Method*, p. 23.

36. The principal landmarks: 'Problems of Empiricism' (1965); 'Problems of Empiricism II', *The Nature and Function of Scientific Theory*, ed. R.G. Colodny, Pittsburgh 1970; 'Against Method' *Minnesota Studies in the Philosophy of Science, Vol IV*, Minneapolis 1970; and *Against Method*.

37. The main point here was that the facts empirically relevant for a given theory could often only be unearthed with the help of an alternative. See 'Problems', esp. pp. 174–9. Cf. *Against Method*, pp. 38–46.

38. Advancing a so-called 'pragmatic theory of observation' he argued that scientists could choose as a result of the uninterpreted sentences that they would be motivated to produce in observational contexts ('Problems', pp. 214–5). But as has been pointed out such uninterpreted sentences can hardly provide *grounds* for a choice. See D. Shapere, 'Meaning and Scientific Change', *Mind and Cosmos*, ed. R.G. Colodny, Pittsburgh 1966, p. 61.

39. *Against Method*, p. 21. Cf. M. Bunge, *The Myth of Simplicity*, New Jersey 1963.

40. Ironically this takes him close to the views of some of those linguistic philosophers he loves to hate, e.g. P. Winch, 'Understanding a Primitive Society', *American Philosophical Quarterly*, 1964.

41. *Against Method*, p. 179.

42. Ibid., p. 23.

43. Ibid., p. 27

44. Ibid., p. 23.

45. Ibid., p. 17. (The quotation is from 'Left-wing communism, an infantile disorder', V.I. Lenin, *Selected Works*, London 1969, p. 574.)

46. Ibid., p. 18.

47. Ibid., p. 25.

48. Ibid., p. 196.

49. Ibid., p. 141.

50. Ibid., p. 212. Cf. V. Ronchi, 'Complexities, advances and misconceptions in the science of vision, what is being discovered?, *Scientific Change*, ed. A. Crombie, London 1963.

51. Ibid., pp. 50–4.
52. 'Editors of scientific journals should refuse to publish papers by scientists pursuing degenerating programmes . . . Research foundations, too, should refuse money', 'History', *Boston Studies*, p. 105.
53. *Against Method*, p. 199.
54. Ibid., p. 187.
55. Ibid., p. 297.
56. Ibid., p. 188.
57. Ibid., p. 305.
58. Ibid., p. 297.
59. 'Everyone can read the terms ("progress", "advance", "improvement" etc.) in his own way and in accordance with the tradition to which he belongs . . . my thesis is that anarchism helps to achieve progress in any one of the senses one cares to choose. Even a law-and-order science will succeed only if anarchistic moves are occasionally allowed to take place', ibid., p. 27. Cf. also p. 114.
60. Ibid., pp. 301–3. Cf. also p. 309.
61. Ibid., p. 189.
62. Ibid.
63. Ibid.
64. Ibid., p. 191.
65. Ibid., p. 33.
66. Ibid., p. 175.
67. Ibid., p. 299.
68. Kant; neo-Kantianism; more generally, the whole romantic movement.
69. Especially symptomatic here is his complaint that 'even human relations are dealt with in a scientific manner', Ibid., p. 301.
70. Cf. G. Stedman Jones, 'The Marxism of the Early Lukács', *New Left Review* 70.
71. It could usefully be complemented by J.R. Ravetz, *Scientific Knowledge and its Social Problems*, Oxford 1971.
72. Cf. J.S. Mill, *On Liberty*, Ch. I, reprinted in *Utilitarianism*, ed. M. Warnock, London 1973, p. 138.
73. D. Hume, *A Treatise on Human Nature*, ed. L.A. Selby-Bigge, Oxford 1968, p. 415.
74. G. Lukács, *Lenin*, London, 1970, p. 92. Lenin's insistence upon the need for revolutionary theory is well-known (though not it seems to Feyerabend): 'Without revolutionary theory there can be no revolutionary movement. This idea cannot be insisted upon too strongly at a time when the fashionable preaching of opportunism goes hand-in-hand with an infatuation for the narrowest forms of practical activity' (*What Is To Be Done?*).
75. Ibid., pp. 99–100. As it is likely to enjoy a certain vogue on the Left it should be perhaps said explicitly that, with one exception, *Against Method* neither owes nor contributes anything to Marxist theory. The exception: Feyerabend's concept of the uneven development of the sciences and of the differential historical temporality of their layers, which he has gleaned from historical materialism. For the rest, references to Marx and Lenin are best regarded as opportunistic ploys designed to appeal to those 'temperamentally opposed to the old ideas and the standards of learning connected with them'.
76. Galileo Galilei, *Dialogue Concerning the Two Chief World Systems*, Berkeley 1953, p. 328. Quoted in *Against Method*, pp. 55–6.
77. For Popper 'theories are . . . free creations of our own minds, the result of an almost poetic intuition', *Conjectures and Refutations*, p. 192. And we are free at any moment of time to break out of the frameworks imposed by our theories ('Normal Science and its Dangers', ibid, p. 56).
78. 'Our science is not knowledge (epistēmē): it can never claim to have attained truth, or even a substitute for it, such as probability . . . *we do not know: we can only guess*', *Logic of Scientific Discovery*, p. 278.
79. Kuhn in fact formulates in a number of places a set of criteria, including accuracy of predictions, number of problems solved, and so on which he says would enable an observer 'to tell which [of two theories] was the older' T.S. Kuhn, 'Reflections on my Critics', in

Lakatos and Musgrave, *The Growth of Knowledge*, p. 264. Cf. also 'Postscript', *Structure of Scientific Revolutions*, p. 206. Yet he draws back from saying that the one which does better in terms of these criteria *is* better (which *need* not of course be the newer – Kuhn's evolutionism leads him to ignore the possibility of historical regression). This is partly because of his failure to see any alternative to a correspondence theory of truth. But partly also because of a persistent metaphysical ambivalence that characterizes his work: he cannot make up his mind if he is a realist or an idealist (or rather he is trying to be both). Thus he says he is convinced that we must learn to make sense of sentences like this: 'though the world does not change with a change of paradigm, the scientist afterward works in a different world' *Structure of Scientific Revolutions*, p. 121. But Kuhn has not done so. Once we recognize the necessity for both, and the irreducibility of, the intransitive and transitive dimensions in the philosophy of science we can, however, transcribe, without strain, the sentence as follows: 'though the [*natural*] world does not change with a change of paradigm, the scientist afterward works in a different [*social*] world'.

80. Opposed to empirical realism is *transcendental realism* which may be defined as the thesis that the objects and relations of which knowledge is obtained in the social activity of science both exist and act independently of human beings (and hence of human sense-experience). See my *Realist Theory of Science*, ch. I.

81. The problem of induction arises from a corollary of this, *viz.* that laws are confirmed or falsified by their instances. For a discussion of the problems that arise from this principle see R. Harré, *Principles of Scientific Thinking*, London 1970.

82. See E.H. Madden, 'Hume and the Fiery Furnace', *Philosophy of Science*, 1971.

83. See e.g. N. Maxwell, 'The Rationality of Scientific Discovery', *Philosophy of Science* 1974.

84. *Against Method*, p. 32.

85. G. Bachelard, *Le Nouvel Esprit Scientifique*, Paris 1934, p. 13.

86. See esp. L. Althusser, *For Marx*, trans. B. Brewster, London 1969, and L. Althusser and E. Balibar, *Reading Capital*, trans. B. Brewster, London 1970.

87. See *Objective Knowledge*, p. 20.

88. *La Philosophie du Non*, Paris 1940.

89. Bachelard said in 1927: 'The problem of *error* seems to me to come before the problem of truth, or rather, I have found no possible solution to the problem of truth other than dispelling finer and finer errors'; and later (in 1949): 'if one poses the problem of error on the plane of scientific errors, it emerges very clearly . . . that *error* and truth are not symmetrical, as a purely logical and formal philosophy might lead one to believe'. See *Marxism and Epistemology* pp. 54–5.

90. See e.g. K. Popper, *Logic of Scientific Discovery*, p. 18 and his *Objective Knowledge*, p. 34.

91. F. Dagognet, *Gaston Bachelard, sa vie, son oeuvre*, Paris 1965, p. 59. Quoted in B. Brewster 'Althusser and Bachelard', *Theoretical Practice 3–4*, p. 35.

92. *Le Nouvel Esprit Scientifique*, p. 11.

93. London 1964.

94. *Marxism and Epistemology*, p. 15.

95. Ibid., p. 157.

96. G. Bachelard, *La formation de l'esprit scientifique*, Paris 1938, p. 61.

97. *Marxism and Epistemology*. p. 98.

98. Ibid., p. 28.

99. *Le Rationalisme Appliqué*, p. 5. Cf. *Marxism and Epistemology*, p. 60.

100. *Marxism and Epistemology*, pp. 139–41.

101. Ibid., p. 143.

102. Ibid.

103. This is particularly evident in his concept of the 'epistemological profile'. See *The Philosophy of No*, New York 1968, p. 36.

104. *Marxism and Epistemology*, p. 82.

105. Ibid., p. 26.

106. G. Bachelard, *La Dialectique de la Durée*, Paris 1936, pp. 63–4.

107. G. Bachelard, *Le Matérialisme Rationnel*, Paris 1953, p. 142.

108. E. Meyerson, *La déduction relativiste*, p. 206.

109. *Le Matérialisme Rationnel*, p. 141.

110. *Marxism and Epistemology*, p. 137.

111. *La formation de l'esprit scientifique*, p. 61.

112. *Le Nouvel Esprit Scientifique*, p. 13.

113. Ibid., p. 9.

114. 'It can be said that there is no purity without purification. And nothing better proves the eminently social character of contemporary science than the techniques of purification. Indeed purification processes can only be developed by the utilization of a whole set of reagents whose purity has attained a kind of social guarantee', *Le Matérialisme Rationnel*, p. 77.

115. Cf. P. Duhem, *Aim and Structure of Physical Theory*, part I, ch. IV.

116. F. Engels, *Anti-Dühring*, Moscow 1969, p. 25.

117. *Marxism and Epistemology*, p. 140.

118. Cf. L. Althusser, *Lenin and Philosophy*, trans. B. Brewster, London 1971, p. 57.

119. V.I. Lenin, *Materialism and Empirio-criticism*, New York 1970, esp. ch. 5, sections 1–3.

120. *Lenin and Philosophy*.

Chapter 4

1. See my *A Realist Theory of Science*, Ist edn Leeds, 1975, 2nd edn, Hassocks and New Jersey, 1978 esp. Chapter 2.

2. See G. Buchdahl, *Metaphysics and the Philosophy of Science*, Oxford, 1969, p. 3.

3. *A Realist Theory of Science*, esp. Chapter 1, Section 3.

4. Ibid., especially Chapter 2.

5. G. Lukács, *History and Class Consciousness*, London 1971, p. 110.

6. See G. Bachelard, *Le Matérialisme Rationnel*, Paris 1953, p. 141.

7. D. Hume, *Dialogues Concerning Natural Religion*, New York, 1948, p. 7.

8. G.W.F. Hegel, *The Phenomenology of Mind*, London 1949, p. 250.

9. See my *A Realist Theory of Science*, p. 40.

10. T.S. Kuhn, *The Structure of Scientific Revolutions*, 2nd edition, Chicago 1970, Chap 2.

11. See P. Strawson, 'Truth', *Proceedings of the Aristotelian Society* xxiv, 1950, reprinted in G. Pitcher, *Truth*, New Jersey 1964, p. 38.

12. Cf. R. Harré, *The Principles of Scientific Thinking*, London 1970, p. 194.

13. Cf. E. Durkheim, *The Rules of Sociological Method*, New York 1964, Chapter 1.

14. See my *A Realist Theory of Science*, p. 182.

15. See L. Wittgenstein, *Philosophical Investigations*, Oxford 1953, esp. p. 193.

16. N.R. Hanson, *Patterns of Discovery*, Cambridge 1963, Chapter 1.

17. F. Dretske, *Seeing and Knowing*, London 1969, Chapter 3.

18. R. Harré, *The Principles of Scientific Thinking*, p. 195.

19. K. Marx, *Capital* Vol I, London 1961, p. 307.

20. K. Marx, *Grundrisse*, London 1973, p. 255.

21. Cf J. Mepham, 'The Theory of Ideology in Capital', *Radical Philosophy 2* (1972), p. 18.

22. Cf M. Godelier, 'System, Structure and Contradiction in Capital', *Socialist Register 1967* reprinted in ed. R. Blackburn, *Ideology in Social Science*, London 1972, esp. pp. 337–8.

23. Cf Chapter 3 above, esp. p. 32–3.

24. N. Geras, 'Marx and The Critique of Political Economy', *op. cit.*, ed. R. Blackburn.

25. See my *A Realist Theory of Science*, esp. Chapters 1 and 2.

26. Ibid. esp. p. 171 ff.

27. See L. Kolakowski, *Positivist Philosophy*, Penguin 1972, p. 173.

28. For a critique of this conception of human beings see: N. Chomsky, 'A review of B.F. Skinner's *Verbal Behaviour*', *The Structure of Language*, ed. J. Fodor and J. Katz, Prentice-Hall, 1965; and R. Harré and P. Secord, *The Explanation of Social Behaviour*, Oxford 1972, esp. Chapter 2. Its roots in 17th century political thought are examined by C.B. Macpherson, *The Political Theory of Possessive Individualism*, Oxford 1962.

29. D. Hume, *Essays Moral and Political*, eds. T.H. Green and T.H. Grose, London 1875, volume 2, p. 68.

30. K. Marx, *Poverty of Philosophy*, New York 1963.

31. Cf. J. Habermas, *Knowledge and Human Interests*, London 1972, p. 71.

32. See eg. C.G. Hempel, *Aspects of Scientific Explanation*, New York 1963, esp. chapters 9 and 12.

33. See R. Keat, 'Positivism, Naturalism and Anti-naturalism in the Social Sciences', *Journal for the Theory of Social Behaviour I*, 1971.

34. See W. Outhwaite, *Understanding Social Life*, London 1975.

35. See M.B. Hesse, *The Structure of Scientific Inference*, London 1974, p. 4.

36. See esp. P.K. Feyerabend, *Against Method*.

Chapter 5

1. See P. Winch, *The Idea of a Social Science*, Routledge & Kegan Paul, London, 1958, esp. pp. 114–15.

2. Ibid., esp. pp. 108, 124–5.

3. Especially R. Harré, *The Principles of Scientific Thinking*, Macmillan, London 1970; R. Harré & E.H. Madden, *Causal Powers*, Blackwell, Oxford 1975; and R. Bhaskar, *A Realist Theory of Science*, 2nd Edition, Harvester Press, Hassocks, Sussex, and Humanities Press, New Jersey 1978. Cf. R. Keat, 'Positivism, Naturalism and Anti-naturalism in the Social Sciences', *Journal for the Theory of Social Behaviour*, 1971, I. pp. 3–17; R. Harré & P.F. Secord, *The Explanation of Social Behaviour*, Blackwell, Oxford 1972; and R. Keat & J. Urry, *Social Theory as Science*, Routledge & Kegan Paul, London 1975.

4. See my *A Realist Theory of Science*, esp. chs. 1 & 2.

5. Ibid., ch. 2, sect. 4.

6. Ibid.

7. See R Harré, *Principles of Scientific Thinking*, esp. ch. 2; and M. Hesse, *Models and Analogies in Science*, University of Notre Dame Press, Indianapolis, 1966, esp. ch. I.

8. Cf. N.R. Hanson, *Patterns of Discovery*, Cambridge University Press, Cambridge, 1965, esp. pp. 85ff.

9. See *A Realist Theory of Science*, p. 182.

10. K.R. Popper, *The Open Society and its Enemies*, Vol. II, Routledge & Kegan Paul, London, 1962, p. 98.

11. I. Jarvie, *Universities and Left Review*, 1959, p. 57.

12. J.W.N. Watkins, 'Historical Explanation in the Social Sciences', *British Journal of the Philosophy of Science*, 1957, 8, reprinted as 'Methodological Individualism and Social Tendencies', *Readings in the Philosophy of the Social Sciences*, ed. M. Brodbeck, Macmillan, New York, 1968, p. 271.

13. Ibid.

14. J.W.N. Watkins, 'Ideal Types and Historical Explanation', *British Journal of the Philosophy of Science*, 1952, 3, reprinted in *The Philosophy of Social Explanation*, ed. A. Ryan, Oxford, 1973, p. 88.

15. Cf. A. Danto, *Analytical Philosophy of History*, Cambridge University Press, Cambridge, 1965, ch. XII, and S. Lukes, 'Methodological Individualism Reconsidered', *British Journal of Sociology*, 1968, 19, reprinted in A. Ryan, *The Philosophy of Social Explanation*.

16. J.W.N. Watkins, 'Ideal Types', p. 91 and 'Methodological Individualism', p. 273.

17. Ibid., p. 278.

18. D. Hume, *A Treatise on Human Nature*, ed. L.A. Selby-Bigge, Oxford, 1968, p. 415.

19. D. Hume, *Essays Moral and Political*, Vol. II, ed. T.H. Green & T.H. Grose, London, 1875, p. 68.

20. Cf. S. Kotarbinski, 'Praxiology', *Essays in honour of O. Lange*, Warsaw, 1965.

21. J.P. Sartre, *Critique of Dialectical Reason*, New Left Books, London, 1976, Book II, ch. I and Book I, ch. 4.

22. There are, of course, non-, and even anti-individualist tendencies in Weber's thought (see e.g. R. Aron, *Philosophie Critique de l'histoire*, NRF, Paris, 1969); just as there are non-, and (especially in *The Elementary Forms of Religious Life*) anti-positivist strains in Durkheim's (see e.g. R. Horton 'Levy-Bruhl, Durkheim and the Scientific Revolution', *Modes of Thought*, eds. R. Finnegan & R. Horton, Faber & Faber, London, 1973).

23. Cf. R. Keat & J. Urry, *Social Theory*, ch. 5, and B. Ollman, *Alienation*, Cambridge University Press, Cambridge, 1971, esp. chs. 2 & 3 respectively.

24. See especially P. Berger & S. Pullberg 'Reification and the Sociological Critique of Consciousness', *New Left Review*, 1966, 35, and P. Berger & T. Luckman, *The Social Construction of Reality*, Allen Lane, London, 1967.

25. Berger and Pullberg, 'Reification', pp. 62–3.

26. Ibid., p. 63.

27. Ibid.

28. E. Durkheim, *The Rules of Sociological Method*, Free Press, New York, 1964, p. 2.

29. Berger and Pullberg, 'Reification', p. 60.

30. Ibid., p. 61.

31. Ibid., p. 60.

32. *Rules of Sociological Method*, pp. 1–2.

33. This is of course the fundamental insight of the hermeneutical tradition in the philosophy of social science. Cf. W. Outhwaite, *Understanding Social Life*, Allen & Unwin, London, 1975.

34. Marx, perhaps, comes closest to articulating this conception of history: 'History is nothing but the succession of the separate generations, each of which exploits the materials, the capital funds, the productive forces handed down to it by all preceeding generations, and thus, on the one hand, continues the traditional activity in completely changed circumstances and, on the other, modifies the old circumstances with a completely changed activity', K. Marx & F. Engels, *The German Ideology*, Lawrence & Wishart, London, 1965, p. 66.

35. Cf. Lévi-Strauss, *The Savage Mind*, Weidenfeld & Nicolson, London, 1966, cf. 1.

36. The internal complexity and interdependence of social structures does not mark a *necessary* difference with natural structures. For some comments on these limits see the 'Postscript to the Second Edition' of my *The Possibility of Naturalism*, 2nd Edition, Harvester Press, Hemel Hempstead, 1989.

37. See R. Harré & P.F. Secord, *op. cit.*, esp. ch. 5.

38. *A Realist Theory of Science*, p. 113. Cf. also M. Polanyi, *The Tacit Dimension*, Routledge & Kegan Paul, London, 1967, ch. 2.

39. *Rules of Sociological Method*, p. 2.

40. Although Durkheim used a causal criterion to establish the reality of social facts on a collectivist conception of sociology, the same criterion can be used to establish their reality on a relational one. (There is no special difficulty, as e.g. the concept of spin in physics shows, in ascribing reality to relations on a causal criterion).

41. According to Marx, human beings 'begin to distinguish themselves from animals as soon as they begin to *produce* their means of subsistence', *The German Ideology*, p. 31. 'The first premiss of all human existence and therefore of all history [is] the premiss . . . that men must be in a position to live in order to be able to "make history". But life involves before anything eating and drinking, a habitation, clothing and many other things. The first historical act is thus the production of the means to satisfy these needs, the production of material life itself', ibid., p. 39. ('The first historical act' must of course be understood in an analytical, not chronological, sense.) Cf. also: 'In all forms of society it is a determinate production and its relations which assign every other production and its relations their rank

and influence. It is a general illumination in which all other colours are plunged and which modifies their specific tonalities. It is a special ether which defines the specific gravity of everything found within it', K. Marx, *Grundrisse*, Penguin, Harmondsworth, 1973, p. 107.

42. The problem for Marxism has always been to find a way of avoiding both economic (or worse technological) reductionism and historical eclecticism, so that it does actually generate some substantive historiographical propositions. It is a problem of which both Marx and Engels were aware. Thus as Engels was at pains to stress: 'According to the materialist conception of history, the economy is the ultimately determining element in history. [But] if someone twists this into saying that it is the *only* determining [one], he transforms this proposition into a meaningless, abstract, senseless phrase. The economic situation is the basis, but the various elements of the superstructure . . . also exercise their influence upon the course of events . . . and in many cases preponderate in determining their form. There is an interaction of all these elements in which, amid the endless host of accidents, the economic movement finally asserts itself as necessary.' (F. Engels, Letter to J. Bloch, 21 September 1890, *Marx–Engels Selected Works*, Vol. II, Lawrence & Wishart, London, 1968, p. 692.) But how are we to conceptualize this ultimate necessity? Marx provides a clue. Replying to an objection he concedes that 'the mode of production of material life dominates the development of social, political and intellectual life generally . . . is very true for our time, in which material interests preponderate, but not for the middle ages, in which Catholicism, nor for Athens or Rome, where politics, reigned supreme.' But Marx contends 'this much [also] is clear. That the middle ages could not live on Catholicism, nor the Ancient World on Politics [alone]. On the contrary, it is the economic conditions of the time that explains why here politics and there Catholicism played the chief part.' (K. Marx, *Capital*, Vol. I, Lawrence & Wishart, London, 1965, p. 81 n.) Althusser has attempted to theorize this insight by saying that it is the economy that *determines* which relatively autonomous structure in the social totality is the *dominant* one. (See L. Althusser, *For Marx*, Allen Lane, London, 1969, and L. Althusser & E. Balibar, *Reading Capital*, Verso, London, 1970.)

43. But is the notion of a 'field' that exists only in virtue of its effects any stranger, or *prima facie* more absurd, than the combination of principles of wave and particle mechanics in elementary micro-physics, now reckoned a common-place?

44. *A Realist Theory of Science*, Appendix to ch. 2.

45. Ibid., ch. 2, sect. 4.

46. Cf. P. Duhem, *The Aim and Structure of Physical Theory*, Atheneum, New York, 1962, pp. 180–90.

47. If true, this would have an analogue to the domain of social psychology in the conscious technique of 'Garfinkelling' (see e.g. H. Garfinkel, *Essays in Ethnomethodology*, Prentice-Hall, New Jersey, 1967), and perhaps in the role played by psychopathology in the development of a general psychology.

48. Consider, for example, the way in which the mass unemployment of the 1930s not only provided the theoretical dynamo for the Keynesian innovation, but facilitated its ready acceptance by the relevant scientific community.

49. Cf. e.g. A. Giddens, *Capitalism and Modern Social Theory*, Cambridge University Press, Cambridge, 1971, Postscript; and G. Therborn, *Science, Class and Society*, New Left Books, London, 1976, ch. 5, part III.

50. See e.g. I. Lakatos, 'Falsification and the Methodology of Scientific Research Programmes', *Criticism and the Growth of Knowledge*, eds. I. Lakatos & A. Musgrave, Cambridge University Press, Cambridge, 1970.

51. Thus the transformational model of social activity implies that it is a necessary condition for any adequate theory of a social system that the theory be capable of showing how the system reproduces or transforms itself. A priori considerations of this sort can be used to criticize particular social theories. See, for example, M. Hollis and E. Nell, *Rational Economic Man*, Cambridge University Press, Cambridge, 1975, esp. ch. 8 for a criticism of neo-classical economic theory along these lines.

52. K. Marx, *Capital*, Vol. I, ch. I.

53. N. Geras, 'Essence and Appearance: Aspects of Fetishism in Marx's *Capital*' *New Left Review*, 1971, 65, reprinted as 'Marx and the Critique of Political Economy', *Ideology*

in Social Science, ed. R. Blackburn, Fontana, London, 1972, p. 291.

54. See *Capital*, Vol. I, p. 537 and *Capital*, Vol. III, p. 798 respectively.

55. Cf. N. Geras, in *Ideology in Social Science*, ed. Blackburn, and J. Mepham, 'The Theory of Ideology in Capital', *Radical Philosophy* (1972), 2.

56. C. Taylor 'Neutrality in Political Science', *Philosophy, Politics and Society*, 3rd series, eds. P. Laslett & W. Runciman, reprinted in A. Ryan, *The Philosophy of Social Explanation*, shows clearly how theories (or 'explanatory framework') do in fact secrete values. Unfortunately, however, by not specifying any criterion for choosing between theories, he leaves himself open to the interpretation that one should choose that theory that most satisfies our conception of what 'fulfils human needs, wants and purposes' (p. 161); rather than that theory which, *just because it is explanatorily most adequate*, and capable *inter alia* of explaining illusory beliefs about the social world, best allows us to situate the possibilities of change in the value-direction that the theory indicates. Taylor thus merely displaces, rather than transcends, the traditional fact/value dichotomy.

Chapter 6

1. I would like to take this opportunity to acknowledge some debts. First, I have benefited greatly from discussions with Roy Edgley on this and related topics. Secondly, I owe much to the stimulus of the pioneering work of Jürgen Habermas in this field, even where (as will be obvious) I come to rather different conclusions. Thirdly, I am indebted to the writings of Alasdair MacIntyre, who did perhaps more than anyone else in the 'analytical' tradition to open up the possibility of a historical treatment of moral and practical philosophies. Finally, this present paper developed out of another 'Emergence, Explanation and Emancipation' presented at a conference organised by Paul Secord under the auspices of the University of Houston in December 1979 (and forthcoming in *Explaining Human Behaviour*, ed. P. Secord, London 1982). I am extremely grateful to the participants at that conference, and at the seminars where I have read drafts of this paper, for their criticisms, questions and comments; and in particular to William Outhwaite for sharpening my thinking on the nature of an explanatory critique of consciousness in natural science.

2. See my *A Realist Theory of Science* 1st ed. Leeds 1975, 2nd ed. Harvester Press, Brighton and Humanities Press, New Jersey 1978, and chapter 2 above.

3. See my *The Possibility of Naturalism*, 1st ed., Brighton and New Jersey 1979, 2nd ed., Harvester Press, Hemel Hempstead 1989.

4. M. Scriven, 'Truisms as the Grounds for Historical Explanation', *Theories of History*, ed. P. Gardiner, Free Press, New York 1959; and P. Achinstein, 'Explanation', *American Philosophical Quarterly Studies in the Philosophy of Science*, ed. N. Rescher, Blackwell, Oxford 1969.

5. See my *A Realist Theory of Science*.

6. See N.R. Hanson, *Patterns of Discovery*, Cambridge University Press, Cambridge 1958; R. Harré, *The Principles of Scientific Thinking*, Macmillan, London 1970; and M.B. Hesse, *The Structure of Scientific Inference*, Macmillan, London 1974.

7. See *The Possibility of Naturalism*, p. 129.

8. See e.g. J. Habermas, *Theory and Practice*, Heinemann, London 1974, pp. 16ff.

9. Cf. A. Collier, 'Materialism and Explanation', *Issues in Marxist Philosophy* Vol. II, ed. J. Mepham and D.H. Ruben, Harvester Press, Brighton 1979, p. 37 and the unpublished essay by M. Westlake referred to there.

10. Cf. A. Giddens, *New Rules of Sociological Method*, Hutchinson, London 1976, p. 121 & passim.

11. See *The Possibility of Naturalism* and chapter 5 above.

12. A. Giddens, *Central Problems in Social Theory*, Macmillan, London 1979, p. 56.

13. See *The Possibility of Naturalism*, ch. 3.3.

14. See e.g. J. Elster, *Logic and Society*, Wiley, Chichester 1978, Ch. 5, and E. Ullman-Margalit, *The Emergence of Norms*, Oxford University Press, Oxford 1977.

15. See *A Realist Theory of Science*, Ch. 1.

16. See e.g. C. Taylor, 'Interpretation and the Sciences of Man', *Review of Metaphysics* 25(3), 1971 (reprinted in *Critical Sociology*, ed. P. Connerton, Harmondsworth 1976).

17. J. Habermas, *Knowledge and Human Interests*, Heinemann, London 1972, p. vii.

18. G.W.F. Hegel, *The Phenomenology of Mind*, Allen & Unwin, London 1949.

19. See M. Polanyi, *Personal Knowledge*, Routledge and Kegan Paul, London 1958, Ch. 4.

20. See *The Possibility of Naturalism*, esp. Ch. 4, Sections 3 and 4.

21. See R. Bernstein, *The Reconstruction of Social and Political Theory*, p. 203.

22. See *Knowledge and Human Interests*.

23. See H.-G. Gadamer, *Truth and Method*, Sheed and Ward, London 1975.

24. See C. Taylor, 'Neutrality in Political Science', *Philosophy, Politics and Society 3rd Series*, eds. P. Laslett and W. Runciman, Blackwell, Oxford 1969 (reprinted in *The Philosophy of Social Explanation*, ed. A. Ryan, Oxford University Press, Oxford 1973).

25. If 'ought' implies 'can', the non-trivial implication of a power is a presupposition, not an entailment, of the ought-statement; which depends upon a theory (i.e. 'factual knowledge') of the agent and her circumstances.

26. See R. Hare, *Freedom and Reason*, Oxford University Press, Oxford 1963, p. 108. The title has been (in my opinion, unconvincingly) disputed – see e.g. A. MacIntyre, 'Hume on "is" and "ought"', *Philosophical Review 1959*, reprinted in A. MacIntyre, *Against the Self-Images of the Age*, Duckworth, London 1971. (The vexed passage in Hume is *A Treatise of Human Nature*, ed. L.A. Selby-Bigge, Oxford University Press, Oxford 1965, III, i.1, pp. 468–70.)

27. K. Marx, *Capital vol. I*, Lawrence and Wishart, London 1965, p. 505.

28. A. Giddens, *New Rules of Sociological Method*, p. 159.

29. See R. Edgley, 'Reason as Dialectic', *Radical Philosophy* 15, 1976, and 'Marx's Revolutionary Science', *Issues in Marxist Philosophy Vol. III*, eds. J. Mepham and D.H. Ruben, Harvester Press, Brighton 1979.

30. See e.g. D. Bloor, *Knowledge and Social Imagery*, Routledge & Kegan Paul, London 1962, Ch. 2.

31. An explanatory critique in the natural sciences could be represented as follows:

$$\text{I.S.1}' \quad \text{(i) } T > P. \quad \text{(ii) } T \exp I(P_N) \rightarrow \text{(iii) } -V(S_s \rightarrow I(P_N)) \rightarrow \text{(iv) } V\phi_{-S_s}$$

32. See J. Austin, 'Performative-Constative', *La Philosophie Analytique* 1962, trans. by G.J. Warnock in *Philosophy and Ordinary Language*, ed. C. Caton, University of Illinois Press, Urbana 1963 (see esp. p. 30).

33. J. Searle, 'How to derive "ought" from "is"', *Philosophical Review 1964*, and *Speech Acts*, Cambridge University Press, Cambridge 1969, Ch. 8.

34. See L. Colletti, 'Marxism and the Dialectic', *New Left Review* 93 (1975).

35. F. Engels to P. Lafargue, 11 August 1884, *Correspondence Engels–Lafargue*, Paris, p. 235.

36. *Early Writings of Marx*, Harmondsworth 1975, p. 422.

37. Is the present direction of argument necessarily incompatible with a substantive utilitarian ethics? Yes and no. The utilitarian tradition has generally been willing to concede that a world with more possibilities is CP better than one with less, so that supposing that a happy or healthy man could make himself miserable or ill (not that he would – in virtue of his state – of course normally want to) but not vice versa, Bentham and Mill would be bound, on this kind of ground alone, to approve an emancipated as better than a non-emancipated state. But could they approve the kind of measures substantive depth theories indicate as necessary for the *transition* to such states? I doubt it. In Kantian terms, one could say that although they might will the end, it is highly unlikely that they could will the means in all but the most improbable circumstances.

38. See J. Habermas, 'Towards a Theory of Communicative Competence', *Inquiry 13* (1970).

39. See R. Harré, *Social Being*, Blackwell, Oxford 1979.

40. See my 'Emergence, Explanation and Emancipation', *Explaining Human Behaviour*,

ed. P. Secord, Oxford 1982 and my *Scientific Realism and Human Emancipation*, Verso, London 1986, Ch. 2.

41. See *Writings of the Young Marx on Philosophy and Society*, ed. Easton and Guddat, Anchor Books, New York 1967, p. 212.

Chapter 7

1. G.W.F. Hegel, *Science of Logic* vol. 2, London 1969, p. 56.
2. Marx to Kugelmann, 6 March 1868.
3. Marx, *Capital* vol. 1, 2nd ed., Afterword.
4. Marx to Engels, 14 January 1858.
5. Marx, *Economic and Philosophical Manuscripts*, end of Third Manuscript.
6. Marx, *Capital* vol. 1, ch. 1, sec. 2.
7. Marx, *Capital* vol. 1, 2nd ed., Afterword.
8. Marx to J.B. Schweitzer, 24 January 1865.
9. Marx, 'Chapter on Capital' in *Grundrisse*, Notebook V.
10. Marx to Lassalle, 16 January 1861.
11. Engels, *Anti-Duhring*, pt I, ch. 13.
12. Engels, 'Dialectics' in *Dialectics of Nature*.
13. K. Marx, 'Theses on Feuerbach', *Early Writings*, Harmondsworth 1975.
14. Marx and Engels, *German Ideology* vol. 1, pt III.
15. Marx, *Economic and Philosophical Manuscripts*, 3rd ms.
16. Engels, *Ludwig Feuerbach*, sec. 2.
17. A. Gramsci, *Selections from the Prison Notebooks*, London 1971, p. 465.
18. J.-P. Sartre, *Literary and Philosophical Essays*, New York 1967, p. 237.
19. S. Timpanaro, *On Materialism*, London 1976.
20. See Bhaskar, *Scientific Realism and Human Emancipation*, London 1986, p. 116.
21. See Bhaskar, *A Realist Theory of Science* 2nd edn, Hemel Hempstead 1978.
22. See Bhaskar, *The Possibility of Naturalism*, 2nd edn, Hemel Hempstead 1989, ch. 3.
23. Marx and Engels, *German Ideology* vol. I, pt I.
24. Marx, 'Theses on Feuerbach', 6th Thesis.
25. Marx and Engels, *German Ideology* vol. 1, pt I, sec. 7.
26. Marx and Engels, *The Holy Family*, ch. VI pt. 2.
27. Marx, *18th Brumaire*, sec. 1.
28. Marx, *Capital* vol. 1, Preface.
29. Ibid., vol. III, ch. 48.
30. Marx, *Value, Price and Profit*, pt VI.
31. Marx, *Capital* vol. 1, Preface.
32. Ibid., vol. III, ch. 48.
33. Marx and Engels, *German Ideology* vol. I, pt 1, A.
34. Ibid., Preface.
35. Marx and Engels, *German Ideology* vol. I, pt. 1, A.
36. G. Lukács, *History and Class Consciousness*, London 1971.
37. K. Korsch, *Marxism and Philosophy*, London 1970.
38. A. Gramsci, *Selections from the Prison Notebooks*, London 1971.
39. K. Korsch, *Marxism and Philosophy*, London 1970, p. 42.
40. Gramsci, *Selections from the Prison Notebooks*, London 1971, p. 462.
41. G. Lukacs, *History and Class Consciousness*, London 1971, p. 27.
42. Ibid., p. 170.
43. Gramsci, *Selections from the Prison Notebooks*, London 1971, p. 465.
44. Marx, *Poverty of Philosophy*, ch. 2, sec. 3.
45. H. Marcuse, *One-Dimensional Man*, London 1968, p. 257.
46. In M. Horkheimer, *Eclipse of Reason*, Oxford 1974.

47. J. Habermas, *Knowledge and Human Interests*, London 1971.
48. Marcuse, *Eros and Civilization*, Boston 1955.
49. See T. McCarthy, *The Critical Theory of Jurgen Habermas*, London 1978, p. 111.
50. T. Adorno, *Negative Dialectics*, London 1966.
51. *Praxis* vol. I, p. 64.
52. G. Della Volpe, *Logic as a Positive Science*, London 1980, p. 198.
53. Della Volpe, *Rousseau and Marx*, London 1978, p. 200.

Chapter 8

1. L. Wittgenstein, *Philosophical Investigations*, Blackwell, Oxford 1963, para. 115, Cf. PMN p. 12.
2. Cf. J. Habermas, *Knowledge and Human Interests*, London 1972, p. 308.
3. The Davidsonian theory is elaborated in *Essays on Actions and Events*, OUP, Oxford 1980, especially Essays 1, 7 and 11. For a critique of it, see RTS, pp. 140–1.
4. Thus there is another story to tell about 'reference' besides the one told in Chapter 6 of PMN, albeit one whose most interesting development postdates the book, namely as a story of the 'search and find' activities of scientists looking for and exploring the novel entities and structures posited by scientific theories. (See e.g. I. Hacking, *Representing and Intervening*, CUP, Cambridge 1983 and R. Harré, *Varieties of Realism*, Blackwell, Oxford 1986.) This kind of story presupposes that science has definite procedures as well as determinate results; and that it is a material practice as well as a theoretical discourse.
5. See A. Donagan, 'The Popper–Hempel Theory Reconsidered', in W. Dray, ed., *Philosophical Analysis and History*, Harper and Row, New York 1966.
6. See M. Scriven, 'Truisms as the grounds for historical explanation', in P. Gardiner, eds., *Theories of History*, Free Press, New York 1959.
7. See A. Chalmers, 'Bhaskar, Cartwright and Realism in Physics', *Methodology and Science* 20, (1987) and 'Is Bhaskar's Realism Realistic?', *Radical Philosophy* 49 (1988).
8. OUP, Oxford 1983.
9. W. Sellars, *Science, Perception and Reality*, Routledge & Kegan Paul, London 1963, p. 173, cited in PMN p. 199.
10. Cf. W. Outhwaite, *New Philosophies of Social Science*, Macmillan, London 1987, ch. 2.
11. See *The Structure of Scientific Revolutions*, University of Chicago Press, Chicago 1970, p. 121.
12. See A. Kojève, *Introduction to the Reading of Hegel*, Basic Books, New York, 1969, p. 156.
13. *Meaning and the Moral Sciences*, Routledge & Kegan Paul, London 1978, p. 20.
14. Cf. Outhwaite, *New Philosophies of Social Science*, pp. 31–5.
15. W.V.O. Quine, 'Designation and Existence', in *Readings in Philosophical Analysis*, eds. H. Feigl & W. Sellars, New York 1949, p. 50.
16. W.V.O. Quine, 'Three Grades of Modal Involvement', *Ways of Paradox*, Random House, p. 174.
17. See his *Meaning and the Moral Sciences*, p. 25 discussed in PMN pp. 284ff.
18. In a way nothing is more significant for understanding the political (in a broad sense) impact of Rortyism as a phenomenon than the implications of the doctrine that revolutionary change (whether in the sciences, the arts or the socio-economic-political world generally) cannot be rational.
19. Blackwell, Oxford 1975. See also A. Sayer, *Method in Social Science*, Hutchinson, London 1984.
20. For instance, in what F. Dretske, *Seeing and Knowing*, Routledge and Kegan Paul, London 1969, Ch. 1, has called 'epistemic perception'.
21. There is some retrospective irony in this in view of Wittgenstein's famous aphorism about lions' talk: 'If a lion could talk, we could not understand him'. See *Philosophical Investigation*, II vi (p. 223).

22. K. Marx, 9th and 10th Theses on Feuerbach, *Early Writings*, Harmondsworth, 1975, p. 423.

23. 'If we could convert knowledge from something discursive, something attained by continual adjustment of ideas or words, into something as ineluctable as being shoved about, or being transfixed by a sight which leaves us speechless, then we should no longer have the responsibility for choice among competing ideas and words, theories and vocabularies' (PMN, pp. 375–6).

24. Rorty sometimes uses a special sense of it (discussed in section 5 below) in Part 3, where it is counterposed to hermeneutics.

25. I. Kant, *Grundlegung zur Metaphysik der Sitten,* translated as *The Moral Law,* Hutchinson, London 1948, p. 119.

26. See P. Manicas, *History and Philosophy of the Social Sciences*, Blackwell, Oxford 1987, p. 307.

27. *The Idea of a Social Science*, Routledge and Kegan Paul, London 1958, p. 115. See also PMN p. 348.

28. This expression is taken from R. Rorty, 'Posties', *London Review Books* 3 September 1987, p. 12. It signifies here roughly the transition from epistemology to linguistic philosophy – the 'linguistic turn' (the title of an important collection of essays Rorty edited, University of Chicago Press, 1967). What I have been calling the 'epistemic fallacy' (see p. 147 above) is now expressed in a linguistic form as the definition of being in terms of our discourse about being – the 'linguistic fallacy' (see PON pp. 133, 155–6).

29. In this context it is worth bearing in mind Rorty's rejection of the concept of human nature. 'Humanity' does not have 'a nature over and above the various forms of human life which history has thrown up so far' (CC p. 13). It would surely be wiser for Rorty to argue not that there is no such thing as human nature, but (i) that it always manifests itself in some historically specific and mediated form and (ii) that it is and must always be known under some historically particular – and therefore potentially transformable – description.

30. Note the similarity with the Renaissance theme of man as the being which is the 'genus of all empirical genera', '*creatura commune*', '*oculus mundi*' or '*anima mundi*'. See L. Colletti, *Marxism and Hegel*, Verso, London 1973, Chapter XI.

31. 'Letter on Humanism', in *Philosophy in the 20th Century*, eds. W. Barret & H. Aiken, New York 1961.

32. There is some irony in the fact that the successful strong poet (or utopian revolutionary) would thus realize the goal of, of all discourses, philosophy.

33. Though Rorty does sometimes imply the contrary: 'Any seemingly random constellation of . . . things can set the tone of a life. Any such constellation can set up an unconditional commitment to whose service a life may be devoted – a commandment no less unconditional because it may be intelligible to, at best, only one person' (CS p. 12).

34. Even if the epistemic fallacy is now committed in a linguistically transposed mode.

35. Of course Rorty would probably acknowledge this – but there is more than a hint of methodological individualism in PMN (see eg. p. 206).

36. Rorty's argument that the difference between the 'kooky' and the 'revolutionary' (PMN p. 339) or 'fantasy' and 'genius' (CS p. 14) is the difference between ways of speaking which, for various contingencies, just happen to 'catch on' with other people or 'take' in the community overlooks the point that, for instance, existential and other claims in the intransitive dimension, successful predictions under repeatable conditions, formal proofs, demonstrations of anomaly resolution (amongst a bundle of historically discernible criteria) have to be satisfied in a revolutionary situation in science before intellectual progress can be definitely said to have occurred. There is reason, albeit often disguised, in intellectual revolutions; and such reason does not impede, but is shown, in part, in its poetry.

37. However, Rorty tends persistently to exaggerate the degree of 'Kuhn-loss', that is to say the extent to which subjects are changed, problems are set aside or displaced rather than resolved, anomalies are repressed or forgotten instead of being cleared up or normalized, in scientific and more generally discursive change. (In this his practice is at one with his theory.) In consequence he tends to underestimate the extent to which reference is maintained (or agents continue to 'talk about' the same thing) through change.

Chapter 9

1. First edition, Leeds 1975; second edition, Harvester Press, Hemel Hempstead, 1978.

2. See *Scientific Realism and Human Emancipation* (henceforth SR), Verso, London 1986, p. 30.

3. Macmillan, London 1970. See especially chapter 4. See also RTS pp. 168–9, n. 39.

4. *Principles of Scientific Thinking*, p. 2 & passim.

5. See my *The Possibility of Naturalism* (henceforth PON), 2nd edition, Harvester Press, Hemel Hempstead 1989, p. 133.

6. Blackwell, Oxford 1980. See e.g. pp. 158, 374–7.

7. See Chapter 8.3, especially p. 159, above, for Rorty's anti-naturalistic fallacy.

8. See SR chapter 1.3 and 'On the Poetics of Social Transformation and the Limits of the Linguistic Paradigm', *Making Social Psychology*, ed. T. Ibanez, Barcelona forthcoming.

9. And e.g. my 'Forms of Realism', *Philosophica* 15 (1), 1975.

10. W. Sellars, *Science Perception and Reality*, Routledge & Kegan Paul, London 1963, p. 173.

11. See T. Benton, 'Realism and Social Science: Some Comments on Roy Bhaskar's "The Possibility of Naturalism"', *Radical Philosophy* 27 (Spring 1981) reprinted in *Radical Philosophy Reader*, eds. R. Edgley & R. Osborne, Verso, London 1985; and A. Chalmers, 'Is Bhaskar's Realism Realistic?', *Radical Philosophy* 49 (Summer 1988). I reply to their criticisms in my 'Postscript to the Second Edition', PON.

12. It follows from this that the reappraisal of the problem of naturalism essayed in PON logically requires complementary studies from a multiplicity of scientific (and indeed non-scientific, such as literary, dramaturgical) perspectives. See PON, p. 168.

13. See A. Giddens, *Central Problems of Social Theory*, Macmillan, London 1979. For some differences see my 'Beef, Structure and Place', *Journal for the Theory of Social Behaviour* 13 (1), 1983, p. 85.

14. Here a substantive variant of the linguistic fallacy – the analysis of being in terms of language – is at work (see PON pp. 155–6). Or we could say that there is a double linguistification in the research process – once at the level of method – at what Outhwaite calls 'epistemic constitution' – and the second time at the level of objects of investigation – Outhwaite's 'ontological constitution'. See W. Outhwaite, *Concept Formation in Social Science*, Routledge & Kegan Paul, London 1983, p. 69 & passim.

15. For example, in studying the life-cycle of an organism.

16. For ontological reasons, as distinct from the well-rehearsed epistemological ones which apply even in laboratory situations (see SR p. 36).

17. See A. Collier, *Scientific Realism and Socialist Thought*, Harvester Press, Hemel Hempstead 1989, chapter 4.

18. See T. Benton, 'Realism and Social Science', p. 19.

19. See the discussions in A. Sayer, *Method in Social Science: A Realist Approach*, Hutchinson, London 1984, chapter 6 and P. Manicas, *A History and Philosophy of the Social Sciences*, Blackwell, Oxford 1987, chapter 13.

20. See W. Outhwaite, *New Philosophies of Social Science*, Macmillan, London 1987, p. 34.

21. Ibid., p. 53.

22. See the exchange between E.O. Wright and M. Burawoy in *Berkeley Journal of Sociology*, vol. XXXII (1987).

23. Strictly, less than this is sufficient for that (see SR p. 179).

24. Forthcoming Verso, London 1989. See A. Collier, *Scientific Realism and Socialist Thought* for an illuminating comparison of the Althusserian and critical realist positions.

25. Published in English in *Philosophy and the Spontaneous Philosophy of Scientists*, Verso 1989.

26. See L. Althusser (and E. Balibar), *Reading Capital*, Verso, London 1970, p. 40 & passim.

27. Compare, despite the continuing formal materialism of his later works, his unrelent-

ing hostility to ontology – e.g. in 'The Transformation of Philosophy', *Philosophy and the Spontaneous Philosophy of Scientists*. This is a hostility shared by Habermas. Both remain in the thrall of the epistemic fallacy – for all their desire to escape the ontic fallacy of Cartesian fundamentalism.

28. Cf. e.g. H. Ottman, 'Cognitive Interests and Self-Reflection', *Habermas: Critical Debates*, eds John B. Thompson & David Held, Macmillan, London 1982, chapter 4 & J. Whitebook 'Reason and Happiness', *Habermas and Modernity*, ed. R. Bernstein, Polity Press, Cambridge 1985, part 2, chapter 2.

29. J. Habermas, *Knowledge and the Human Interests*, Heinemann, London 1972, p. 314.

30. See e.g. P. Anderson 'The Affinities of Norberto Bobbio', *New Left Review* 170 (1988). For a recent realist – in the sense of 'critical realist' – view of politics see J. Isaac, *Power and Marxist Theory: A Realist View*, Cornell University Press, Ithaca 1988.

31. Cf. Marx: 'It is as ridiculous to yearn for a return to an original fullness as it is to believe that with this present emptiness history has come to a standstill. The bourgeois viewpoint has never advanced beyond this antithesis between itself and the romantic viewpoint and therefore the latter will accompany it as its legitimate antithesis to its blessed end', *Grundrisse*, Pelican, Harmondsworth 1973, p. 162.

32. See my forthcoming *Philosophy and the Idea of Freedom*, Blackwell, Oxford 1989 and my planned collection of essays on recent and contemporary Marxists (including Althusser and Habermas) and the new idealists, provisionally entitled *Philosophical Underlabouring*.

Name Index

Subject Index